To Roy,

SWEET TURF,
SUNDAY MORNINGS

You'll never walk alone!

Mark

by MARK HIGGITT

IN MEMORY of Tracey Wall and Lindsay Dingley,
the kind of women without whom Sunday football
wouldn't be allowed to happen anywhere, and Dad,
who lit the flame

Published by Many Heroes
Copyright © Mark Higgitt 2015
ISBN 978-0-9933003-0-1

CONTENTS

All action pictures by Aaron Manning

FOREWORD

SEVEN'S TOO YOUNG TO DISCUSS the idea of roots with your grandson. But it's old enough – I think – to gently introduce the notion that where he's come from will one day feel as important as where he's going.

That thought crossed my mind as he and I played a game of 'who'll-blink-first', us or the red traffic light staring back through the embers of an early spring Saturday evening. In front of us, the signpost jabbed one finger ahead to the M5 south, the way home, and another to the Black Country.

Ah, the Black Country.

I pointed to the latter, the green light glowed, and we drove straight on – but not before I'd promised that, one day, we'd turn left instead and head down Memory Lane.

When we do, I know which streets we'll explore first.

The one where his great-grandmother was born almost 94 years before.

The one where his great-grandfather first kicked a ball, a few hundred yards up the road, a few years after that.

Either side, we'll disappear down others, the streets I stumbled along way back in 2001 – long before he was born – during a year in search of those same roots, an odyssey wrapped around the fortunes of a bunch of Sunday footballers, long-lost cousins (possibly) who are bound by something that runs much, much deeper than the Ten Yard Seam that shaped their landscape and their families' lives for generations.

I wrote a diary of that year, for reasons that will become clear in what follows. It never made it into print but, when that Memory Lane day comes – before we pack our sandwiches and lick our lips at the prospect of faggits and pays – I'll dust off these scribblings to acquaint him with those Sunday heroes and villains, the kind of men who make the spirit of these few lines as true now as the day they were written…

> In Wednesbury town, a clock whose name
> is coupled with its cocking fame,
> was yearly held by custom's right
> a wake where colliers met to fight,
> where bulls were baited, torn, abused
> and dogs were killed, which much amused
> those sturdy knights of coal and hammer
> who scoff at peace and joy at clamour

Those sturdy knights of coal and hammer, who scoff at peace and joy at clamour. Let's head back to the turn of the century and introduce them to you, too….

1 VINDALOO

I'M SORRY TO START WITH A FART, but that's how it happened. I heard it before I saw the farter, a pale, shuffling man wearing a baseball cap, blue denim jeans and a matching denim jacket that, presumably, had been a lot tidier before he'd passed out in the early hours.

The fart, I'd hazard a guess – hazard in more ways than one – lasted three sluggish steps, a weary rasp with a short, wet burble as its finale, the worrying hint of a follow-through. I can still hear it, and it still makes me feel faintly queasy.

A dark-haired woman was following him, petite, but with a look of disgust that seemed less to do with the odour he was trailing than the amount he'd farted since being scraped off a floor a few minutes before. He reached the touchline, a yard or two from me, and halted, wobbling, a man trying desperately hard not to fall off a cliff.

"Have you finished?" she asked. He took a breath, and so did I.

"Not yet," he muttered. I moved. Rude, I know, but not as rude as venting the rotting remains of 12 pints and a vindaloo on a complete stranger.

Thirty yards to our right, a handful of men in scarlet-and-black shirts, black shorts and black stockings, and a handful of others in assorted polo tops and jeans, were kicking in at goal. Well, some were.

If I say Germany 1 England 5, you'll understand why one gangly youth with a Number 1 cut was rushing round trying to re-enact Michael Owen's Munich hat-trick. What he lacked in poise and the assassin's touch he made up for with blind imagination and a scattergun, giving a running commentary as he went. He only stopped, on his knees, out of breath, when the last ball was bouncing in the road, a rusty railing away, where Cinder Bank meets Simms Lane, on the way north from Netherton to Dudley.

I wondered how many grown men were doing the same on the green fields of England at that very minute, and wished I were one of them.

"You made it," the voice was familiar, though we'd only spoken a couple of times, once on the phone, once in the pub. Three times, actually, but we'll come to that.

I twisted and Jezz Dingley, Yew Tree Rangers' secretary, extended an arm. His handshake was brief, but firm.

"We'm going to struggle here," he pulled a face, and I recognised the dialect. It wasn't the pitch he was talking about, though it could have done with a short-back-and-sides. Still could. It wasn't the weather. The Black Country was basking like anywhere else that early September Sunday morning. The trouble was players.

"Scratch side. Holidays, other things. Some on 'em ay decided what they'm doing."

I was impressed, though, and relieved. A month before, this day had been in doubt. After finishing their second Warley & District Sunday League season with promotion to Division 1, despite finishing sixth in Division 2, Dingley's most optimistic stab had been that nine players would sign on. I gazed down the pitch and counted 13 Yew Tree shirts. The figure wasn't hard to reach, seeing it was a warm-up that lacked movement. Then he told me that the morning's opponents, Barrel, had played three or four friendlies already. This was the first time Tree had pulled their kit on.

A struggle? The first 10 minutes of Yew Tree's new term were. They were as rusty as the railings, and the early shot a Barrel defender hoofed off his line had less to do with tactical precision and skill than the lucky end of a messy, mass schoolboy drift down the right while acres of space went begging on the left.

Then the ball arrived with Barrel's Number 8, unmarked 20 yards out at the other end, and – a loop and a dip later – the bottom pitch at Hillcrest High School and Community College had seen its first competitive goal of the season. It happened that quickly. I'd had no expectations, one way or the other. But Jezz Dingley had.

"Told you!" he muttered, and stalked off.

I'll be honest from the start. As the ball headed back to the centre-spot, the blue men of Barrel joyous, the scarlet of Yew Tree looking among each other for blame or inspiration, I had a moment of dread. In the context of the morning – surrounded by people I didn't know, but united with them by the shape of the ball and more than a century of unspoken tradition – the dread was brief but, after 15 years away from the whiff of embrocation and last night's ale, disconcerting. It was that the rest of the season would take its lead from there.

For four, long minutes, it came back. The slow, melancholy descent into autumn. The damp. The mist. The wind and rain of early winter, the clinging, knee-wrenching mud of a Christmas that promises only a hip-jarring freeze in new year, and a season that's over in all but name long before the first snowdrop pushes through. All that. Then Yew Tree equalised and I was snapped out of my doubt.

I was watching a man at the bus stop at the bottom of Simms Lane when the yell came, and I turned to see a player spread-eagled in the Barrel area, 100 yards away. By the time I'd picked out the victim – Tree's Number 9, a rangy, blond centre-forward called Scottie – he was holding the ball, waiting for the referee to stride 12 yards from the goal line and scrape his studs where the penalty spot should have been. Only the Dudley Metropolitan Borough Council groundsman hadn't left one.

Scottie made no mistake from the scuff and the gleam from his new Adidas boots was matched, for a second, by the warmth of his team-mates' celebration – though neither outshone the glow of his Mediterranean tan. Suddenly, life didn't seem so bad, not on the fringes of the Yew Tree gathering.

Unsurprisingly, Barrel's Number 4 saw it differently.

"Come on lads," he shouted, "we'm fucking shit!" The motivational moment unwittingly set a trend for the coming months and prompted the visitors' manager to dig deep for something more constructive. From 10 yards beyond his back four, where he was acting as linesman – no new-fangled terms like 'referee's assistant' here – he put his finger on the problem. "All I can see is arses running away from the ball," he yelled. "Treat it like a bottle of perfume. Welcome it!"

Tree took the goal as a sign of better things to come, and began to dictate the shape of the play. Shape may be too strong. It suggests a structure or system. This was more of a thick Banks's Bitter formation, an overspill drawn to whichever corner of the table the ball happened to be, a similarity that occurs to me with hindsight.

I retreated from the touchline – one fart too many perhaps, or simply the need to stand back and watch in wide-screen – and strolled in the sun around the pitch.

I'd done half a lap when a high ball was floated from the left wing towards the Yew Tree area, and the man at the bus stop stood upright. The ball dipped as it flew, then it dropped like a stone. The Yew Tree keeper had one eye on it and the other on Barrel's Number 9 arriving, unescorted, on the edge of the six-yard box.

"Challenge for the fucking thing!" a Tree defender (loose description) shouted. Sadly, the ball was already in the net.

Even now, I can close my eyes and replay the scene. The call's always late, and the keeper never answers back, mainly because his head's in his hands. Then he drops that as well. The voice that echoes across Baptist End belongs to a dark-haired woman in her mid-20s, standing among the contingent of subs, mates, mickey-takers and sundry bystanders. Some are laughing, some are cringing, others are unmoved, deadpan, the kind of poker faces that come with shock or a total lack of surprise. I didn't know which and didn't have the chance to find out before she yelled again.

"Tell him to fuck off," then "it was 'im who lost the fuckin' thing in the fust place."

The ball was heading back to the centre circle, when the keeper found it in him to answer, though "Leave it out" was a little feeble, it seemed to me. And to her.

"Don't be a prick," she went on. "Stand up for yourself!"

I looked up the line. The rest didn't flinch. I looked at the road. A bus was slowing towards the shelter, but the man waved it past and sauntered closer to the railings.

Half-time came. A chance to regroup, consider the situation, suck an orange or have a fag. It was also a blessing for a Sunday hoofer, bereft of breath, blistered of foot and solemn of pledge that he'll take pre-season seriously next time. In the centre-circle, a crew-cut man in his late 40s, dressed in blue, glanced at his black, steel-capped boots, then spoke. Most of the others put something in their mouths and ignored him.

"Their Number 7 and Number 8," he pointed down the pitch, even though Barrel were up it, "they'm running it."

He was right. Seven was tall with a curly mop. He wore his shirt outside his shorts, his socks at half-mast and an arrogant expression to go with his arrogant, confrontational manner. Eight was different. To start with, he was short, stocky, tidy and called Errol. Both could play a bit.

"I want someone up their arses all the time," the manager looked around his men, but he didn't suggest who, and no one volunteered. So he moved on.

"You make a pass and stand there admirin' it. Every throw-in's up in the air. It ay what we talked about." This was the result of talking?

Then Jezz Dingley walked over, smouldering.

First, he demanded that they encourage each other. Then he set the tone by using the words 'no' and 'application' in succession, jabbing a finger at the keeper, and blowing his stack over "an honest mistake… don't slag 'im off".

"The problems are 'ere," he jabbed again, at the grass, by which I assumed he meant midfield. "We've got 45 minutes to put it right."

Too right, I thought, but I wasn't thinking of league points.

I glanced to my right and saw a middle-aged woman with greying hair and the stern look of concentration or dissatisfaction. She was too old to be a girlfriend or wife of someone on the pitch, so I guessed she was a mother. Maybe the second-half would reveal the son, though I couldn't help thinking that watching this, for all the pleasant warmth and the occasional breeze, was taking loyalty too far.

As the huddle broke up, one of the non-playing throng tapped a mate's shoulder. He had the lean, close-cropped Black Country look you'd expect to see coming back from an old Black Country welterweight in a book of old Black Country photos.

"Get 'im out of the game and you'll win it," he nodded at Errol. The boxer's name was Rob Wall. I'd met him once already. I learnt the keeper's identity at the same time as the ref, when he laid both hands on the ball soon after the restart, outside the area. I was next to Dingley when it happened.

"We'm in the shit," he nodded, a pained look of despair or acceptance on his face. But the ref only took the keeper's name. Which was Phil. Still is.

"If you'd given him red, I'd have appealed," Dingley advised the official when he next ventured near the line.

"I asked him to pick a card," he smiled back. It was a Sunday morning, after all.

Not just any Sunday morning, though.

A never-to-be-repeated Sunday morning.

A Sunday morning after the night before.

And a long, lazy summer.

So, when the beer wasn't winning, when they weren't beating themselves, both sides were defeated by the pitch. The dull thud and occasional thwack of limb on limb brought little flashbacks. One late, fatigue-fuelled crunch would be followed by a loud crack soon, surely, and my money was on Tree's stout, flame-haired left-back, a man who embodied everything that lithe team-mate Scottie didn't. They called him Ginger, which was as accurate as it was unoriginal.

The Chaucerian language that followed his moments of madness or rage was aimed as loosely as a mouthful of spit at a chainshop furnace. It was mostly intended to absolve him of responsibility for what had happened.

I knew "we'm" was Black Country for "we are", that "bay" meant "am not", and that "day" doubled for "did not" and "doesn't", because my Dad hailed from the other side of Rowley Bonk, the tall ridge that separated the two valleys of this old industrial landscape. But most of what Ginger uttered or shouted needed an interpreter.

I did look on with the feeling, however, that this curious figure – the picture that appears when the last fold in a game of Consequences is turned – would loom large in the months to come, if the first match of my season wasn't also the last.

For the record, the game ended 4-4, a sequence in which Tree's ragged defence twice gifted Barrel the lead, then watched the compliment returned. Tree's third came from that heady Sunday morning mix, a quick winger, a tired full-back, and a cross that dipped late. I followed the scorer's wheeling celebration run across the goalmouth, arms outstretched like an aircraft, until my eyes alighted at the bus-stop. The bloke was still there. And there were two more with him, watching.

They stayed there as another bus slowed, then drove past. They stayed as Phil the Keeper redeemed himself with a brilliant save, after Yew Tree either relaxed or tired. It's hard to say which. But they'd gone by the time Scottie fizzed a shot over. It was rising as it cleared the railings, 20 yards away. If this were a scene from Barry Hines' *The Blinder*, the ball would still be in orbit. But this wasn't fantasy football. It bounced once on the Cinder Bank tarmac, struck the front of a passing ambulance and rebounded towards Dudley.

By continuing with whatever their Sundays had in store, elsewhere in the Black Country, those two old fellas missed Jezz Dingley's snarl as Barrel scored their fourth, and they missed the penalty, 10 minutes from time, that cancelled it out and restored the smile to the club secretary's face. I wasn't sure who scored the penalty, and didn't really care – beyond the fact that it appeared to coax the farter one step closer to consciousness – because I was certain the ref had already played 146 of the scheduled 90 minutes anyway.

Four-all, then. Ironically, the same score as the first big game I ever saw, at The Hawthorns, a few short miles the other side of the ridge, on Saturday, April 11, 1966. West Brom vs Arsenal. Tony Kaye, Clive Clarke, Ian Lovett, Bomber Brown, Bobby Hope and Jeff Astle were playing for the Baggies, though the years might be playing tricks. I don't remember the sequence, but I recall being thrilled by the fact that more goals seemed to be scored in the flesh than they did on a 19-inch Bush TV. The next game I saw was 0-0.

The score this Sunday morning was of no consequence to me for its own sake. It wouldn't shape my week, as it would have 20-odd years before, if I'd been heading for the shower with steam spiralling from my boots.

"Harborne next week," Jezz shouted to me as the onlookers dispersed, more sober than they'd arrived but planning, I had no doubt, to put that right.

I said "Yeah", I confess, with little conviction. It didn't fool me, so it probably didn't fool him. He turned round and, like a bad day on *One Man and His Dog*, tried to round up enough men to take the nets down. Some were as disinterested in that as they'd apparently been in the outcome of the game, or in playing to the peak of their Sunday morning ability, as if habit alone had made them tie their laces.

Maybe Germany 1 England 5 was already more than any red-blooded, working class Englishman had a right to expect for one weekend, a season even, or a lifetime. I looked at the expressions on their scarlet faces – sun-scorched, blood-soaked as their bodies screamed for air – suggested that, like their performance, the lager would lack its sharp edge. And the Sunday roast would be blander than they'd like as well. And there'd be a whole week in the factory before they had a chance to put it right, if that were part of the deal, of course.

Me? I sauntered to the car and pointed it south, gazing lazily at buildings that had seen better days, lining a High Street that could say the same.

Harborne next week. Perhaps I'd allowed the intoxicating Munich glory to monkey with my expectations. Perhaps I'd simply forgotten that, to enjoy the good days, you had to suffer the bad. That occurred to me as I headed from Netherton to home.

The car's long been my sanctuary, a retreat, a place to contemplate alone. This time, waiting for red to become green outside the McDonald's drive-in at Halesowen, the good-day bad-day thought was chased by this: What am I doing here?

What was I doing there? The week gave me the chance for some honest reflection, so I'll tell you all I could tell myself as I wove through suburban Birmingham towards Selly Oak seven days later. The simple answer's this.

Football, Black Country, people, though not necessarily in that order. A season following an out-of-date A-Z around the Warley & District Sunday League, blindly trusting that whatever happened would bring some kind of reward from ordinary lives.

If you're feeling deeper, perhaps you can explain how fate piled three books on my bedside table and triggered this voyage of discovery. What put Nick Hornby's *Fever Pitch* on top of JL Carr's *How Steeple Sinderby Wanderers Won the FA Cup* and JB Priestley's *English Journey*? What vein emerged in the first, a 90s homage to football fanatics, then threaded through a soccer fantasy, and finally came to rest in the heart of a chilling study of 30s Britain?

I'll return to Steeple Sinderby later and leave it at this, for now. If Hornby's study of obsession – not just Arsenal – had been a reminder to me of days long gone, in one shocking *Journey* chapter about the Black Country, Priestley was as good as whispering in my ear "look beyond the pitch, here's your landscape, your heritage".

My landscape? It sounds very *Field of Dreams*, now I see those words speaking back to me from the paper, though maybe there's a little Shoeless Joe in there too, somewhere.

I'd slugged away for points on rain-swept Rowley hillsides, from time to time, in my own middling career. It was also where Dad was born, his playground till he was 16 and the war came. Yet he'd never taken us back, as dads often feel the need to do, apart from Uncle Len's funeral. Whether that was time, a lack of transport, or because he regarded it as another life, I wasn't sure. All I knew, as he prepared for a cancer operation, was that it was calling. Corny, yes, but also true.

I'd hung up my boots six days, 11 hours and 35 minutes before my younger daughter, Katie, was born at the start of the 1985 season, intending to take them down again once she was sleeping through. I never did. I never bade my team-mates farewell, never crossed the thresh-hold of a dressing room again. Never felt the high that follows a line of embrocation. So, even if they didn't know it at the time, Yew Tree had a lot of making up to do.

From them, I was hoping for rekindled memories. Mazy runs, the sweetest passes, last-ditch tackles, a word of anger, or a sporting gesture. A Beckham free-kick, a Charlton rocket, the last goal I ever scored, a 35-yard screamer against Ringspanners. You know? Perhaps you don't. Moments of magic that flow from the feet of a superstar every week, but once a lifetime from those of a mortal, apart from that wonderful No Man's Land between snooze and sleep, where anything can happen, must happen, and often does. Disgusting habits in the showers. Life played out over 90 minutes every Sunday morning, and again afterwards, in pubs, at kitchen sinks, and anywhere between. Such things. Sights and sounds. Poetry and motion. Not too much to ask for. Surely.

So here I was, in Selly Oak, where this particular Sunday's landscape was a sports ground nestling between big, red-roofed detached houses on a leafy lane leading to the QE Medical Centre and the University of Brum campus. Netherton it wasn't. Isn't. South-west Second City. It was the closest Yew Tree would come to playing in Europe.

The sky was blue, the breeze was keen, the leaves were rustling, and there was a hint of autumn in the air. Altogether, a good day to be out playing football.

The green wooden pavilion wall had 'student pricks' sprayed on it in yellow. I had a hunch it wasn't a sign pointing to where they were kept, but a cheap declaration of contempt for the beer-swilling learning classes who'd frequent this part of the Second City again in a couple of weeks, when the last of their 26 weeks annual holiday ended.

The once-mighty Moseley Rugby Club's colts were training, learning how to ignore the ball, yet carry on with the game, while their parents held a fund-raiser, barbecuing burgers. At the top of the field, a team was warming up in a professional manner on the world's narrowest soccer pitch. The distance from touchline to penalty area was two yards. An inswinging Aunty Mabel corner could have cleared the playing area's full width without bouncing, assuming the linesman held her Zimmer while she swung her boot.

There were faces among the Trees I didn't recognise from the Barrel game, a setback in my plan to slot a column of names next to a column of shirt-numbers. Mind you, the list from eight days before was an incomplete mish-mash of nicknames that would require an interpreter, then a psychologist, to explain. I didn't see who won the toss but, as Harborne lined up to play down the pitch, with the breeze behind them, I had a fair idea.

Let's deal with the highlights first. In the second minute, a Harborne boot hoofed a Yew Tree shot off the line. That's it. For the next 88 minutes, it was one-way torture.

It might seem strange, having started with a fart on the edge of a soccer pitch, to suggest removing the ball and ask you to imagine that a virus had been responsible for the horror of what followed. It could hardly have been less destructive. Likewise, it's possible to take away the goalposts and the goal-line, yet still pinpoint the seconds when worst fears came true. Just as I could choose not to tell you the score without underplaying the scale of the slaughter we were to witness.

It didn't occur to me at the time, but the blokes around me this breezy day would shape my life for the next year, at least. So you can imagine how painful it is to admit that even the most ardent, football-hating XXXabbering would have recognised the moment when the suffering should have been ended. Assuming you've reached this far by realising – like Hornby – that the Beautiful Game's a metaphor for life, you can pick the moment you'd have stepped in and administered the lethal injection.

Let's start with Phil Tucker. He still wakes in the night, sweating coldly, XXXabbering like a traumatised idiot. The aerial assault did it, B52 carpet-bombing in B15, though this ordnance did hit its target. It was pitiful to witness and, in its awfulness, easy to miss the innocuous moment that triggered it.

A little lad called Tigs, whose mother couldn't have known he was out playing with the big boys, had replaced Ginger at left-back. He was neat, confident, aware of what was around him and looked to have all the time and space in the world. He also had his head screwed on. So, knowing it was safe to do so, he conceded a throw-in close to the half-way line, when Harborne tried to hit the angle to the corner flag behind him, rather than try to play his way out of trouble. Close to the half-way line. That's crucial.

Harborne's Number 9 picked up the ball and wiped it on his shirt, as if he was going to hit the penalty area, 40 yards away. As if.

It's important to say, at this point, that there was a dip on the edge of Tucker's six-yard box. As the projectile speared out of the blue, he ran in to the depression, meaning his desperate leap to punch the bomb clear started from a patch of grass six inches lower, at least, than his legs were expecting. If he'd fallen into a grave, it couldn't have been funnier.

"We'm second best," Jezz Dingley sighed, the first in a ceaseless string of "we'm this" and "we'm that" and "we'm the other". I thought second best was an optimistic view. Five minutes later, another long throw, this time from the left, was half cleared – an improvement of sorts – but, this time, the Yew Tree defence charged out to catch Harborne offside and missed a man running from deep. The old ones are the best.

Tucker's dad was on the line, a big man with red cheeks, a rumbling voice with an echo chamber somewhere near his belly, and a smile that looked permanent.

"We'm going to get a lesson," he said to me, but only because I was nearest. A week before, Dingley had said something similar about the same time. What was also clear was the fact that Tree needed poise, someone to test the turning speed of the home defence, a pace akin to the No 11 Outer Circle bus. A Beckham comes to mind. Ann Widdecombe would have been a start, but they had neither. Their luck was spent.

I'd already learnt a new name when Tree's captain hobbled off. Tigs moved to midfield, Ginger went to left-back. As their team-mate lay on the turf, cautiously removing his boot, another sub bent over him, casting a shadow which, even allowing for refraction, could have done with losing a couple of stone.

"Mitch, does it hurt?" he asked. Mitch looked up and nodded.

"Hah! Mitch has broken his leg!"

The Harborne followers stared, and so did I.

"Bastard," was all Mitch muttered back. Then he laughed.

Another piece of the jigsaw soon appeared. I'd heard about Gavin, a lad whose disciplinary record had been so bad the season before that, but for a case of mistaken identity, the Warley & District Sunday League would have banned him for good.

He hadn't played against Barrel because he and his brother, Craig, were in a bowls tournament. Bowls? It's possible to be passionate about bowls. I intend to be, one day. I pondered that double-life he clearly led as he was penalised for a petulant foul in the centre-circle. The ref pointed to the scene of the crime, but Gavin didn't budge. It was the closest he'd been to the action all morning. When the ref glanced away, he tried to kick the ball. I was surprised he recognised it. Unfortunately, he missed. He jabbed again. And missed. The third flick worked. Predictably, the ref reached for his pocket. It was more than Yew Tree's Number 11, 20 yards away, could take.

"Fucking hell, ref," he yelled. "That's petty, isn't it? You're not on telly now."

A minute on, Harborne's Number 9 launched another salvo, this time from Mars. The panic in Tree's defence was palpable. The dip in Tucker's six-yard box was sinking deeper too. And the breeze was stiffening.

It wasn't long before the name of Tree's right-back went in my book when Dingley told him not to argue after he'd floored a Harborne man in the area. Yode, a solidly-built man in his mid-20s, I'd say, with a hunched run and a radiator rammed down each sock, disagreed with the decision. He was the only one. Penalty.

The half-time inquest began quietly. Paul Gennard, the manager, told them there was no communication. He'd spent the half saying very little himself, so he was right. They nodded, but said nothing. Then the previous week's half-time voice of reason, Rob Wall, piped up. He talked of "wanting it". Gennard picked up the theme, sort of.

"What have we turned up for? I'm sick and tired of standing here watching it!"

It was a worrying admission, given the season was but eight days old.

"We've talked about two-touch. What's happened?"

Two consecutive touches would have been a start.

The second-half was as painful as the first. As Dingley complained that no one was talking or organising defence, no one talked or organised it. And panic was spreading.

I didn't mean to make snap judgements about them, just as I hoped they weren't sizing me up, but I had Jezz down as an engineer. Something said he was accustomed to taking things apart, sorting them, putting them together again and expecting to see a spark. Why else would a secretary make more noise than the manager? Seeing things go wrong, yet being helpless when a spanner needed wielding, clearly didn't suit him.

Then anger was added to panic. By the time I saw the opposition's hefty Number 6 in a heap, clutching his leg, the apparently reasonable Rob was walking away, chased by half of Harborne. With a speed sadly lacking so far, six Trees raced after them.

If the ref could have dug a hole with his pencil, he would. Mind you, at £16 a match, I'd have thought twice about putting my nose in the way. Thus it was a woman on the line who screamed "Go and look at the player, don't get involved in a fight".

In my life, this kind of thing has happened with stomach-churning regularity. I was next to a Harborne sub, gazing in a direction that might have suggested I was making eye contact, when he offered an opinion, loudly. He had a face like a robber's dog, black, angry eyes, a waist the size of Brum's inner ring road and the height to match. His point was this. If the ref didn't wave red, he'd knock the ref's head off.

He began to look at me and I'd have agreed, if he'd asked. Eventually, the ref beckoned Rob... and booked him. I twitched and moved. Then Rob was substituted.

"I'm sorry about that," he trudged up, shook his head, rolled his socks down and took a swig of juice. "I don't normally get involved in that sort of thing."

I'd no reason to doubt him. He didn't look like someone who'd hit his late 30s with a black record, though what did I know? And what did I care? For now, the flash of anger and the regret didn't tell me much about him, because I was more concerned that the Robber's Dog was glaring at us both. I did the only thing I could. I went.

"Twenty two pints or two pints?" Paul Gennard said to me a few minutes later, much further down the line. For a second, the manager had lost me.

"They want to play football. We want to have a drink," he rubbed an index finger beneath his greying moustache. He had the look of a young Michael Elphick about him, of the Boon era, not the walrus *EastEnders* Harry Slater period.

Harborne wanted to play football, Tree wanted to have a drink? I wasn't in a position to comment, and I'm not sure he expected me to. He looked at the ground and turned his back to the action. It's hard to talk to strangers at a time of grief, so I made a multi-purpose "u-huuh" noise, and sauntered even further down the pitch towards the corner flag.

One of Tree's contingent was there playing with his lad. He pointed up the slope to Tuck, and recounted the keeper's best game, when he was so drunk he didn't know where he was till half-time. Still, he caught everything. He laughed, and I laughed too. Pity he hadn't downed a skinful the night before. With five minutes to go, game over, and the Trees moaning loudly about the smallest decision, Harborne broke the nominal offside trap again. Tucker was rounded, again, and, when he stood, he was limping.

Five-nil. Someone had probably passed away in the QE Hospital, a couple of hundred yards away, during the previous two hours, but no one had here. Five-nil, though, can feel like the death of a close friend. At the very least, a bad car crash.

"What can you say to them?" I asked Jezz Dingley as the final whistle blew.

"Nothing. They know they played bad."

We watched the Trees drift back to the green pavilion and, out of the blue, he pointed out those who could have made it in the game they loved, and why. It was sad, truly sad, as squandered talent always is. Then he listed those who drank together, and always had. My card was marked. I mentioned Paul's 22-pint lament and asked where you drew the line.

"You can't," he insisted. "These guys work 39 hours a week, and that's how they want to spend their leisure time."

I turned to leave, dispirited, for the second time in eight days, and said goodbye.

"We'm at home next week. Cup," he caught me before I could blend in to the foliage. "You gonna come?"

You gonna come? It was the natural successor to "What am I doing here?"

I knew there were millions feeling the same as I did, asking themselves the same question, as they always did after a Sunday morning pasting, returning home to wives and mothers who'd be wondering the same thing. Regret at a wasted morning rippled out from here to Bearwood, Wolverhampton, Cannock, Liverpool, Glasgow and all points of the compass. And a ripple of joy, too, of course. That was the thing.

You gonna come? In my search for mazy runs, I'd found a disjointed bunch of blokes in need of something inspiring, anything, to go with their readiness to charge around together at the end of every grinding week. I'm guessing that was as true for them as it was for me.

More than that – fuelled by the welcome Jezz Dingley and his mates had given a stranger – was a hope that, if I did find myself back in Netherton a week later, at some point, they'd prove they weren't completely out of their depth. You don't know how much I hoped for that.

2   IT AY JUST 11 AND 11

ANOTHER MORNING LIKE HARBORNE, another gloomy drive home, would have made watching the next one harder. But that wasn't the only reason my spirits needed lifting. While my first drive up here had been in a state of World Cup afterglow, my second was in the aftermath of the Twin Towers, the Pentagon and a field in Pennsylvania.

I didn't expect to be thinking this but, as I slowed for the speed camera signs at the foot of the climb up Haden Hill, I did wonder whether football was what we should be doing, that weekend. My first attempt to write this paragraph picked up the thought. In such circumstances – horrific, but distant and beyond our control – is the Beautiful Game the first thing we should worry about, or the last?

It's neither. It's a sport, not a statement. So here we were.

Gornal Bush were a big side with Lakes AFC written across the broad backs of their tracksuit tops as they warmed up, a clue that they'd either changed their name or borrowed some kit. The Trees were milling about. I looked for signs of the touchline support that had surprised me in its size and tone against Barrel and Harborne. But, today, there was only the bloke who'd told me the tale of Tuck's greatest game a week before, his little lad, and a woman as Tree's Number 5 ran towards the empty line, hoisting his shirt.

"Nothing like a bit of loyal support," he laughed. "They've fenaged after last week."

"D'you think it's the weather, Bran?" she asked.

"No," he reached into the kit bag. "We wuz shite."

He found a can of freeze spray, lifted his shirt again and winced.

"Spray me back will you, cock?"

She obliged, and he jogged back to the D to join Jezz Dingley's pre-match talk before they gathered in the centre-circle, where the other supporter picked his little boy up and both teams bowed their heads. For 60 seconds, the only sounds were the Sunday morning traffic rumbling past, and a blackbird singing on the railings that separated the pitch from a strip of ravaged land reclaimed by nature.

Did any of the players dwell on the horrors of Tuesday, September 11? Maybe. Maybe not. Wolves had drawn 2-2 with Stockport the day before. The Baggies had put four past Man City. While Tree were on their own voyage of discovery in Division 1 of the Warley & District Sunday League, the two bitter rivals were desperate to end long years of exile from the top flight. So maybe a handful of Trees – the ones who hadn't renounced their old gold or navy blue-and-white birthright for claret-and-blue or red-and-white as impressionable schoolboys – were thinking of the promised land. Maybe it was the 90 minutes to come, or maybe it was New York. Whatever, for the first half-hour, kicking down the slope, with four changes to the side stuffed by Harborne, Tree were a different team.

I watched two chances go begging in the first five minutes, then set off round the pitch, watching Jezz Dingley prowling the far touchline. If he paced like this when the mud came, he'd gradually disappear into a trench 20 yards long and the width of a pair of broad, Black Country shoulders so that, by February, only the top of his head would be visible – that and, occasionally, his flailing arms.

I already knew he was a man who didn't stand still long, or remain quietly philosophical about what happened on the pitch. So our conversation was more a series of half-sentence thoughts fragmented by action. Like a run Scottie didn't make.

"He's played for Stourbridge, Bromsgrove, Halesowen. He'll score goals for you."

Like the reshuffle to the starting line-up. Picked on the basis of last week's match?

"No, who's available. We'm three short. One lad's had to go to the airport. Mark. Tall lad. Three on holiday."

Like the lad who looked like one of Tree's two right-backs.

"Dave Taylor. New Road lad. He worn't gunna sign. Supposed to be midfield."

"Unlucky, Mitchell," he shouted as the captain went close, then an aside, "They'm brothers, Scott and Mitchell", then another yell, "Good defending that was, Mitchell".

Mitch was your rugged jeans advert type, a George Clooney to his brother's beach-loving Leonardo DiCaprio. He'd recovered from his Harborne ankle injury, and he was running things. On a greasy surface, in a shifting breeze, he saw possibilities that hadn't featured before. He just needed someone to tune to the same frequency.

It wasn't the most riveting game, but not the dullest, for all the disjointed passages where neither side summoned enough poise or purpose in the drizzle to keep the ball for more than three or four passes. I ambled off again and, when a loose shot hit the Simms Lane railings, broke into a jog, took the ball on the rebound, rolled it to the right, flicked it with the outside of my left foot and volleyed it to the keeper. He moved five yards to his right and picked it up. Some things you never lose.

An old fella was leaning on the railings, an unimpressed look lurking in the creases that turned his face into a 3D map of this place, spider-vein B-roads starting nowhere and going nowhere, living archaeology that showed how a hard life could leave its mark, a warning to the kids kicking a ball.

"I can't understand how no one's scored," I muttered.

"They ay gunna score at this rate," he said. And he was right.

The half ended goal-less. Manager Paul Gennard was on holiday, so Dingley mustered the players in the centre-circle and doled out the orange segments.

"For 25 minutes we was wonderful, really was," he told them. "The last 20, we ay been in it. We'm giving it away. We'm rushing. No one wants the responsibility,"

Dad once told me about the first time he took Mum to a Black Country pub, in the early 50s. He knew how to show a girl a good time. Some old-timers were playing dominoes in one corner. They grew louder and louder until, eventually, with each sharp word, she feared the worst. He insisted she was witnessing a conversation, not the preamble to murder. But she wouldn't have it.

I mention this to explain how I recognised the signs as half-time went on. Everyone was jabbering at once, like this: "Am I talking to meself?" "We're going to have a couple of subs. Robin's struggling, I want you to go centre-half." "You'm no good?" "I'll give it a couple." "Give it a couple." "Bass. Left side of midfield. Work hard. Plenty of balls, okay?" "When you put 'em under pressure, like I say, they gi' the ball away." "If anyone makes a remark on the sideline, ignore 'em. You get on wi' yer own job." "Does that include you?" "No, you take notice of me...."

Jezz paused, some of his men took a last drag, one ran for the bushes, another removed the joke-shop orange-peel grin from his mouth, and others laughed at him.

Jezz turned and pointed the lino's flag at one of his subs.

"I've done it already," the player turned his back.

"By the way," he finished as they dispersed, the flag still in his hand, "we doh play offside any more."

Puce, three minutes later, he yelled: "Everything's gone out the bastard window!"

It had. Gornal's Number 6, a slightly-built Asian lad on casters, had won the ball in midfield and glided through Tree's defence before picking his spot. Tuck might as well have been standing by the old bloke at the railings.

Eventually, I'd see the Trees for who they were, themselves, but not yet. To begin with, I'd see these men for who they weren't, the mates I'd played with, the legends of small, smelly dressing rooms and village pubs, the ones who didn't know when to play the ball to feet, or when to pass into space, the ones who shirked tackles, the ones half-a-yard late for a half-chance that went begging, or the ones who never yielded, who stood up to be counted, who knew where the ball was going, and went there first.

In other words, the blokes you could depend upon, the ones you couldn't, the ones you'd want alongside you in a scrap, the ones who'd go missing. If you've played, you can fill in your own names. If not, maybe you can wonder which one your lad or dad was.

So, when Tuck's brother Kevin – the dad who'd picked his lad up for the minute's silence, the sub who'd just replaced Mitch – restored Dingley's smile, two minutes later, by nodding the last ricochet of a bagatelle in to Scottie's stride, 12 yards out, I saw Nigel Davis in an Alcester Town shirt. One-apiece. The rain stopped.

A minute later, Yew Tree's Number 10 bundled Gornal's pint-sized keeper into the net. The ref blew. The guilty party was a barrel-shaped, crew-cut man answering simultaneously to the names Stan, Scurve and Craig. He had the air of a Staffordshire bull terrier chasing a meat-wagon. It was Stan, then, but I saw Womble Bisp.

"Penalty?" Scottie threw his arm up, laughing, but it might have been Martin Bradbury, 25 years before. The ref saw the joke, but not the keeper. He was counting his legs. Gornal's Number 7 didn't either. "Up it five!" he yelled. "Up it five!"

The next 40 minutes lacked nothing in huff and puff, but everything in rhythm, poise and thought. The Gornal players didn't appear to know what 'it' or 'five' were, so 'up it' they did not. From where I watched, though, 'it' had become dire. Then, like a scratchy 30s movie, the direness became strangely compelling. So bad it was good.

It had its moments, to be fair. Like when Ginger kicked his winger up in the air, and Stan went down like he'd been shot, no Gornal player within touching distance. The visitors'

Number 7 went to the rescue of both, asking the ref not to book the flame-haired loony at left-back, then breaking away to clear the cramp locking Stan's leg while the Trees showed their concern with another "Hah! Stan's broken his leg".

There was nothing from my past to use as a yardstick when the Gornal manager sent his first sub on, though. He was seven feet tall and shoe-horned into kit stitched for someone at least a foot shorter. He gave his name to the ref while the Trees stood, jaws gaping, praying he'd jog to someone else. In the end, he took station in front of the home back four. I couldn't see what expressions Yode, Gavin, Bran and Ginger were wearing, but it would be forgivable if they'd trumped a little nervous wind.

It wasn't long before the Big Mon collided with the ball 15 yards out and crashed a header against the angle. In the mêlée – some defenders trying to block the goal-bound ball, others more wisely not – one Gornal player ran into a post and collapsed beside the grounded Tucker. The rebound dropped straight into the keeper's lap.

Then the Big Mon scored. There's little point building the tension. They knew he was going to, I knew he was going to, and you knew it too. Big blokes nearly always score, in my experience, when they have a lump hammer on the end of their right leg.

The longer it stayed 1-2, the more I realised – in my private 70s and 80s flashback – how many bad games I'd been partly responsible for, the more I winced inwardly and the more I craved this one finding inspiration, as if – by association – it would also rewrite once-forgotten moments. The closer the final whistle came, the further away salvation seemed, yet the match ended 4-3, so that shows you how little I knew about this bunch, and how I'd forgotten that a game can turn in the blink of an eye.

I have two mates – Dave Plim and Martin Bradbury – who watched the 1979 Arsenal-Man United FA Cup Final on TV. Four minutes from time, they were sitting comfortably, and so were the Gooners at 2-0 (Talbot, Stapleton). Then United won a free kick and the phone rang. Plimmy ran out and Gordon McQueen's boot brought United hope. The cheer from the front room signalled the moment. Wrong number.

Two minutes later, Steve Coppell sent Sammy McIlroy away, and the doorbell went. The little girl from up the road – presumably told to find something to do – wanted to take the dog for a walk. Another roar. McIlroy had equalised.

Plimmy rushed in, 86 minutes of his life disappearing down the pan, but thankful for extra time. He grabbed Bramble, then the lead, and United's Gary Bailey missed a cross. So did Plimmy. Alan Sunderland didn't. Three-two. How we laughed.

It's shaped many a decision about leaving a match early. So, although Tree's comeback was unexpected, at least I saw it.

There are only a couple of incidents I remember from the 90 minutes. A moment after Gornal took a 2-3 lead, Kev Tucker rolled the ball into an empty net from six yards. The keeper – already pasted by Stan – collapsed, gripping his hip, while Tucker raced off towards the line, attempting something gymnastic, and failing. His dad had been talking about the Harborne game as the shot went in.

"Only 29," he nodded at Kev, and I nearly accused him of lying, because he looked 40. "Bad knee. Bad since he was 16. Stopped Conference sides coming in for him."

I felt a twinge. Bad knee. These days, they have a fancy name for it. I looked it up on the internet that night. It said: "Osgood-Schlatter (say: oz-good shlot-ter) disease is one of the most common causes of knee pain in young athletes. It causes swelling, pain and tenderness just below the knee, over the shin bone (the tibia). It occurs mostly in boys who are having a growth spurt during their pre-teen or teenage years. It's most common in young athletes who play football, soccer or basketball. Osgood-Schlatter disease usually goes away with time." Usually, but not always. Osgood I knew, but it didn't say who Schlot-ter had played for, if you were wondering.

I digress, and I confess. From the depths of direness, tension had emerged. Gornal's Number 7 was screaming things like "If we don't shoot, we don't know", and "Put some snow on it". Stan's call for Tuck to "Take some bastard off it", when he kicked from his hands, was poor by comparison. At 3-3, touchline talk had switched from Ginger's failed Saturday night fumble to the prospect of a golden goal.

A minute into extra time, the ball arrived at Dave Taylor's feet, 20 yards out. A moment to compose himself was called for, maybe another to run over the trigonometry, and then a breath to shoot. But he hesitated for three or four seconds, his mind swamped with possibilities, and he hit the ball tamely at the keeper. More of a back-pass, really. Dingley threw his hands in the air and let out a strangled cry.

"He didn't know whether to pass it, sit on it, fart on it…!"

Unsurprisingly, Tree's record was about to extend to P3 W0 D1 L2.

Ten minutes into extra-time, Phil Tucker spread himself twice in a split-second, first denying the lad on casters, then the Big Mon. It was more than Stan could take.

"Put the flag up!" he yelled at his team-mate running the line, his face purple.

"Gavin was playing him on," the lino shrugged, a clue to where he felt the balance between honour and honesty lay.

"It doesn't matter, just put your flag up!" Stan screamed, doing the same.

A minute on, he was ripping his shirt off.

"You run your bollocks off and they don't give a fucking bollocks," he screamed, adding "Fucking arseholes!" for good measure. Gornal had headed the winner. A soft goal. Not the first and, I suspected, not the last.

Stan didn't stop to explain who 'they' were, and it didn't seem my place to enquire. He stalked off up the hill without stopping to help take the nets down.

Rob walked into the changing room a few minutes later, defeated, but evidently less so than his pal. Stan put his arm round the Old Mon's shoulder.

"I'm sorry about that. I day mean it, like. I just lost me temper," he admitted.

"I can understand," Rob nodded, trying to extinguish the flames. "You worked hard out there. You was loosed down again, mate. I understand how you feel."

"I know," Stan said, trying to cool down, but not succeeding. "I'm so pissed off…." And he started again.

I found that out a week later, as Rob sipped the top off a pint of Banks's and slid me a J20 across the table in the Smoke Room at the Yew Tree, a snug, purple-upholstered sanctuary in a stout 50s pub set amid 60s semis and bungalows, high above the scattered lights of Merry Hill Shopping Centre.

The drive up had shown me a different Black Country, different as places sometimes are lit by the moon and street lamps. The Halesowen Road was quiet, houses and factories looking as if they'd been lined up in the chill autumn night air, empty, ready for Wednesday. The landscape was littered with evidence of the generations that had shaped this place – red bricks, soot-rimmed chimneys, Walter Somers, the factory at the heart of the Iraq supergun affair, the Boilermaker Arms – but there was little sign of those who lived here now.

I'd been in this nicotine-stained, windowless Smoke Room before, one sunny Sunday lunchtime, a couple of months earlier, when I'd sat with Jezz Dingley to explore what a season with Yew Tree Rangers might hold, and whether they'd have me. Within a few minutes that day, Rob had arrived and shaken my hand. Phil and Paula Tucker turned up a few minutes after that, then Paul Gennard.

The outlook hadn't been bright. Dingley had had six players signed, yet the league required a squad of at least 16. He wasn't that optimistic of signing many more, either. The name on most lips had been Gavin Skidmore. Only the Outlaw Josey Wales had notched more victims in the previous season. The pitches of the Warley League were littered with the remains of so many broken bodies that the league wouldn't let Gavin sign again. But, if he didn't, how many others would?

This room was also where Jezz, Rob and a few others had started Yew Tree Rangers a year before, after the secretary's wife at Albron gave manager Dingley the shove the night a 4-1 win put them top of the table, a conversation which went "You'm sacked!", "Yo cor sack me. Yo doh pay me!" So this room had history.

The Dortmund-Liverpool Champions League game echoed from the Bar. Sky TV. We talked Warley League instead. I'd opened a notebook, but I nudged it past the Apple & Mango and the scratchings. The questions I needed answering weren't the ones I'd jotted on the page. They weren't the kind you asked a stranger, your host, not yet anyway. Questions like "Are you going to be worth watching?" or "Will you ever be better than this?" This wasn't the time, or the room.

"It's a shame we'm having this conversation now, as opposed to two seasons ago," Rob raised the subject himself, drawing on a cigarette and sipping from a tankard bought by his lads and kept behind the bar. "We'd won Division 3 and it's more or less the same team really. We was saying the other day, our preparation ay changed at all. Saturdays, we do what we do. We managed to win Division 3, by eight points. This year we've gone up again, and some of these lads, it's a bit tough for 'em. We could've done with another season in Division 2 and had a settling down period.

"We had three or four players last year, and they made the difference. There was more football in 'em. Some of the lads, they've still got a kid's way of looking at it. I'm 37. Towards the end of me career. If you're involved, you don't see so much of it. But if you're on the side, some of it looks terrible." I didn't disagree.

"We can give as good as we get, but the bottom line is that we *am* a footballing team. Believe me, all we're out for is a laugh. We stick together, we go out drinking together. Some of 'em work together. So they'm… it's like one big family."

I asked him to tell me more, and he picked up where Jezz's touchline briefing had tailed off, starting with Phil Tucker.

"Phil," he said, and my mind went to the eighth minute at Harborne, to Tuck's run to meet that throw-in, to the dip in the six-yard box, to his leap to clear it from a patch of grass six inches lower than his legs were expecting. If it's possible, it was funnier thinking about it again than when it had happened. Now, though, I could laugh out loud.

"I've known Phil a few years. He started out as centre-half, for the Liberal Club. He's been in goal five or six years. Phil's about 30." He paused again and, this time, my mind went to the Barrel game and Paula's 'Don't be a prick' suggestion.

"His only fault, as I see, is decisions… whether to come off his line or stay. These kind of decisions. And command his area a bit more. But that's the only thing… And he don't talk. Keepers, you need 'em screaming all the while. The good keepers do. But, Phil… he ay bad. We give him a bit of stick. Occasionally, he'll go down and it's through his legs. 'Oh, no!' You know what I mean? But… shot-stopping he's good at. And he's brave." He took another sup, lit another cigarette.

The teamsheets so far had been an unexplained collection of first names, surnames and nicknames that had travelled with these blokes most of their lives and were fixed as firmly as the broad shoulders of their stock. Like Yode.

"Yode? I've only known him last season. He's about the same age as Ant, about 25. He played at school with 'em, and at Netherton Colts through the age groups."

"Ginger?"

"Ginge is actually a good player. He was on Leeds' books. If it's a back four, I prefer Tigs there, I must admit. He keeps goal-side, whereas Ginger tends to drift. He leaves his man, the ball comes through and then he's chasing him, you know. He's the same age, 24 or 25."

"Fiery."

"He is, isn't he?" He laughed and supped and sucked on his cigarette. "There's one or two, they'm out for a laugh, and he's one of 'em. He's a top lad."

Not as desperate to win as Stan, though.

"But, then, Stan loses his rag and throws his shirt because of the likes of Ginger."

A pattern was emerging, and I thought back to Harborne again, to Paul Gennard's second-half lament, as Yew Tree were pulled apart. Twenty two pints or two? "They want to play football. We want to have a drink".

"This is the hard part," Rob nodded. "You've got six or seven, it's 100 per cent. There's Ant, meself, Stan, Mark, he's the same. The will to win. Gavin, Craig, his brother…. Yoder, he's up for it. Phil in goal. He don't mean to do these things."

I mentioned Mitch, the man who seemed to see the things others didn't.

"Good player, isn't he? He plays for Dudley Town, with his brother, Scott. Bass wants to do well because it's us lot. But Scott..." another pause, "... If we've got 100 per cent commitment, Scott's got 80. Saturdays, he'll have the hundred. Mitch is different, 100 per cent commitment all the time. That *is* just Mitch."

"What about Yosser?" I'd watched him twice now.

"Young Yosser? Tell you what, his ability is unreal."

"If he was three stone lighter," I said, but Rob finished my sentence, "... he'd be at a higher level. All these tricks. His brother's even better. They'm both called Yosser. There's Yosser and Yosser.

"Gavin's committed," I offered. He laughed and blushed.

"Gavin's only problem, and you're going to say it's mine, is discipline. Most of it's his own trouble, moaning at the ref and linesmen. He gets himself into trouble, but his commitment... and he's fit. He doh carry no weight. I like Gavin. Good player."

I described my view of the defender's Harborne yellow card.

"Sometimes it's not the tackle, it's what he says after. He's in his face. 'That worn't a foul!' Niggle, niggle. After 15 minutes of that, you'm on the wrong side of the ref. We had to write a letter to the league," he went on, and the pre-season poser Jezz Dingley had outlined emerged. "The league banned him. Apparently, they'd got one sending off against Gavin, and he worn't even sent off! Their mistake."

A Tree family photo was developing. Kev and Phil Tucker were brothers. Phil was married to Paula. She was Gavin's and Craig's sister.... Rob picked up the thread.

"Scott and Mitchell, they'm brothers. Me and Ant, I'm married to his sister, so we'm brother-in-law. You know big Ant?" – I didn't – "You've got Gavin and Craig. Stan and Mark, they'm brothers. Dave Taylor's their cousin. It's unreal, like.

"Their mum comes to watch every Sunday too," he added. "Lin."

"Grey anorak?" I asked. He nodded and stood up to ring the bar bell. I stuck with Vitamin C and asked about his job.

"I work on the roads, putting gas into houses. Mainly in the Birmingham area. Most of the lads have physical jobs. Which seems strange, doesn't it, to do a physical job all week, then play football?" I wasn't so sure. "On the shovels, sweat coming off me nose. Without training, you're already training. You'm using your legs, your back.

"You work all week, you've got to do this, you've got to do that, whatever, the pressures at home – not pressures, but general life. Then, Sundays, you get together, you have a laugh, try your best. Well, some of us do. And if we win, the joy of winning. In 40 years time, we'll all be playing bowls together, or crib!"

"Or watching your kids playing..."

"... or their kids. It goes on and on and on. My lads play. All three. The wife, her keeps running round, dropping him here, and him there. Me dad had one lung out when he was young, but he still went to games me uncle was playing."

The tradition was continuing. Young James, Dan and Aaron often watched dad.

"They love the banter, they know the lads as mates. They love it."

And they were all following in dad's boot-steps too. Aaron, the youngest, had been playing a year. When he started, they struck a deal, a pound for every goal he scored. It lasted until he bagged 11 in a 13-2 win and Rob had another idea.

"Every goal I score, give me 50 pence. Every goal you score, I'll give you a quid."

One week, before the falling out Jess had mentioned, their old team Albron were playing at Halesowen. At 2-7, they were awarded a penalty, and Rob put the ball on the spot.

"Our babby'd finished and he come running over and he shouted at me 'Dad! I scored three!' The secretary said 'Your dad's scored five… and he's got a penalty'."

Aaron did the only thing he could.

"Jezz, don't let Dad take it!"

Rob scored, but Aaron was up by the end of the season.

Our chat went on. For two hours, maybe more. We talked about Rob's wife Tracey, treasurer to James' team, Yew Tree Rangers Youth, about Dan playing for Netherton Colts, and about Aaron signing for a team in Dudley. We talked about James telling a teacher he wouldn't fill in for two mates at district trials, because he didn't want to be third choice. Fourteen going on 24. About him maybe joining the police force, after a year on the shovels with dad, to shape him up, "grafting alongside real down-to-earth, basic people, so he'll be able to understand what makes a working man tick".

And we talked about the links between past and present, about an old boy called Lenny who'd taken Rob under his wing as a young mechanic, passing wisdom down the line. All the little tricks. Football's the same.

His folks used to push him in a pram to watch his Uncle Roger play for Parkdale. Now they'd watch Rob in the morning and, in the afternoon, one of the lads.

"They love it. 'Look, he's gone off again, just like our Roger!' It's as though there's something that's been put there by older generations."

Roger's dad – Rob's maternal grandfather – had grown up in Netherton. His hands had helped to strike Titanic's anchor chain, and he'd had three brothers, enough evidence in Rob's book to add weight to the theory that there's a football gene.

"It's law, ay it?" he added, a question that asked 'Do you think like me?' rather than 'Am I right or wrong?'

He'd long since described the fields down the hill from the pub – where his mates had their pitch, and their street team played the street from Lodge Farm – by the time Liverpool drew in Dortmund. And the noise in the Bar had long since subsided to a murmur by the time I looked at my watch. Rob laughed.

"Our Aaron, he come back from school the other week and said 'Dad, d'you mind if I support Liverpool as well?' I said 'Yes'. He says 'No. D'you mind if I support Liverpool as well, 'cos me mates do'. 'Yes'. He said 'Well, d'you mind….' 'Yes!' Five mates support Liverpool, and he must have felt the pressure. 'Wolves are crap'.

"It's like me dad. He supports the Baggies. Me Uncle Roger, he supports the Villa, me cousin supports Wolves, and I support Wolves. Late 60s, through the 70s, one week we'd go up the Albion, next week Villa, then the Wolves. Our neighbour, he used to stick his head over the fence and shout 'Up the Wolves!' It's in yer head at five or six. I can remember saying 'I support the Wolves'. It's making a statement.

"I used to be Georgie Best mad, even though I support the Wolves. I'd always got a Man United shirt, white collar, Georgie Best boots, lace up at the side. Even when I score today, I always try to take the keeper on, drop my shoulder, and try to walk it in. Then I come out of the goal going 'Georgie, Georgie, they call him the Belfast Boy'.

"Ginger, he'll score a goal now at five-a-side and he'll go 'Bergkamp!' because he supports Arsenal. 'Bergkamp!' He's never been there. It's just a name to him. Yosser supports Arsenal. That's it nowadays, ay it? Following mainstream. But that's football. From Sundays, to Juventus, to England, whatever. It ay just 11 and 11. It's families and communities. It just extends out... A team finds you. It's brilliant, ay it?"

3 OVER THE TOP

BEYOND THE RAILINGS, IN GREEN LETTERS, on a white noticeboard emerging from the last trace of early mist, I read 'Hillcrest Community College', then 'Proud of our Success'. As this was a Sunday morning, 'Proud of our Excess' would have been nearer the mark. Barrel, Harborne, Gornal Bush. Drawn, lost, lost. Enough said.

I'd left Baptist End seven days before with a sinking feeling. Then I'd shared the Smoke Room with Rob Wall, and the outlook had changed. Harborne had been bad, Gornal worse, but something burned deep inside him and it had warmed me, so maybe I wouldn't step straight out of the Yew Tree into the Last Chance Saloon. Maybe.

There were still questions I hadn't been able to ask him, though, a sign that my quest was worthwhile. And there it was, beyond the bus-stop, stout, a little care-worn but with an air of permanence. The Hope Tavern. Any metaphor in a storm.

I'd aimed to watch from now on with sensors tuned to Rob Wall's view that "For six or seven, it's 100 per cent every week", but with question marks on the others. The next three games would sort them out, though I'd only see two of them.

The first was against Midfoam in the first round of the West Bromwich Albion Cup, not that I knew it as I strolled up the line during what's loosely termed as a 'warm-up', my face now drawing a nod of recognition from most Tree followers, even if few of them knew what was going round my head.

So, Tuck was quiet and occasionally wobbly, Gavin and Bran were Regan and Carter, Yode was a Tonka Toy, and Tigs was tiny. Yoss was plump but blessed, Stan emotional, Mark committed, Mitch talented, Scottie tanned, and Rob injured.

Then there was Ginger. The left-back looked like the result of Bart Simpson's one-night stand with a rugrat. He was running round with his backside hanging out of his shorts. Actually, backside's too genteel. His arse. The vile moment only ended when he ran to a loose ball, yelled "Bergkamp!", and blasted it a mile over the bar.

Scott Gennard was on the line, talking with two others about the length of the slash up Posh Spice's dress on *Parkinson*. They only broke off to hurl abuse at Ginger.

I paused to ask them who Yew Tree were playing. They didn't know.

I asked them which cup it was. They didn't know that either.

Ginger jogged up to quiz Scott about his love life and, for a moment, I had a flashback as the gentle breeze drifting down from the Rowley Hills blew the strangely intoxicating smell of liniment at me, closely followed by the sickly-sweet trace of last night's aftershave.

In my search for the 100-per cent men, the game produced little to rouse. So I was pondering the relative merits of a three or four-star car wash on the way home when Mark Horton, Tree's Number 4, won possession on the edge of his area and passed the ball wide down the right. He didn't leave it there, and I still thank the Lord he didn't, for it had the air of a something he intended to finish himself, 60 yards away, if he could meet his date with destiny.

I'm still uncertain whether it was the lope of his stride down the hill, or the fact that most people fell silent as he advanced, but there was a painful inevitability about what was unfolding before our eyes. As the cross was cut back from the byline, he turned from a young gazelle to an old man watching the No 42 pull slowly away from the bus-stop, knowing he didn't have the legs to catch it. The ball swung over and dipped towards the far post. He launched himself to intercept, horizontal, arms tucked into his side, aerodynamically-efficient, but not aerodynamically-efficient enough, like a half-finished Exocet.

He hit the ground, nose first, and slid through the crusty ripples of last year's goal-mouth mud to a halt by the far post. The ball had long gone. He picked himself up and began the long trek back, his gallantry honoured by the laughter ringing in his ears, waving two fingers at a touchline suggestion that someone ought to collect him in a car.

The sun had vanished and I was wandering past Paul Gennard when Tree's new keeper made a hesitant dash to intercept a through-ball. There was no danger, not from where I was standing. But, a yard to my left, the manager shook his head.

The keeper in Tucker's place was young but familiar to the rest. They called him Chubbs. In the pre-match kick-in, he'd dropped the ball twice, tripped over it once and missed most of the shots fired in to test him. Nerves, maybe. Or maybe not.

"It's going to be six," I'd heard someone say. "He's gunna have one o' them days."

Now Paul Gennard was muttering "We've got to get another keeper". It was the start of a recurring theme. The next few minutes saw the start of another when a Midfoam defender leathered the ball into the bramble-covered no man's land beyond the pitch. Jezz sprinted to grab the stepladders, scaled the railings and began probing the thorns. Gennard and Dingley. The two men who drew the Trees together, somehow, every Sunday, yet watched what followed from opposite sides of the pitch. In the space of two minutes, the faces of bemusement and despair had become fixed in my mind.

Two minutes after that, so had another. Yode, Tree's rugged, no-nonsense right-back, took a boot in the face. He went down, stood up and wobbled. The more he wobbled, the more he insisted he was fine. Yode, a man for whom work surely involved knocking down brick walls. One of Rob Wall's 100 per cent men.

Dingley dropped the ladders, sprinted to his first-aid bag, dashed back up the Cabbage Patch and did something with a sponge.

Neither he nor Yode had regained their composure before Tree went ahead when Ginger, little legs pumping like Thomas the Tank Engine, ran on to a pass from Tigs and chipped the keeper from 18 yards. One-nil. He ran along the line, arms swirling, gurning, clearly pleased, with his mates in pursuit, doing the same. Scrappy turned to happy.

A minute on, the lead doubled when Tree's Number 9 found poise and netted a rebound. He looked like he'd been dragged through a hedge backwards, then dragged through it again, forwards. Possibly the scruffiest player I've ever seen.

"What's his name?" I asked Jezz Dingley.

"They call him Opple," Jezz said. "Bass's mate."

That was it. Two-nil. It should have been five. Still, a win's a win. And a cup tie safely negotiated, too. I breathed a sigh of relief.

About the time the next game kicked off, I was 400 miles and almost a century away, on the Somme, watching a wreath being laid at the grave of an Unknown Soldier of the Worcestershire Regiment, a private whose body had been found by workmen digging a cable trench six years before. It was one poignant moment among many on a five-day trip with my close friend and newsroom colleague John Phillpott in search of clues that might take us a step closer to discovering his identity, 85 years on, we hoped. Still do.

By the time the Bengals match action ended, John and I were in the infamous Sunken Road, near Beaucourt, standing in the footprints of a handful of men of the 1st Battalion Lancashire Fusiliers who'd been filmed minutes before going over the top at the start of the Battle of the Somme. We crawled up a steep, slippery bank and stared at a small wood about 200 yards away across No Man's Land, to where a German machinegun had been waiting at 7.30am on Saturday, July 1, 1916.

I was holding a copy of a frame of that film as we walked through Beaumont-Hamel Cemetery, half-way between the Sunken Road and the German line, a few minutes later, pausing at grave after grave of Fusiliers, men aged 19, 20, 24, the engravings on each headstone reading as a caption to the image immortalised 10 minutes before these men had gone over the top, 10 minutes before they were ripped apart running head-on into a wall of fire.

Jezz's e-mail was waiting for me when I arrived home. It told me two things. First, he'd either been ill or day-dreaming the day his English teacher did the spelling test that included 'hat-trick' and 'wrapped'. Second, and most important, it brought good news.

From: Jeremy Dingley
To: Mark Higgitt
Sent: Monday, October 01, 2001 2:52 PM
Subject: Yew Tree v Walsall Bengals 30/9/01

Hi Mark hope you've enjoyed your holiday in France. Some good news to report. We have finally won a league game. The score was 4-1, against Walsall Bengals, but it wasn't easy. We went in at half time 1-0 down. We should have had it all rapped up by half time. Second half we played a little better but could not score. Then came the turning point. We brought two subs on Robin & Bass on for Stan & Opple, up front. Then we brought Meese on for Justin. With about 20 minutes left Gavin scored the equaliser. Then the oldmon (Robin) produced some magic, by scoring an hatrict in 6 minutes. Hope you don't mind me sending this. Look forward to seeing you, JEZZ.

A league win to follow the cup victory. I'd missed it, but I'd been right to stick it out, after all. That night, I played the tape of my chat with Rob, about a bunch of men who'd grown up in each other's pockets, who left family behind every week, and fought over 100 yards of stud-scarred earth, then went home again, eventually. Sons of Netherton, doing what sons of North West Lancashire were doing that same day.

Almost 85 years before, it could easily have been their great-grandfathers' faces frozen in time in the Sunken Road, then left behind where they fell. Mind you, if such a film had been run on, my guess was they'd have found something to argue about before going over the top.

My tatty A-Z and I had seen many places in 25 years, but we nearly parted company the next weekend. Not all thoughts in my Ford Escort sanctuary were about soccer or Jezz's blood pressure. Not all about the Twin Towers, either, or Liverpool. Some had been scarily close to the meaning of life. On the Rood End Road, though, passing the same factory a third time, the Big Question was neither sporting nor philosophical. It was: Where the hell's West Smethwick Park?

I eventually found it, a patchwork of tree-lined paths and pitches set amid leafy roads flanked by tidy 30s semis which, to my eyes, looked like homes where the Black Country had first tried to grow a middle-class. Having found it, I drove past most of them twice, looking for Pitch 5. By the time I glimpsed Tree's scarlet-and-black stripes playing George Celtic's green-and-white hoops, the game had started.

I saw Tuck first. He looked unhappy. Then I saw the sling.

"Injured?"

"Ah. Broken collarbone," he nodded in a kind of tut, unable to shrug his shoulders.

"How d'you manage that?"

"Trying to stop a fight."

"How did that happen?"

"Gavin and Craig. Last Saturday night. Social club at Wollescote. They wuz 'aving a row."

"What about?"

"Som'at saft. Might as well have let 'em carry on. I tried to separate 'em and fell, and all the weight went on me shoulder. I got up, me shoulder was here." He lifted his left hand level with his right ear.

"Good night then?"

"Ah!"

"What did Paula say?"

"She worn't too bad after we'd gone down the hospital. Three in the morning we came out."

He was done for the season, waiting for the bone to be pinned, but he still ran down the slippery bank to fetch the ball, one-handed, when it went into touch. The back of my knees went funny every time it flew past after that, so I raced to fetch it myself.

The Tree side had picked itself, as I recall. Scott and a couple of the others were in Blackpool, Rob had gone down with a virus the night before, and Mitch Gennard, the manager's son, was injured. Even Jezz was at work.

Mitch sauntered up the touchline, protected against the chilly breeze by a T-shirt. How Tree could have done with him. Nevertheless, as half-time approached, a strange wave of optimism arrived with the sun. I should have known better.

Apart from being the Bart Simpson's illegitimate son, I should mention that Ginger had the touch of a Gazza about him. Not so much the sublime balletic ability to conjure space from nothing, because someone who runs like Thomas the Tank Engine could never have Swan Lake as a backing track, but more the tendency to thumb the self-destruct button when life seemed so good.

Three minutes before the top was due off the orange-box, with Tree a goal up, he made a niggly attempt at a tackle 10 yards inside his half. The Celtic player shrugged him off, so it wasn't even a good foul – not a suggestion I'd make if Dad was around because, naturally, there's no such a thing. The whistle blew, but Ginger turned and red mist descended. Effing off, though, wasn't something the man in black planned to do, despite Ginger's suggestion. My heart sank and my blood simmered.

"We'll be lucky if this is a yellow," Paul Gennard quietly shook his head. Luck didn't come into it. Red. Mitch didn't turn his head as the left-back passed, but he did offer an opinion.

"Twat, that was," he said.

Ginger: "What was it for?"

Mitch: "Still a twat."

"That'll be 20 quid," Mitch's dad added for good measure.

On the line, Stan and Mark Horton's mum Lin was fuming too. She was simmering as the players ended the first-half, and coming to the boil as they stubbed out their fags, discarded orange peel and adjusted their bits a few minutes later.

"He shouldn't have been in the side anyway," she steamed and pointed at Ginger. "He turned up late." We'd return to the theme before the week was out.

Ten minutes after the restart, the shamed left-back's mobile went. We heard one side of the conversation.

"At the football," he said, then, "Cos I bin sent off. The ref said I swore, but I day."

"Only told him to fuck off," Mitch said without taking his eyes off the play.

"Well, I said 'Fuck off'," Ginger conceded, "but not to him. It wor even a foul!"

Wisely, he steered clear of Lin. She was far from happy, anyway. Stan had fallen over on the pitch not long after Ginger's rush of blood and younger son Mark had heckled his brother from the line.

"You can stop that," she scolded. "At least he wants to win."

"I want to win," he answered back, "but he's always laughing at me."

"Act like a man," she ordered, and he did.

Two-nil wouldn't have flattered Tree, but the second goal never came. Instead, five minutes on, Celtic's Number 8 picked up a loose ball 18 yards out. Chubbs, Tree's new 17-year-old keeper, stepped forward a pace, the lace of his right boot undone, and planted his feet. That's where they stayed. One-one.

Tree's response, however, was startling – and two more recurring themes were added to the growing list. First Yosser mesmerised three Celtic players with a drag-back and shimmy that lacked only *Putting on the Ritz* as its theme and released Meesey. The bulky, head-down midfielder, a bit-part player so far, danced a few steps of his own, socks at half-mast, shirt flapping, and unleashed a drive I never imagined to be in his gift. It cannoned off the angle. The keeper, heroic until now, smacked his head on the post and wobbled along the line before sinking to his knees. He was still wobbling when Yosser flicked the ball up and volleyed from 30 yards a moment later. The ball brushed the bar. Casual beauty. You'd have paid to see it.

"It'll go to extra time if it stays like this," Paul Gennard rubbed a hand across his stubbled chin, and two thoughts occurred to me. First, there were weary legs among his men. Second, extra time? I'd been under the impression this was a league match.

Whatever, like me, he really should have known better. With five minutes left, Chubbs parried a speculative shot and was helpless as the rebound was side-footed home by a prowling man in hoops. The young keeper hadn't played badly, but he sank to his knees, dejected. Not as dejected as Stan, predictably.

"You play your guts out for 90 minutes and, because that twat gets sent off, we lose," he yelled at the final whistle and scowled at Ginger.

It was hard to disagree but, with his mood a little raw, not the time to say so. Instead, I watched him stamp past his mother. So did she. Just as she'd watched him stamp round all morning.

I didn't know at the time, but Birmingham County FA's guess was that between 50,000 and 60,000 players were registered within its region. It meant an incredible amount of broken wind, bad language and flabby arses had been aired on the parks and playing fields of England's industrial heartland that weekend. Enough, perhaps, to fill The Hawthorns and Molineux, with a little to spare for Villa Park – though there were some who'd have started in Aston and left it at that.

As far as Ford Escort thoughts go, this one occurred to me as I drove past a sign for Rood End Road, in Oldbury. Lin Horton exposed herself to more than her fair share of this every Sunday. What, in the reign of Sam, possessed her?

4   THE WORKING MAN

ON THE WAY TO LIN HORTON'S, THERE ARE ROADSIGNS saying you've entered the Black Country. Like you've crossed a border.

Ignore them. The Black Country isn't a place, because it doesn't appear on maps. It's not a region, either, because it has no boundaries. If it's anything, it's a presence, something to be felt, a state of mind. Whether you're there or not is based on trust because, if you ask him, the Black Country's wherever a Black Countryman says it is.

It wasn't discovered, and it wasn't declared. It emerged slowly from the Ten Yard coal seam, a rich, carbon backbone fleshed with limestone, ironstone and clay beneath the rolling hills and fields of north Worcestershire and south Staffordshire. When the Industrial Revolution brought canals in the 1780s, it was consumed by the filth that belched from its hell-fire iron foundries and grim chain and anchor shops. The people who gave it life saw it for what it was, as they do today. Black country. It seemed reasonable. There, a history lesson in around 150 words.

Netherton's as Black Country as anywhere can be. Halfway between Dudley and Brierley Hill, its name comes from the Anglo-Saxon for "the lower settlement". For the first villagers, that was a hillside in the shadow of a Saxon church. By early Victorian times, most were scraping a living making chains and nails in backyard furnaces. Many families were large, drawn from the fields, earning starvation wages. Death often came a-knocking, especially for children. Homes were cheaply built and health was poor. Competition for work in a booming population witnessing invention after labour-saving invention was harsh, and violent. The canals carried barges in laden with the raw materials, and took the finished products out again. When the railways came, they did the same.

The heritage of heavy industry survived until the 70s. Then it hit hard times again. Now it looks tired and forgotten, if you catch it on a bad day. Content and forgotten, on a good.

Netherton's town centre hasn't changed much in the past hundred years. Where the landmarks up from Old Hill in the early 1900s would have taken me past Newton's (the fancy draper), Pargeter's (the grocery), Hingley's Chain & Anchor Works, Talbot's (boot and shoe maker) and Roberts (pawnbroker) – among dozens of other butchers, bakers and fork-handle makers – my drive to Lin's home substituted places like Panny's Palace (chip shop), Wilf Gilbert (bookies), Netherton Labour Club opposite, the Newspapers and Convenience Store, and the Saxon Motor Company.

Though the landscape around and beyond the buildings flanking the Halesowen Road and Cinder Bank had changed dramatically, the geographical and psychological ground covered by Stan's directions to the family home had stood the test of time, as near as matters. It went like this: "Turn right into Swan Street at the Hope Tavern, left at the bottom by the White Swan, down to the roundabout by The Lion."

Their neat 60s terrace, disappointingly, could have been on any suburban estate from

Croydon to Carluke. A part of me was hoping it would be old enough to boast a ghost or two. The last Black Country house I'd set foot in was my Uncle Len's, at his funeral. I can remember the hall, because it was the only room I went in. He was laid out in the front room. It was a dark day, in every sense.

Stan was laid out in the Hortons' front room, too, signed off by the hospital from night shift duties as a medical supplies supervisor in Leicester, a commuting Black Countryman. He'd wounded his hip as well as his pride against George Celtic. The way he'd gone down, the rhino that hit him must have started its run-up in Langley.

Mark was sprawled on the sofa with his girlfriend, Sam, recovering from a day designing central heating systems. Man United were playing Olympiakos on TV. Champions League. Sky TV. Mega-money. We call it progress. Discuss.

"You play your guts out and, because that twat gets sent off, we lose," Stan had said on the Sunday. Lin had said nothing. Quiet and composed beside the pitch, I'd looked down the line, at times, and wondered whether this would have been like looking at my grandmother, 70 years before, a gran I'd never known, a mother of eight boys, all footballers, and wife to a man who'd helped run Oldbury United.

Lin sat me down in the back room, tutted, then walked in to the kitchen to make tea. I was gagging for a mug-full, but I heard the chink of best china.

"It was league, so we'm right down, ay we?" she said, talking about three points thrown away. "We'm about third or fourth from bottom.

"It was that Ginge, worn't it?" she called. "If Paul had kept to his agreement… Like Carl Evans says, what happened to 'If you ay here for the time, you don't play'? He worn't there. He phoned our house and our Brian says 'Well, if you ay gone, I'll run you over to see if they'm there'. He'd already phoned and told Mark he was borrowing Mitch's van. So he got a taxi from this house to Mitch's to get the works van to get over there. Well, it's wrong. He should've put Justin on instead of Clark – that's his name, Ginger. And Paul says he made a mistake. Which cost us the game."

It was a hell of an opening, but I shouldn't have been surprised. Before the Midfoam match, I'd seen her watching two teams on the wrong pitch. It had taken her minutes to realise that her boys weren't there, let alone the fact that no one was wearing black-and-scarlet shirts. It had occurred to me then that her whole married life might be based on the error of turning up at the wrong wedding and thinking 'Seeing as I'm here, I might as well get married!'

This evening went the same way. Trying to follow her was like watching a tornado rip through a ping-pong ball factory. For an hour, Ginger was rarely far from her lips, once she'd spared a thought for the other Craig, Gavin Skidmore's brother, who'd ploughed a thankless furrow after Ginger's red card.

"He ran his heart out," she said, and I liked her for noticing because, as every midfielder knows – I'd been one – his job's thankless when the full-back behind him has told the ref to eff-off. Then she added: "Mind you, he can be a little cow bag, too, when he starts."

Ginger, then. In no particular order of importance, three examples – starting with how long her lads had played in the same team.

"They was at Albron, wor they? It was a shame 'er spoilt that," she paused, referring to the woman who'd tried to sack Jezz the night a victory had put their old team top of the division. "All right, I like to watch, but I wouldn't interfere."

"That was over Ginger," she said, an early indication that he was automatically the prime suspect for anything unexplained and unsavoury, the disappearance of Shergar, for instance, or the unexplained second gunman on the grassy knoll.

And, when I carelessly wondered how long Stan's moods lasted after a bad day.

"He goes for a drink, he comes home. Well, this Sunday, he come home early because he was in pain. He must've been, 'cos he's come home at half-past two. He turns round and says 'That bloody Ginger....'"

"What would you have done if he was your lad?"

"I'd have told him off. I know my kids won't swear... all right, they swear. But I don't think they'd go that far. Everybody loses their rag, but you don't say that to the ref! You might say that under your breath, but he shouted it. Everybody heard!"

And this, when I asked why the person who moaned the most was the first to tell someone else to 'Let it go'.

"I don't know. At the end of the day, they'm all good lads. Mind you, Ginger, it's got nothing to do with football, he went on holiday with our kids. He was going out with my niece. A couple of days in, he wanted to come 'ome. So, instead of letting him come 'ome on his own, my nephew come 'ome with him. Just 'cos he wanted to get back to my niece! They fell out in any case."

Somewhere in between, it became apparent why football was a religion in the Horton household. The engraved trophies filling the cabinet behind me – "the top un's the babby's, the bottom's the Big Un's" – was the biggest clue. Mark had done better than his brother, including a season with the Baggies that he'd hated because they hadn't let him play his way. I'd only known him a few weeks, but that didn't surprise me.

"He day like that," she said, and twisted in her chair.

Now, at 20, when he put his mind to it, he was a good player, desperate to win, but not as desperate as Stan. I'd mentioned the half of their veins that was pumping beer, and she'd shared her view of the balance in a working man's life.

"When they've been toiling all week, you can't say Saturday nights are out," she nodded, "but my kids always turn up. They don't like to let their team down.

"He was 23 the other day, Craig," she said, to prove the point. "You know he had that terrible weekend last weekend?"

I hadn't noticed any difference.

"That's why. 'Cos he was 23 and they had to go and celebrate."

"What makes you go every Sunday?" I asked. No one else's mother did. She smiled.

"I done it since they started. I had to go in the morning to see Mark, and in the afternoon to see Craig. When they both played Sunday afternoon, it got hard."

"Was football part of your life with your dad?"

"Me dad liked football but, having three girls, he'd got no chance, had he?"

"Did he play?"

"I don't know. You'd have to ask him. I know he liked cricket. And he supported Aston Villa. That's all I know. In this house, it's all Wolves."

"My Dad's Albion."

"We hate Albion. Our Craig, he's got Wolves tops upstairs. Mark used to support Villa, but he's gone over to Wolves. We bought one a Villa ball and one a Wolves ball. He's still got it in the box."

For a second or two, I thought she might drift down Memory Lane, but she didn't. She harked back as far as her boys did, a factory worker with a truck-driver husband.

"When you watch a game on a Sunday, what are you going to see?"

"I want 'em to win! I get ever so excited. I don't know why, I just do."

"How do you follow the game? Have they developed your understanding of it?"

She hesitated, so I used the pause to take a breath.

"Well, it's offside I don't understand. Why can't you just go on into the goal? Like five-a-side?"

"D'you understand what they're doing? The movement, the positional play?"

"All I know is one of them plays at the back, and one up front. Even if my two kids are absent, I'll still go and watch. I like the whole team. They'm a good lot of lads."

"Why d'you think football's important to your two?"

"Enjoyment. They'm lads. If I remember, Mark got Netherton Colts, his age, going. He put a notice up at school. Justin went, and Scott. Meesey was with Mark up Castle High, and they was in the school team. They enjoy it. Their dad comes occasionally, if it ay too far to go."

"What does he think?" I asked, but that was when she really started to lose me.

"They call one another names. It's harmless fun."

"Did he play?"

"Yes he did."

"Was he good?"

"I cor tell you. He played with Paul Gennard, I think. I had to go up the school one day, the same lads from the same school playing for the same team. The teacher says 'That's all they talk about, the football'. I said 'What d'you expect?'"

I sipped another mouthful of tea. On the touchline, I'd wondered what went through her mind. I had no more idea on a Sunday than I did as she talked, a mother exposed to the highs and lows of ritual male behaviour, and now trying to explain why. I sipped again and that was when it dawned on me. Jumpers for posts. In the park.

"I was thinking on Sunday," I went with the flow, such as it was, oblivious to where Ginger might appear next but, frankly, past caring.

"When Yew Tree went a man down, Celtic still had four marking Craig. So you'd got two men over. I'd have put Craig into midfield, Justin up front."

"That coloured bloke running the line kept shouting 'Why've you got four on one?'," she folded her arms. The door squeaked.

"Mum!" Mark shouted. "I've been in since five and I haven't even had a drink!"

"Get lost!" She pulled the door shut. "They'm playing up… I'm sorry, but I'd have put Justin on instead of Ginge. If he couldn't have turned up on time, he don't play. And I'll tell you something else I don't agree on. Training. If they can't train, why play? All right, some on 'em has to work, like Craig, when he's on lates. But, if he can get back, he'll try his hardest." So Ginger had missed training too.

Training. That was on Thursdays, at Hillcrest, one slice of a weekly football routine that also took in Tuesday nights, Sunday mornings and any match on TV between.

"Do they ever go to Molineux as well?"

"They was going to have a season ticket," she said, "but they thought they'd wait and see if they got up."

Then I found myself saying "My mum hated it when I stuck my boots in the washing machine", and asking "What do yours do?"

What do yours do? I was carefree, careless. Look, no hands! She'd broken me.

"I usually washes 'em in a pillow case. I takes the strips out the bags. If I don't, they'm there a week. Come Sunday, 'Where's me boots?' I says 'You know where they am. Your bags are in the cupboard, your shinpads are with the towels'."

And so it went. Lin Horton in her stride, the mother's view of Yew Tree Rangers, Ginger, Life and Football.

For the record, it also included attitude and consistency: "We ay a positive team, am we? If you've noticed, every week, it's a different team. We keep changing it, one for this, and this and that."

Bass and Opple: "When I first seen 'em play, I thought they was a load of shit!"

And Paul Bowen: "He's another," she laughed at the sound of her opinion. "I ay over-keen on him either."

And there was Carl Evans too, the eternal substitute, Meesey's cousin. How many more branches on the Yew Tree family tree?

"Trouble with Carl is he's asthmatic. He's out of breath all the while." I don't think that's breaking any medical confidences.

"Final question," I ventured. "If you were picking the team…."

"Don't ask me to pick the team…."

"…. what would your idea of the best team be? You can pick your lads."

"My lads would be in, first pick. Robin'd have to be in it. Bran. Mitch. Yode. I don't know about goalkeepers because… Scott. They'd definitely be in my team."

"That's seven. Four more to go."

"Them'd definitely be in. Justin. And Tiggles. I know he's small, but he gets in."

"Two more."

"I don't know, really. Meesey, 'cos he's got the build, ay he? And then there's Gavin and Craig, another two good 'uns as well."

No Ginger, then?

"Definitely wouldn't be Ginge. I wouldn't let Ginge play for us no more if it were up to me. Ginger, no way!"

No Ginger, then.

An hour or more after we'd started, I was on her doorstep, running Stan's pub landmarks in reverse through my mind, thanking her for the tea, listening to her say "I don't know whether that was any help or not", gauging the strength of the rain, and asking if I'd see her on Sunday. Stupid question.

"If my lads are saft enough to play in it," she said, "I'm saft enough to watch in it."

Saft? The next couple of games proved it. Mist shrouded the first, the closest Tree had to a derby, against Netherton Hillcrest. In fact, closer. Tree were at home, but they'd have been at home if they'd been away anyway, because Hillcrest paid the council a small fortune for the privilege of using the same cabbage patch.

Saft? It was cold, too, as they gathered outside the dressing room and waited for Jezz to turn the key and give them shelter. That's probably the point where I'd have invoked Osgood-Schlatter and offered to take charge of the oranges. Mark Horton had turned up in T-shirt and shorts. Stan was in a T-shirt too.

Lin and Brian Horton were on the touchline, with Sam, in anoraks not T-shirts, hands buried deep against the sharp morning air, trainers wet from the damp pasture, chilblains coming on nicely.

On Five Live's *Sportsweek*, the *London Evening Standard* sports editor had been asked about Liverpool manager Gerard Houllier's Anfield heart drama, the day before, and the stresses of managing a top club. They were paid handsomely, he replied instinctively. The rest of us had to work for a living.

The working man, then. Jezz Dingley toiled in a factory. He opened the dressing room door but had barely picked up the kitbag before he was body-checked in the rush. Paul Gennard drove for a living. He arrived five minutes later and, I presumed, set about providing words of wisdom. I say 'presumed' because this sanctum wasn't mine to visit, yet. I could have given the team talk, though. So could Lin Horton. Third or fourth from bottom. A defeat today wouldn't do.

The working man. Rob Wall spent 40 hours a week digging trenches. He emerged first. I mentioned last week's bug and he pointed to his belly. He shouldn't be playing, "but....", and shrugged his trench-digging shoulders.

The working man. Tuck was a wood-machinist. When he could work, that is. He'd been to hospital twice for an NHS op on his shoulder. The first was cancelled. He'd gone back on the Thursday. He'd have a pin in for two years minimum, 10 at most. He'd always struck me as a man who had life's trials sussed. Even if that wasn't the case, he had Paula close by, ready to tell him. Thanks to her saft brothers, if they'd had a 'This is Hillcrest' sign above the dressing room door, it would be a couple of months before he'd be able to reach up and touch it, for good luck.

As befits a cabbage patch, the grass was tufty, three or four inches long in places, so ideal for Sunday football. Stan wanted to kick a ball about, but he'd have jarred his sore hip trying to walk in it. Tigs ran in it and his legs disappeared altogether. He was wearing 2, but playing left-back. No Ginger. He hadn't turned up. No Number 3 shirt either, only wild accusations he'd taken it with him after being sent off.

So much for the working man. What about the stresses of management?

It was to be a disjointed morning.

"Have you played the same two in the middle of the back four in successive games?" I asked Jezz, pointing to Bran and Mark as they struggled to deal with the second or third cross in as many minutes. I'd taken my ritual stroll round the pitch earlier than normal. He was in his ritual place, alone on the far side.

"Ah, last week," he said, though they hadn't. "All last season. Chemistry day work."

Tuck's dad, John, had been in the middle of telling me about his 59th birthday, the day before. He stopped to offer a view. "Bran was our player of the year last year.

"Twin brother's birthday today," he went on. "Born 28 hours apart. I were born 2.40 on the mornin', and our Alan worn't born till six next mornin'. Twenty-eight hours!"

Twenty-eight hours. I looked at my watch. On the pitch, Rob and Opple had gone close, otherwise the first touch wasn't good and the passing was wayward.

"What's going wrong here, Jezz?" I asked. The stresses of management.

"Finishing," he admitted, sounding like the 13th man in a queue for a 12-man life-raft. "We can't finish. Don't talk. Communication. We say it week in, week out."

I wished he was being unduly pessimistic, but he wasn't.

"Are you where you thought you'd be?"

"No, not really. I was hoping we'd be up the top. There's no reason why we'm down there. We're about third or fourth from bottom."

"How many teams?"

"Twelve. But I'm a bit worried. The Bengals game's been called off today. If they've dropped out the league, then we'm second from bottom. We'll drop more points because we beat 'em. They lost 11 last week. They only had nine players."

So what would make a successful season now?

"Survival."

The stresses of management. Bran hoofed the ball clear at some point, no finesse, just brute force, a left boot to the brambles. I somehow knew what was coming.

"This is doin' my head in. None of that lot'll fetch it," Jezz jabbed a finger at the far line, where the subs were laughing at his expense.

I watched him. If Jezz hit the deck at half-time, there wouldn't be a doctor on stand-by and an eminent surgeon poised to flex his fingers. The best we could have done was a road-digger to open him up, a central-heating engineer to fiddle with his pipes, and a plasterer to fill the crack afterwards. And someone to write the obituary. Me.

His problems, and Paul Gennard's, were stacking up. Yode was out for six weeks after pulling a groin against George Celtic. Stan was out for four, Mitch for another two or three, or four. Brother Scott had finished, having moved clubs on a Saturday. They should have had five subs, but Ginger had decided not to turn up. Sulking, they said, but who was I to know.

At 2-2, the half-time whistle was a blessing. As I crossed the centre-circle, I heard the ref say "Evenly-matched game, the right spirit. I'm enjoying it". It confirmed most of what I'd been brought up to believe about refs and opticians, but it was a slender ray of light. Maybe Jezz and I had it wrong. Maybe, in the great scheme of things, Division 1 of the Warley & District Sunday League was only ever meant to serve up this kind of football. Steve Bull was never going to turn up at Hillcrest and pull the Number 9 shirt on. Becks was hardly likely to drop a 50-yard pass on Opple's head, 12 yards out, open goal. Maybe we were expecting too much.

The stresses of management. Paul Gennard tried to gee them up at the interval. His advice went "Stop Errol playing, you've killed their game," to which Craig Skidmore added "Stop his clogs". It wasn't up there with "All I can see is arses running away from the ball… treat it like a bottle of perfume", but it was the best today. He usually barely uttered a word, so there was a kind of eloquence in his simplicity.

Otherwise, all Paul had in return was Carl and Bass arguing about who'd run the line in the second-half. Carl pointed the flag at Bass. Bass walked away. Carl dropped it to the ground. The rest laughed. End of half-time team talk.

"Are you doing how you thought you would?" I asked Paul as the whistle went.

"We'm doin' better, ah," he said, and rubbed a finger across his chin. "It was criminal, last week. We should've got the points. I know the potential of the players. It's getting them to do it every week. Keeping off the piss would be a start, though that'd make no difference. You know what I'm saying?"

"What's your idea of a successful season from here?"

"Finishing top two, or winning it," he said, then "winning a cup", and finally "holding our own, 'cos we've come straight from Two to One. We ay really strengthened the squad. I should like another back-four player really. Because, half the time, they're guaranteed a place. You know what I'm saying?"

His words were interrupted by a moment of déja-vu. Mark Horton had laid the ball out right and set off on a run down the pitch which, with every lope towards the road, brought flashbacks of the Midfoam game, the gazelle-like run, the legs turning to nutty slack, the desperate finish and, most of all, the miss.

This time, sinking slightly at the knees as the yards took their toll, he rounded the keeper – a buck-toothed man around five-feet-seven called Flapper – and shaped for the shot. But the ball took the slightest of hops off a divot on the edge of the six-yard box. Too late, however, for his leg was swinging. We watched the ball cannon off the outside of the post and away for a goal-kick. How they laughed. Again.

I should have listened to the ref, really. Soon after Mark's fruitless charge towards Flapper, Tree took a lead they never relinquished, and it ended 6-2. It prompted a sight I hadn't seen in five matches so far, Stan smiling.

"Right, off to the ale house!" he yelled as the final whistle echoed down Cinder Bank. At the top of the hill back to the changing rooms, he bellowed "Mum, lend us a tenner for the pub". A mile away in Dudley, the land of Duncan Edwards, hundreds of women turned, instinctively.

The after-match shower scene wasn't mine to visit either, not yet, and neither was the Yew Tree. Daft as it sounds, I was waiting until I was asked, a yardstick to whether I'd really been accepted or not. Whatever, something also told me that a tenner wouldn't slake Stan's thirst. And I doubted whether he'd be home much before supper.

The *Special Report* on Five Live's came from the plains of Afghanistan, exploring the effectiveness of America's post-September 11 humanitarian air-drops. The wind whistled. Five's man had seen jam in one crate of aid. Jam? It had been supplied by a company in Brooklyn, he said. Two weeks before, he'd visited an apartment there and met the family of a man who'd been a janitor on the 102nd floor of a World Trade Center tower when one of the planes hit the 90th.

While the reporter talked, a boy was trying to buy rations for his family, with 400,000 Afghanis in his hand. Sounds a lot. It's about tenpence. A few minutes later, with Stan's cadged tenner already dented, no doubt, I paused at lights in Halesowen, opposite a McDonald's drive-in. It was packed. You know what I'm saying.

5 ME SAIRVUNT MOSIZ IZ JED

I KNOW WHAT YOU'RE THINKING. Why did the Trees turn out each Sunday, if they apparently enjoyed it so little? I wondered the same until, one day, I found this:

> In Wednesbury town, a clock whose name
> is coupled with its cocking fame,
> was yearly held by custom's right
> a wake where colliers met to fight,
> where bulls were baited, torn, abused
> and dogs were killed, which much amused
> those sturdy knights of coal and hammer
> who scoff at peace and joy at clamour

Wednesbury might have been a few miles north of Netherton but, suddenly, it made sense, and not just about the Trees. I recalled a tense TV afternoon when Dad and I had seen Andre Kanchelskis run the length of the pitch, twisting spines, ball and toe linked by an invisible thread, before walking it into the net. I gasped. Dad went off on one about the winger running to the crowd, shirt swirling round his head. In Dad's eyes, and maybe his heart, he couldn't stop the one tainting the other. How many similarly joyous moments had he spared himself over the years? It angered me even to guess.

I wish now that I'd read the poem before the Barrel match, but I hadn't.

The names Causeway Green Road and Titford Road rang a tiny bell as I wrestled with the A-Z, this time through Langley, in search of Londonderry. I'd parked on a leafy road between 30s council and 60s private housing, where one Black Country suburb runs into another, when it came to me. Dad.

I didn't know much of his childhood until he was diagnosed with bladder cancer. Shameful, really, to spend so long not really knowing your dad, but I guess I'm not alone. Anyway, shuttling between fear and optimism, he found a little space for being wistful and jotted down the odd memory. He'd intended to fill a couple of sheets but, like Forrest Gump, his jog became a marathon. Within weeks, he'd stitched his memories into a picture of the 20s in which places like Uncle Ben's Bridge and Titford Lake are locked in an eternal winter. The dank cold, and the lung-choking smog conjure blue-greys and mushy-pea greens, but mostly dull browns.

This day was different. From now until April, a warm, low sun and a gentle breeze would be a gift. If there's a first day of autumn, this was it. Hitchcock, though, would have filmed it in black and white. The thought came in hindsight, but the seeds were sown as I wound the window down, and something disagreeable began to emerge from every dark corner. It was only a football match. But a heavy hand was guiding it.

First, Ginger walked past with Stan and Mark, towards shops up the hill. The stride was urgent and their heads were down. I pulled a fleece over three tops. They were in T-shirts. If Mark was playing, he was leaving it late.

Minutes later, the team trotted through the dew without him. He wasn't the only thing missing. The usual chat and banter was missing too. When he finally appeared, he drifted slowly down the far side of the pitch, towing a black cloud.

Lin had a dour look. It reminded me of Mum, the day her Christmas chocolates vanished, and my twin brother let me take the blame. Found guilty, yet innocent. Rough justice. It's taken 35 years for that to come out, but I feel a weight lifted.

If Lin's look was dour, Jezz's was menacing and Paul Gennard's spelt pure gloom.

The pitch was heavy, and quickly cut up. The ball didn't know whether to die with the first bounce or fly off a patch of fast grass. Predictably, the mood among the visitors grew darker with every mis-controlled ball and misplaced pass. I lost count of those in the opening minutes. Heavy legs. Heavy hearts. Mine was lined with lead.

On another day, I'd have laughed when the Sandwell Borough Council man drove up and threatened to call everyone off unless Barrel paid the rent. Funny now, but not then. The captain ran over in his Toon stripes, short sleeves, Blue Star logo, 200 miles from the Tyne. He asked someone for his car keys. I half wished they'd gone missing, then all of us could have gone home. But some twonk found them.

There was worse. In the first game of the season, Barrel's Number 7 had stood out. Not for his curly mop. Nor for wearing his shirt outside his shorts, or socks at half-mast. What I recalled from the sun-kissed 4-4 was his arrogant expression, his arrogant strut and his confrontational manner. Today, he'd already taken Craig Skidmore out by the time he was booked for a chop on Meesey. It wouldn't be his last.

Yew Tree were one up by then. Opple had met Mitch's defence-splitting pass in one stride and rifled past the keeper in the next. Ten minutes on, they'd squandered two more chances. Then Meesey lost possession playing a short pass. If this evil pitch had, effectively, laughed in his face, it was clutching its ribs as the ball moved left, and it was crying helplessly as Chubbs felt the breeze in its wake a second or two later. One-one.

Gavin Skidmore had the look you expected to see in a sepia-tint picture, a man in his early 20s, I guessed, with a tiny Babe Ruth stride in his first few steps. He broke into something longer only occasionally, because he usually laid the ball off early. When he dispatched Barrel's Number 8 with a robust tackle, it was time to drift and wonder.

I halted on the far side, with Mark, Ginger and Stan 30 yards away on one side, and Jezz 20 yards away the other, a buffer zone, without UN protection. Grass cuttings covered the ground, the last of the year, I mused, with the charred remains of fireworks with names like *Thunderbomb* and *Gladiator* dotted among them. So God did irony as well.

From the sanctuary of the line, Ginger gave the ref his view of Gavin's foul. Stan, too. Jezz waited for the free-kick to come to nothing, then shouted "Stan, let it go".

That's when I recognised the ref as the man who'd sent Ginger off. Strange. He wouldn't put up with Ginge's foul mouth, but Barrel's Number 7 was still there, so violence didn't worry him. If anything moved within five yards of the ball, it was kicked. Someone would be in hospital, come Monday, not walking back in to work.

I strolled past another *Thunderbomb* and met Lin Horton.

"How are you?"

"Not very happy," she didn't smile, but nodded at her "drunkard son". He'd been at Yosser's birthday party the night before, and most of the morning too. Birthday Boy was chugging round in his customary third gear, but Mark had been unable to stand at pick-up time. My mind rewound 10 days, to her proud boast that her lads wouldn't let their team down. Her face suggested she was thinking the same.

Stan had been true to his mum's sense of commitment, at least. He'd taken his kit, even though he was signed off and not insured to play. Ginger hadn't even packed a shinpad, on the other hand. He didn't think he'd be playing. That didn't surprise Lin. I nodded at Mark, trying to make light of a dark moment on a grim morning.

"I thought he might have had an injury," I said to her.

"He will when I get 'im 'ome."

The fringe of the orange-fuelled Yew Tree fag-fart-scratch feast wasn't the place to be this half-time, so I hung around the Barrel team-talk instead, trying to look nonchalant. The Number 6, Justin, was telling his players they were on top.

"We're pissing it," he said, which seemed a little one-eyed to me. Then he turned to his Number 7 and scowled.

"Calm down, Steve," he said. A yard from me, someone suggested Steve was drunk. He said it quietly, but I still left.

That's when the argument started. It involved the Barrel sub who'd run the line in the first-half and a stripling called Liam. The flag handover was the customary signal for Trees to flee, but Liam had volunteered, an object lesson in team spirit that was wasted on the visitors, because they weren't watching.

"You've been told never to run the line again," the sub reminded him. But no one else stepped forward so, faced with a thankless task or handing the flag to a total incompetent, the sub did the only thing he could. He gave Liam the flag.

"I always get it wrong," Liam shrugged as another team-mate ran back, agitated.

"You shouldn't do it," he snapped, aiming his comment at the man who'd washed his hands, "not 'cos you'll get it wrong, 'cos you don't want to be shouted at."

It might have been true, but it was academic. The unburdened man strode off. Instead, I watched Liam point at Tree's goal and say "That's our way, isn't it?"

What followed was predictable. Predictable as in the season so far, predictable in the image of the morning. First, Mitch mis-hit a shot from 18 yards and put Tree ahead, then psycho Steve shoved Meesey away after an innocuous challenge, and Meesey gave him what he wanted, a shove back.

Next, Gavin bawled at Chubbs for dropping a cross. The 17-year-old complained about being complained about, and dropped his head too. Paul Gennard ran past me as the ball went out for a corner, muttering "Let's see if we can defend against this", and watched Barrel equalise – after which Chubbs walked around, kicking mud.

It went on. Mitch was booked for telling the ref he was a joke after more push-and-shove, with Steve. A bit much. But, if the manager's son had been sent off, I'd have willingly called the ref a joke too, found my keys, and paid the fine.

I've walked away from amateur dramatics early, but never a football match. I came close that day. I'd thought the Midfoam win was the moment when the faint whiff of success and the intoxicating stench of embrocation had welded me to Yew Tree Rangers. But I actually passed the point of no return during the next eight minutes.

First, Mitch found Opple with a brilliant through-ball, even if he did look a yard offside. Liam the Reluctant didn't raise his flag. Some team-mates shouted at him, but the rest stood, waiting for the whistle, and watched Opple score. Two-three.

Two minutes later, Barrel's Number 4 hoisted an arm as Rob Wall's long pass found Opple and Gavin free. Gavin spurned the chance to square for Opple's hat-trick. It looked offside to me, so I searched for Liam, but he was gone. In his place, the original linesman was holding the flag up, on tiptoes, turning red. By the time Gavin made it 2-4, he was near a stroke. He hit the pitch, stiff-legged, like a tot whose vocabulary isn't wide enough to express anger.

The ref waved him off, but he stood his ground, yelling: "The fucking thing was up! He was off-fucking-side!"

It was up again, minutes later, when Barrel's joy at nicking a goal back was killed as Gavin restored Tree's two-goal lead. The man holding the flag now was Liam, and his team-mates were shouting. I shook my head and passed more fireworks.

Psycho Steve's substitution had lifted some of the gloom, and Liam had cheered me up no end so, though he'd turned up to play football, the lad's day hadn't been totally wasted. But the heavy heart returned with Jezz's nod in Mark Horton's direction.

"He could hardly stand this morning," the shaven-headed secretary didn't try to disguise the disgust in his voice. "Got in at 6.30."

I looked at Lin and knew how much it had spoilt her day. I looked at Rob, at Bowe, at Craig, and at Bran, still struggling for the move to lift them above mediocre, if only for a few seconds. Instinct would tell them there were around 10 minutes left to earn a feeling of satisfaction that didn't feed off the score alone. I hadn't played for 16 years, but I knew that feeling.

I looked at Tuck on the line, and wondered how they all felt. A party's a party, a Saturday night's a Saturday night. But where did commitment start and end? Where did individual freedom give way to team loyalty and pulling your weight? Did it cease to matter because this was a Sunday morning in Londonderry Lane, not a Saturday afternoon at Molineux? Or because they were 5-2 up? And why had all that resurfaced in me, why had Mark cheesed me off, so long after my last match?

I should have remembered the morning for Tigs' mazy run on 80 minutes, Maradona from half-way, dropping a shoulder here and there, past blokes who'd suddenly found despair in their legs, not energy. The keeper did his best. He advanced. He spread himself. And he picked the ball from the net. Three-six. Game over.

Tigs. I wondered how a talent like his could be languishing in a Warley park. I heard him cough as he ran past, thought of the fag he'd light at the final whistle, and realised some people are only good at setting themselves up for regret.

It started to rain as the minutes ticked away and Bass went on. He was a radio-controlled toy that heads in one direction, bounces off something, rights itself, then sets off in another. Within seconds of arriving on the pitch, he'd missed a couple of chances, prompting Carl, Ginger, Mark and Co to shout "Ref, man coming off!", then tell the sub "You've had your run!"

It made them laugh, but not Jezz. He didn't look like a man whose team had won 6-3. Then Bass missed again, and I found myself by Lin.

"Not a very enjoyable morning."

"He told me he let 'imself and the side down by turning up drunk," was all she said.

From: "Jeremy Dingley"
To: "Mark Higgitt"
Subject: League standings
Date: 22 October 2001 11:49

Mark – If you want to talk to me, any Friday night will do if that's ok with you. The table should be attached to this. (fingers crossed) Getting a little better (I think). Have a nice lie in next week. See you soon. JEZZ

Have a nice lie-in? I would, but I suspected few of Paul Gennard's men would bid British Summer Time farewell with an extra pint or two.

Yode and Phil, both now injured, were by Jezz's red Escort as I walked towards the dressing rooms. A church service was going full tilt in the school hall, a sea of happy-clappy hands swaying behind the mucky, frosted glass that made me queasy. Phil ignored them and looked up, not at heaven, but at the second floor, his old form room.

"I never did me exams," he said, out of nowhere. "Couldn't see much point."

I walked down the hill with Paul Gennard, his men straggling in twos and threes. Bran, Stan and Ginger were in one little group, already cutting Foggy, Compo and Clegg figures. I wondered if I'd ever see them marching together, one day, resolute. The answer was yes, one day, but not this.

Hangman's Tree were one of 39 teams among the 70 in the Warley & District Sunday League with a pub or social club affiliation, so I was hoping they'd used the extra hour as sensibly as the Trees. Then Paul mentioned that they'd won by five the week before, a result that belied their last-but-one place in the table Jezz had e-mailed. So, even though the home side had somehow turned the marvellous, the mundane and the malevolent into fourth behind Khalsa, Harborne and George Celtic, this wasn't a game to take for granted.

When she was six or seven, my daughter Katie came up to me at a family do where she'd witnessed three Black Country great-uncles for the first time.

"Does Grandpa talk a foreign language?" she asked.

"No. Why?"

"Because he's talking to Uncle Jack and I can't understand what he's saying."

I know how she felt. It was hard, at the best of times, to understand what Mark Horton was going on about. When life presented him with more than he could take, though, it was impossible. This day, after his fall from grace, he was sub.

On the line, he said: "The Lord spoke ter Joshua un sed 'me sairvunt Mosiz iz jed. Gerr up un tek the childrun uv Israel oover Jord'n ter the land ahm agee'in um. Be strung un brairve un abbay wot's rit in the buk o' law un yow'll dew well un prospa. Dow be frit cuz ah shull be wi' yer t'elp yer weerevva yow goo'."

To be frank, for weeks, I didn't have a clue what he'd said. Then I came across the *Old Testament* written in Black Country dialect. I read it and replayed the tape a dozen times, and the start of Joshua 1 is as near as damn-it what he said.

He followed it with "Like Liverpool not playin' Gerrard. I ay trainin' again and I ay playin' again". I had more luck with that because "Stevie" or "Gerrard" peppered most of his talk. As he sulked, the others were kicking in, a damp thresh on autumn grazing cared for by Dudley Metropolitan Borough Council. They clocked his abject misery and did what any team-mates would. They told the ref he was running the line.

"I ay gunna and that's the end o' the story," he shouted, and told Yode he could do it as part of his return to fitness. Stan was by him, also clothed in a sub's tracksuit top.

"Tek it in yer stride," he told his younger brother. Lin was five yards away, silent. Mark wouldn't take the flag. Stan refused too, and walked off. Kev Tucker didn't.

Yew Tree won the game 4-2. A sparkling performance to banish memories of Londonderry Lane? Not really. You've probably spotted that most Warley & Sunday District League goals were the result of bad defending. This was no different.

On the other hand, the Old Mon did something I don't expect to see again in my life. Meesey picked the ball from Rob's kick-off knock-back, controlled it with one touch and played a ball through the middle with the next. It was innocuous, until a Hangman defender let it roll under his foot. Rob seized it, settled himself on the clod-riddled pitch and shot beneath the keeper. One-nil. Five seconds. It took longer to describe than it took to score. It'll be on *A Question of Sport*, one day.

Eighty-nine minutes and 55 seconds later, Tree's run had stretched to five wins in six. Minutes after that, I was passing the steel anchor that marked times past in Netherton, just up the hill from a dubious statue of Joe Darby, champion all-round spring jumper of the world, depicted in blocks of silver metal. Joe Darby. Another name from Dad's childhood. The questions I had to ask him were totting up.

Then I pointed the car down the long hill towards home. There was a match on the radio, but I turned it off. I had two things on my mind, one satisfying, the other not.

Mark gave me the smile. He'd spent five minutes warming up, in a world of his own, before he came on for Bass after 50 minutes. Then he'd played his heart out.

A niggling moment, though, had spoiled the second-half. A young lad with the Hangman contingent was handed the flag following a substitution. He took it with a little trepidation, but no sign of ducking out. A couple of minutes later, the sluggish Hangman defenders called for offside, their only co-ordinated move of the morning. He jerked the flag up. The home side yelled their disapproval, most using words of no more than four letters. But he kept the flag high.

"Ref," Paul Gennard shouted, "he's a kid, you've got to do something."

It came out a harsher than Paul meant, but a Hangman player called from the pitch for the other sub to take the flag.

"It's not his fault, he's only a lad," someone yelled back.

"That's why he's going to be shouted at. It's making people angry," the reply came.

The lad had wanted to help. But he trudged off, disconsolate. It was the kind of thing he'd remember for the rest of his days. I will.

I said there were two things in my mind as I drove home. In fact, there were three. The other was Jezz Dingley.

It had been painful watching him being tortured, again, 4-2 or not. If there'd been a high point to his morning, I'd missed it. Of lows there'd been many, but Stan and Mark refusing to run the line in the second-half was the most obvious. Jezz had to run it himself. It meant he hadn't been able to attend to Yosser when the young midfielder slid his bulky frame into a challenge and emerged with blood running down his shin.

"I've had enough being ball-fetcher, trainer and linesman," he scowled as I reached to shake his hand at full-time. "Something has to be done."

6   JEZZ DINGLEY

JEZZ DINGLEY, BALL-FETCHER, TRAINER, LINESMAN and secretary. Something has to be done.

There's a fine line between the fires of anger and passion, and Jezz hadn't yet crossed back to the safe side when I bought him a pint in the Yew Tree, the next Friday. As we supped, I think he slid over.

The last time we'd sat there, a month before the season began, he'd had six players. He was trying to persuade the league to lift Gavin Skidmore's ban, there'd been no time for friendlies, and the club was on the verge of folding. Goodness knows what caused the turn-around. I couldn't help thinking, though, that there must have been moments on some Sunday mornings when he wished the other 10 or so hadn't signed.

I'd seen some of them in the Bar as I walked in from the November cold, the kind of crisp night that carries light and sound across vast horizons. While families had filled the pavements through Halesowen, and fireworks had filled the sky over Merry Hill, Mark, Stan, Rob and Bran were nicking Ginger's chicken and chips and discussing a league position that was infinitely healthier than his diet.

They'd gone from leaking goals and listing survival as their main ambition to counting Rob's Georgie-Georgies and, occasionally, listening to the unfamiliar click of things falling in to place, even if it often still did look terrible from the line.

"They don't realise till they stand with us," Jezz said to me. "Stan come up Sunday and says 'I don't believe we'm this bad'. I said 'Don't think we'm moaning for the fun of it'.

"Every time there's a corner I fear, I do. No one can head it. We switch off. We just stand there," the note in his voice was familiar now. "In here, we don't talk about it. Nine times out of 10, they'm just acting saft."

They say your football team finds you, and maybe they're right. Our pre-season chat hadn't been our first. That had come at Lion Farm, around a year before. The landscape there had once been occupied by a brick and tile works, along with the scree hills and canal arms that went with it. Dad had worked there as a 14-year-old. Now it was a windswept expanse of grass and marshy fringes, echoing to the sound of wheeling seagulls and the distant rumble of the M5.

The team I'd thought about following for a season, Royal Lowes, were playing that day. The pitch was one step from A&E, rock hard where the shelter of bushes had kept the thin, wintry sun from weeks of frost, and rock hard where it hadn't. So was the sideline. The atmosphere was nasty, the humour lacking, the football grim. I sought sanctuary on the far touchline and that's where I found Jezz, a Michelin man wrapped against the icy blast. We talked. We laughed. I turned my back on Lowes and, a few months later, called Jezz to find out what Yew Tree had to offer.

"I'm a very passionate person, where football's concerned," Jezz watched the barman shake a bell, a free demo to show how to grab his attention above the din next door. "I love football. I love to win. But, at the end of the day, I know we ay good enough."

He paused a second, then perked up.

"We am. But it's only a Sunday morning game. When I was a kid, if I had a real bad game, I used to cry, it hurt that much. As you grow up, you think 'How stupid was that?' At the end of the day, I'll be at work on Monday. It's only a game of football. But it was life and death then. It really was."

He was lying. Is, not was.

This was a man who spent Sunday mornings on the move, kicking every ball, making every decision, burning nervous energy, venting the rest with a foghorn that stunned pigeons in Pensnett. He could have been any club secretary, any former player, any young dad, any night-shift worker in any pub in any town or city in the country.

By now, I knew the faces of Rob's 100 per-centers. There were some, I reckoned, who felt like crying, and others who didn't. Those for whom it wasn't just a Sunday morning, those for whom it was. Barrel was bound to surface.

"There worn't a few words said, but there could've been," he admitted. "I'm in two minds about calling a meeting Sunday. Nine times out of 10, it's sorted and Joe Soap here gets the brunt. This time, Joe Soap's going to give them the brunt of it".

As he bounced from one to the other, his voice dropped a note. No edge. The despair turned to a kind of fatalistic weariness.

"Sunday was the pits. We'm losing balls left, right and centre. Another Sunday. I cor do it. So, I might give it three weeks, because Paul ay here. The way I feel, if I ay happy with things Sunday, then I'll ask everybody to come here."

Sunday had been a low point, Yoss injured, first-aid man Jezz running the line because none of the other subs would. I unwrapped a fresh razor-blade for him, then one for myself.

"I cor do nothing. That's my priority. Make sure the kids are all right. What could I do? I ay gunna accept it," he said, and started a conversation, playing both parts.

"Have you got the key to the changing room?"

"What for?"

"I wanna change and go and play golf."

"What happens if someone gets injured and yo ay here?"

He looked at me and paused.

"They don't like being sub. They expect to have subs. But, put the boot on the other foot… We'll probably have a slanging match in here. I had a row with Bran the other week, about goal-keeping positions."

Ah. Goal-keeping. I'd only seen Tuck play a handful of times, and he hadn't looked confident. More confident than Chubbs, though. Watching the 17-year-old was torture. You willed him to play beyond his tender age, yet feared for every cross, turned away in relief when he pulled something out of the bag, and felt what his defenders felt every time the ball went near.

"I'll always stick up for Phil Tucker," Jezz said. "I love the guy. And he takes some right slack off this lot. He's stopped making mistakes. The only reason he makes them is because they won't get off his back. He's frightened. It's happening with Chubbs. I've told him. 'Yo wanna stop listenin'. Why ay you bin to the pub?' 'Oh, I go home and fall asleep'. 'Bollocks! You don't come to the pub 'cos you're frightened to death of that lot. You'm gunna get the piss ripped out of you. Tek it. You let a goal in against Barrel and the first thing you did was look across at that lot. Take no notice'.

"The bank holiday, he played in goal for the kids. He collected the ball and was taking the Mickey. He rolled over and dropped it. I said 'Chubbsie, Rule 19 of football….' 'What's that?' 'Never take the piss until you've got the ball'."

Chubbs or Tuck? Academic. Tuck was out. Chubbs was all they had so, choosing one from the other was hardly a test of his footballing philosophy, or Paul's. Mind you, there was enough among the others to do that. He mentioned two names, Meesey and Yoss, and made an obvious admission.

"They go forward, but they don't come back."

Then he named two more, Mitchell and Craig Skidmore.

"You've got to keep on all the while."

"Tigs?" I asked.

"He's 19. Lives opposite Mark and Stan. He turned up one day. We was Albron then. Bloke came up to me and says 'You know any local teams?' 'What for?' 'Chap's come with us today, like, he's looking for a team.' 'Where d'you play, mate?' 'Left back. Left midfield.' 'Size boot?' 'Nine.' 'Get changed, I'll get you a pair'."

He carried on, quickfire, and related another conversation, playing Tigs first.

"Jezz, I shouldn't be playing, I ay paying subs. Everybody else is."

"I told you. When you got a job, give us a pound a week."

"I cor even afford that."

The Hundred Club and subs were £3.50 a week with a chance to win £30.

"Give us a pound!"

"I cor afford to do that."

"Keep the Hundred Club going, and knock the subs on the head."

"I ay happy. Folks are paying subs, I ay."

"My problem, not yours."

Then he found a job. He gave Jezz £30.

"How much else do I owe?"

"Nothing."

"Thank you."

He owed another £10.

Before the Hangman's game, I'd found Jezz pumping balls, cussing a £17 fine for forgetting to pay the ref before the last home game. Most refs would have let it go. And a report had been sent in late, even though Jezz had delivered it on time.

"It's fucking petty," he'd said. "Seventeen pound's a lot to a club like this."

Cussing £17. It didn't surprise me. Neither did the intensity with which he recalled moments like the Tigs conversation.

I'd have bawled back at him, if I'd been playing, for some of the things he'd screamed at the pitch. Put passion and the heat of the moment together in anyone who cares, deeply, and it'll explode one way or the other, either a stream of old English from the mouth, or a dribble of blood from the ears. But, when he talked of his family, the intensity went.

It's unfair to suggest the obvious, that he knew how much time football took out of their lives, but couldn't stop himself. It was unfair to think it, sitting there, supping with a man I barely knew. But I thought it.

It took me a few minutes to work out that the contrast spoke far, far less about any indifference to hearth and home than it did his obsession with Yew Tree's version of the Beautiful Game. It wasn't the obsession that makes someone shell out for a season ticket to stand on the Tilton Road End. That's easy. It was the devotion that sees you sink your freezing feet into a mudbath on an icy January morning when even Titus Oates would have poked his head over the duvet to declare: "Bugger that for a game of soldiers. I'll have another cup of Bovril and read the *Telegraph*."

So, we talked briefly, matter-of-factly of his divorced parents, family life, his wife Lindsay, his children – Chelsea, who has cerebral palsy, Nathan and Aaron – and left it at that before we were on to his Sunday morning philosophy.

"Put 'em in and 'ope for the best," was his motto. "That's all you can do." Then I asked him if he had a football dream.

"I should like to go all the way and play in the Premier of the Warley League," he said, and I heard the note in his voice drop again, this time to wistful. "And then, if you can get the players and the commitment, then have a stab at the Kiddy League."

It wasn't the kind of dream I was hoping to hear.

Then he said: "I should love to have me own football club. Win the Lottery and say 'I've got a million quid, boing, I'll put it on a club'. Twenty million tomorrow and, well, I'd find a piece of land, Dudley Wood, get the speedway track on, and that middle's our pitch. Know what I mean? Get investors in, make a stand, nice changing rooms. Be in the Warley League."

"Are there any moments on a Sunday morning when that flits through your mind?"

"No."

"There aren't moments when you dream there?"

"No."

"So when do you dream?"

He paused, and smiled as if he'd been caught with his fingers in the biscuit tin.

"When I'm at work."

I'd had him down as an engineer since the first weeks of the season, a man accustomed to taking things apart, sorting them, putting them together again and expecting to see them go, then starting again after a curse if they flat refused to spark.

"What d'you do?"

"We make motor components. I'm just a machinist, really. I put the ball seat into a rocker."

"Repetitive job?"

"Seven thousand rockers a night. Just doing that," he mimed it, "tin in front of me, pick 'em up, drop 'em down the chute. I've got a machine behind me, what they call a large pad. You've got a pad where it comes off the camshaft, you have to grind that to that sort of shape," he moved his fingers, "a convex shape."

"If we're sitting here in June, what d'you think we'll be reflecting on?"

"I should like to win a cup. A cup final day's fantastic. With the teams we've got to play, I hope to be top half of the league. I'd be disappointed if we're not."

"You have as many hard games to come as you've had."

"Tough cookie in a fortnight. Lowes. You know 'em. I'm looking forward to the rest of the season. Well, I am and I ay. Tell you the truth, if what happened last week happens again, I shan't be carrying on."

He needed help but, so far as I could see, not necessarily someone to actually carry the bucket, just someone to offer.

"Paul helps out a lot. Robin does his bit. There's too many 'me, me, me', unfortunately. It's a shame, really, 'cos we've got a really good club."

"I really loved my Sunday football," I said.

"If you don't, what the hell are you doing?" he laughed. "Come January, when you'm up Rowley College, freezing, you know why you love your football."

As he said it, I heard familiar voices in the Bar. There was Stan's, clear as a bell, Ginger's, half-excited, half frustrated at whatever they were doing, Mark's, untranslatable, Rob's, egging them on, and club chairman Ted Terry's, chuckling. I couldn't hear Julie's or Sam's, though they were still there too.

Out of the blue, Jezz leant back and smiled.

"We've enjoyed having you, the lads and everyone," he said. "I've spoken to them, and I was minded to ask if you wanted to join the club."

7   SUNDAY, MUDDY SUNDAY

"JEZZ HAS SENT AN E-MAIL," Maggie told me as I arrived home, four days after goals from Craig Skidmore and Stan had bounced Third Division Abbey out of the second round of the West Brom Cup. "He isn't well. You'd better read it." I did.

From: "Jeremy Dingley"
To: "Mark Higgitt"
Subject: Yew Tree
Date: 07 November 2001 17:23

Hi Mark – Sundays match was a cup game. Their was one league game, which didn't effect us much yet. Barrel lost to Merrivale 4-3.The talk to the players has not yet happened, I will see what happens on Sunday. I hope to see you on Sunday, while I'm writing this to you, I'm waiting for my wife to come back with my eldest son so I can go to the hospital. Not feeling very well (chest pains). – JEZZ

Chest pains? I could believe it. He'd attached the league table, presumably to keep his mind occupied as he waited. That was harder to take in. Tree were third, two points behind Harborne, two ahead of George Celtic.

He hadn't looked happy when I'd left Birchley Park, one of Dad's childhood stamping grounds, that Sunday, which was a shame, given the way our drink, two days before, had ended.

The Trees had used their usual compass to find Chubbs' goal in the kick-in and lost another ball in the hawthorns. Then Stan had refused to run the line, again, and fellow sub Bass had made himself scarce, leaving Ginger to lag 10 yards behind play for the duration of the first-half, disregarding play.

Stan wouldn't have even been on the pitch to score Tree's second, if he'd had his way. He'd been licking his lips for most of the second-half at the prospect of a McChicken Sandwich when Paul signalled for the out-of-sorts Opple to come off. The youngster trotted to the touchline as Scott, Mitch and Carl appeared carrying takeaways.

Anxious to play, but so close to breakfast he was slobbering. Stan begged Paul to delay the switch, then spent the next five minutes casting anxious glances at Scott and Mitch as they ate their breakfasts, then his.

For me, it was reward for a cold, wet morning and a characteristically bitty game. If any of us had known what fate the cup had in store for Tree, the mood might have been lighter. For everyone except Jezz, I suspect.

Late in the first-half, as Tigs' shirt was pulled, I'd sauntered past an unkempt, grey-bearded bloke in a Nike cap, black jacket, blue track bottoms and muddy trainers. He yelled at the ref long after the foul was given and, inviting a stranger – me – to agree with him, gestured at the scene of the crime.

"It was obstruction!" he insisted.

I'm not very good at ignoring such invitations to debate, but I'm utterly useless at telling people what they want to hear, for the sake of it.

"The ball was in playing distance," I shrugged my shoulders. "He was entitled to put himself between the man and the ball."

"Is that right?" he stopped waving his arms about.

"As long as the ball's in playing distance," I nodded.

"I've never understood the rules," the scruffy git replied, and I nodded again. "I'm more interested in the ethos of the rulebook than the framework it provides for the game," he expanded. "I've never considered it as a body of work. For me, it's something that's supposed to encapsulate the spirit of the game."

Fast forward two days again. As I re-read Jezz's e-mail, I wished he'd been with me to hear it. Ethos, framework and encapsulation? They wouldn't have been the same as standing up at an SA meeting and unburden himself by saying "I'm Jezz Dingley, and I'm a soccerholic", but at least he'd have heard proof, first hand, that he wasn't the only one gripped by this vice, or in trying to make sense of the obsession.

As I advanced up the M5 to Netherton, a few days later, I couldn't help pondering the tonking Royal Lowes were likely to hand out on Remembrance Sunday, if the lads weren't on it from the off. Otherwise, Jezz was driving my thoughts.

If he'd pegged it, I don't suppose I'd have been far up the list of people Lindsay Dingley would have thought to call. On the other hand, I hadn't fancied ringing, finding her on the other end and having to ask a subtle question, like whether she'd changed the summer holiday booking to four, not five.

For once, *Sportsweek* wasn't part of the drive. The radio wasn't working, a casualty of war, in a sense, given that car had been savaged by a Greek truck driver en-route to the Somme. The radio had been disconnected while the repairs were done, and I'd put the security code in a safe place. Hence the time to kill.

Remembrance Parade diversions in Astwood Bank sent me past The Oddfellows, our watering hole when I'd played in the Midland Comb. I hadn't seen it for 20 years. Twenty miles on, I watched a young girl in a bright red coat, wrapped against the chilly breeze, skipping with her dad towards a church as hobby-bobbies kept parade roads car-free in Halesowen. Wooden surveyors' crosses standing in watery M5 roadworks had already created their own illusion. All I needed was mud stretching from one side of the Hillcrest pitch to the other and I'd have an embarrassment of clichés to call on. If Paul had signed a sensitive defender called Wilfred Owen, well, I'd have been laughing.

I had a fair idea what Ginger was thinking about during the minute's silence, even though suspension meant he wasn't at the centre-circle. I'd heard him asking for a sniff of Carl's nose, an unsubtle reference to the size and agility of the young lady Meesey's asthmatic cousin had entertained the night before. I'd had a thought that my snapshot of the life of young working Black Countrymen ought to include a first-hand night out. In one, short question, however, Ginger had convinced me that little of it would be reportable. Carl, to his credit, declined to answer. He simply grinned.

On the pitch, others were stretching their quads and some had their heads bowed, spirals of breath drifting skywards. I heard gunfire and turned. It was Ted Terry's spaniel, Robbie, crunching a plastic bottle he'd found littering the pitch.

At the end of 60 seconds, Stan wheeled away, shouting "Come on, boys!"

"If that's how quiet they can be," his mum, hands in pockets, nodded at the hecklers down the line, "we ought to have a minute's silence through the 'ole game."

Somewhere between Frankley and Old Hill, in my idle musings, I'd imagined I was in the commentary box at Hillcrest, microphone in hand, chipping in to a pre-match chat. With Paul *en vacances* and Jezz *hors de combat*, I'd ventured that there'd be a chance of seeing Lin in charge. It hadn't seemed such a daft idea in fantasy, and it still didn't as I twisted to see if Jezz was about to appear on the hill, lugging the balls and first-aid kit. "She won't stand any nonsense, Gary," I'd told the studio, and I reckon they wouldn't. But we'll never know, because Jezz appeared, doing his familiar little half-run, half-walk to the pitch.

I didn't have the chance to enquire as to his health before the game started. If it had been a heart scare, this wasn't the place to continue the recovery, whether football was the obsession that had caused his decline, or the escape from whatever had.

Stupidly, my other fear was that Lowes' manager Craig Barnsley didn't recognise me. He was wearing the green anorak he'd worn that freezing day I'd wandered away from something nasty at Lion Farm, on my recce the year before, and bumped in to Jezz. Mind you, I had the same coat on too. If he did recognise me, it wasn't apparent.

Tree kicked downslope on the pitch by the road, wearing their orange-and-blue first-choice kit for the first time, a colour scheme chosen as much for its similarity to a distress beacon as fashion, if the first minute was anything to go by. Chubbs failed to talk to Gavin as he chased an over-hit pass and fumbled it. The ball slid worryingly close to the post. Gavin blamed Chubbs. Chubbs blamed Gavin, and they were still at it as play went on. I looked at Jezz and tried to gauge whether the wince was connected to what he'd just witnessed, or a pain creeping up his arms. Or both.

The high-explosive opening set the tone. Lowes were as humourless as I'd remembered, led by a gobby forward called Poacher, who spent the 20 minutes before he limped off facing the sideline, swapping insults with the suspended Ginger. The visitors were also aided by a ref who – don't start me off – played to their call and missed some hospital tackles, yet couldn't stop giving indirect free kicks for verbal obstruction.

But Tree gave as good as they took.

They weren't as disjointed as against Abbey.

And they weren't five down by half-time, as I'd feared. They were 3-1 up.

Poacher's demise was the key. The lad who replaced the limping striker had to be 16 to play open-age football, but looked 14, tops, and seven stone, dripping wet. He went to right-back and ran his socks off, but received less support than a young boy needed in a man's game, marking Craig Skidmore. The midfielder was drifting in and out of the game as his concentration came and went. Eventually, Jezz was close to bursting.

"I've been having chest pains all week," he bawled, "now you'm making it worse!"

Whether Craig was running hot or cold, it was only a matter of time before the lad was exposed once too often to his shuffling Hammy Hamster impression.

It took 22 minutes for Tree to score the first. Stan cut inside and rolled the ball right to Craig for a 25-yard shot the keeper could only tip into the net. It took just another three to notch the second, when Mark harried and Bowe turned a loose ball into a high cross. The keeper failed to hold again. Stan was there. Ta very much, like.

Lowes' sole goal came on 35. Chubbs attempted to line up a wall for a free-kick, but left a hole the size of Dudley Castle, and just as impregnable. The young keeper's dive was as futile a gesture as you could fear to see. Jezz went off on one.

"You had two hours to get that wall organised! For fuck's sake!" he yelled at Gavin.

"Jezz, shut up," Gavin yelled back. "We had it sorted."

"It's his fault," his brother added, pointing at Chubbs.

"Why's it always my fault?" the keeper shouted. It had taken seven weeks but, at last, the 17-year-old had found his voice, even if they ignored him.

If there was ever the threat of a bright start thrown away, that was it. Tree attacked from the restart and won a free-kick 25 yards out when Yoss was given a face-pack. Tigs jogged over and curled a majestic shot into the top left-hand corner, the only slice of net he could see. The old bloke leaning on the railings at the Halesowen Road end of the pitch, a bright red poppy lighting the left breast of his blue anorak, smiled.

Three minutes later, Chubbs mishandled a cross and conceded a corner.

"You'm better than that," Bran snapped at him. "Shape up!"

Within two minutes, the keeper raced out to block a through-ball and stood up clutching his hamstring. It's cruel to think it but, so soon after having two fingers pointed, it was difficult to be sure whether the injury was real.

The half ended with Meesey and Lowes' Number 7 squaring up off the ball. The Lowes man pushed him away, and watched the ref pull a yellow card from his pocket. Meesey, the architect of the niggle, shook the enemy's hand.

"It's a Sunday morning, ref, they've shaken," Bran shouted. "Cor we just forget it?"

I'd have been happier to hear the captain say "That was big, Meesey", but he didn't and his team-mate walked away, laughing.

Three-one by half-time, 6-1 by the end, an outcome no one would have predicted as Chubbs limped to his goal at the start of the second period and Jezz muttered "I fear for this half". I knew what he meant.

The sight of Opple – gangly, slightly splay-footed – pulling the keeper's jersey on a minute later was greeted by derision on the line, but the heckles turned to grudging cheers when the striker intercepted a run from deep with ease. He didn't look any more like a keeper than Chubbs, but he seemed to know what he was doing, and the value of his save doubled on 56 when Yosser's Fred Astaire feet mesmerised a Lowes defender into an ill-judged lunge and Tigs threaded the free-kick home from 20 yards. There might be only one David Beckham but, if you'd asked me to cough up to watch a replay, I'd have gladly put my hand in my pocket.

Yosser and Tigs. Both were the right side of 20, both were still young enough to make it. One was too heavy to do justice to his blessed talents, that casual beauty. The other was too small, despite the skipping, gliding run that rarely hinted whether he intended to explode off his left or right foot. It always looked like it was a race to see what blew him away first, a defender or a gust of wind. Neither ever did.

Poacher's eyes had been black on the pitch, the look of a man who's seeking the man who said his mother had a questionable taste in curtains. Now, on the sideline, still limping, he was the same size as Yogi Bear and about as frightening.

"Realistically, there's no way back from 4-1 down, is there?" he turned to Jezz.

He was right. Seventeen minutes later, Craig plugged in to Tree's new confidence and hit a long crossfield ball into Bass' path. Lowes hadn't given up, but they'd slowed by half-a-yard. It was all Bass needed. He flew past his man and fired home.

"That's what I'd have done," groin strain victim Mark Horton shouted.

"If you'd stayed on, it would've hit the pylon!" Carl shouted back.

Stan wrapped it up 10 minutes before time.

"Christ, it feels good to beat these lot at last," the overweight striker smiled as the final whistle blew, though a more honest declaration might have been "Christ, it feels good to have survived 90 minutes". He'd manhandled a Lowes player to the ground moments before Tigs' second. The ref missed it.

Still, there he was, victorious. Lowes, by contrast, were shell-shocked. Their Number 4 was one I remembered from my Lion Farm foray, a brash, intimidating figure then, but a lone voice echoing across the Remembrance Sunday mire as his team had died, yelling things like "Let's finish on a high note!", then "Let's have the last say" and, finally, a plaintive cry on the breeze – "Come on, lads" – as his team-mates ached for the shrill, final blast of the whistle that had sent them over the top, 90 minutes of action before.

After the game, by the dressing room, Ginger turned to Tigs with a grin on his face.

"Make the most of it," he laughed, "I'll be back in four weeks!"

Tigs smiled. So did Ted Terry.

"You haven't got a hope!" the chairman laughed.

Not everyone did though. The nearside front window of someone's Escort Cabriolet was scattered across the ground. Some players banged the Sunday mud from their boots against the brick wall, and some looked at the CCTV camera high on the wall opposite. Meesey did neither. He sat in his car and lit a cigarette. Yosser did both, briefly, as he stripped his shirt off, walked in to the dressing rooms and, two minutes later, walked out again, changed. It was either the shortest shower on record, or he was on a promise.

Ted Terry suggested we head off for the pub, so I went. I hadn't joined them after a match yet. I'd been waiting for an invitation, a test of their acceptance. They were probably waiting for me to invite myself, an indication that I knew how their world worked. Whatever, it seemed a good day to take a further step inside.

So, by 12.30pm, I was in the Gents, answering the call of nature that had become more pressing with every minute of the previous two hours, when Rob walked in.

"No one went out for a drink last night," he said. The shock made my bladder stall. "Stan was in bed by 7.30." Stan? Tucked up before *Blind Date*?

I joined Ted in the Bar – him with a pint of Banks's, me an apple juice – and, out of the blue, he told me he'd dipped into his pocket for £300 to help buy the team kit when they set up, "because the lads have their hearts in the right place".

In ones and twos the others dribbled in, bought a drink, paid their subs – well, some did – and watched the 100 Club draw. As I took it all in, I was introduced to Rob's dad, Ken, a man who looked as at home here as his son. Then Ted went to pay his Hundred Club and the room burst in to 'Happy Birthday'.

He blushed, then stroked his white beard and smiled as they belted out "… happy birthday, dear Santa". A couple of minutes later, I nodded at Rob.

"He looks a happy man," I said to Ted. "I always wanted to do what he's doing, playing until you're 40."

His smile broadened.

"He drinks, smokes. He's as fit as a butcher's dog. Smashing lad, lovely wife, three great kids. The littl'un's team plays on a Friday. Won 12 out of 12."

I looked at Rob again, hands on his thighs, no goals today, but laughing and sipping a pint. It was a chilly November day. Six-one, 37 going on 21, in his favourite pub, dad behind him, mates around him, with his family, sharing the conversation about a game they'd had to win. He looked content to me.

A few minutes later, Stan walked in.

"Rob says no one went out last night," I said to Ted, and gestured at Stan with my glass. "He was in bed by 7.30."

"He might have been in bed," Ted smiled, "but he took some cans with him."

I drove through Astwood Bank on the way home, as I'd done so often on Sunday mornings 20-odd years before. The war memorial had four poppy wreaths against it and maybe 50 little white crosses planted in front. Sunday, muddy Sunday.

I decided to phone Lindsay Dingley the moment Jezz sank to his haunches after the Netherton Hillcrest (away) match on Yew Tree's (home) pitch at Hillcrest, a week after. I wondered how much more the poor bloke could take. Consistently bad would have been better than the relentless roller-coaster, I imagined. The heart attack would come at a game, surely.

The game had been as unremarkable for Tree's abject ordinariness as Lowes, the previous week, had been illuminating for showing exactly what they could do with something less than 80 milligrammes of alcohol in every 100 millilitres of blood. It's unfair to pick on two blokes, but I'm going to. For most if the 90 minutes – though it seemed like 190 – Craig Skidmore drifted in and out of contact with Planet Earth on the left side of midfield, while Mark Horton showed he wasn't a natural right-midfielder in the middle. I expect you're as unsurprised by that as I was. But what could Paul and Jezz do? Very little. The team had picked itself. Scott had stopped playing Sundays, Mitch and Yode were injured, Dave Taylor and Evo had given up.

As I write, it sounds a little churlish to be criticising a bunch of working men who were 3-0 up by half-time, and even worse to mention that Hillcrest's keeper – the buck-toothed Flapper – never took part in the second-half, because his nerves were shot. Jezz had even followed Paul Gennard's characteristically low-key team talk by telling them it was going well. My heart sank as he said this.

"Win this and we'm two points behind Khalsa. Your destiny's in your own hands."

Stan had clapped. Another half like it and they'd be in the pub, laughing. The fool.

Churlish? Within nine minutes, it was 1-3. Within 11, it was 2-3, the first a hopeful cross which dropped beyond Chubbs into the vacant net, the second when the 17-year-old moved his body behind a free-kick (P39, the *Gordon Banks Academy Handbook*) then fumbled it (P42, *Alan Rough's Goalkeeping Made Easy – The Scottish Greats*). We watched it trickle in.

Those sturdy knights of coal and hammer, who scoff at peace and joy at clamour?

Jezz flew off the handle and Meesey told him to shut up. Then they all joined in. Maybe it was the time these blokes had spent in each other's pockets over the years, family, friends, schoolmates. Whatever, it was more than Bran could take.

"This is shit, ay it? Get out of bed!" he shouted.

Ironically, minutes before Chubbs' error, Gavin Skidmore had swung and missed as the ball flew off a divot, the last line of a threadbare defence wiped out by maintenance men who hadn't maintained. Chubbs raced to face the onrushing forward and drew cheers from the sideline by clearing. Cheers. For a few rewarding minutes, it had made a contrast to the previous week's bad-mouthing.

The mood in the pub was subdued afterwards, so much so that, after one of the old regulars asked the first man in what the score was, they didn't ask anyone else. I wasn't too bothered. It made a change from moaning.

Ginger did try to cheer things up by mentioning that Stan had mistaken the washing machine for the lavatory in the wee small hours, while they'd been watching the Lennox Lewis-Haseem Rahman fight at Yosser's. No one laughed.

The win kept Tree second in the league behind Khalsa, but I couldn't see them staying there. Rob sat by me and supped his cider. I nudged him my pork scratchings while they waited for landlady Lin Sanders to appear with the ritual trays of grub.

"Jezz has been talking about chucking the secretary's job in," he said, then paused to consider before adding "but he'll have calmed down soon."

Then word came through that Spenner, the old Albron team-mate who'd had his car raided the week before, had broken his leg. He was 30. Some shook their heads, the implication being that 30 was too old to come back. Rob and I swapped a glance.

"There's a bit old and there's a lot old," Rob said, straight-faced. "We'm a lot old."

"Who you playing next week?" I turned to Jezz when he came in, and my chest jolted. I'd nearly said "Who are *we* playing?" It wasn't quite that fourth-date moment when you catch yourself saying "I love you", but it was close.

He e-mailed me the following Wednesday. Barrel had dropped out of the league. It meant four points and 10 goals had been wiped from Yew Tree's record. He attached a new league table too. Then he listed the coming matches, "away Sunday at that lovely place Lion Farm, Pitch 7", a first-round League Cup match against Tap House, then two "interesting" games against Khalsa, the first at home.

His tone wasn't optimistic but, to me, there were reasons to believe that, somehow, Tree's fortunes had turned round. If things went well, the coming weeks would shape a season that went down to the wire. If they didn't, the weak link in my plan to follow Tree for a season would be exposed. The season would be over, in all but name, well before Craig and Gavin Skidmore dusted off their summer bowls.

As I read Jezz's e-mail, I hoped he saw it the same way. But, to be frank, I wasn't certain he could step far back enough for that to happen.

The day Jezz thought he was having a heart attack, Lindsay had walked into the house and realised something was wrong. He was deathly white and gasping for air.

She left him and went out again to take a couple of Aaron's friends home first. They'd had a football match, but she couldn't drop them at school, because their parents were expecting them at home. That was her responsibility. She wouldn't have liked her children left at school or walking home in the dark. So Jezz had waited.

I'd found him easy company since that first, frozen meeting at Lion Farm. It was hard not to like the man, even if I hadn't been able to fathom how his passion for Yew Tree fitted into home life. When I spoke to her on the phone, one evening while he was at work, I started to think that maybe it didn't.

I pictured a woman with her arms folded but hoped that, 30-odd miles away, there was the hint of a smile in her eyes.

"I hates football, I can't be bothered with it," she told me straight away.

"I take it you didn't meet at a match."

"No. We met at speedway. We used to go the dogs. I'm the dog in trap five! You ask him, that's what he'll tell you."

I mentioned his 'I'm having chest pains' e-mail.

"I came in and he looked white and he was hyperventilating, panicking," she said, and ran through those frightening hours with barely a pause for air. "He was like it when I left him. I cor deny it, he was short of breath. It all came about with him excessive drinking on the Sunday. I dropped him off at the pub, 10-to-three. I'd gone to bed at 10 and there was still no sign of him. He kept me up all night throwing up. He ay told you that, has he? I'd told him not to be sick on the carpet. I made him go to work. He went in on Tuesday, at half-seven. By a quarter-to-eight he was phoning me to tell me he was coming home. He was home by eight. Wednesday I took him to hospital, 'cos I'd had the football first. I could see he ay well, 'cos he hadn't been eating, either. The doctor who seen him, she was great. Her sent his bloods off to see if he'd had a coronary."

The minutes had dragged as they waited for the results to come, not knowing whether he'd gone the same way as Liverpool's Gerard Houllier. Finally, the medics returned.

"It was the drinking and the not eating which had brought on the pains," she explained. "And the panicking. I don't want to sound horrible, but I had to be that night. I have a disabled daughter" – nine-year-old Chelsea, who suffers from mild cerebral palsy after a 26-week birth – "and I'm horrible to her. I have to be. I have to try and treat her normal so that she does things. If I don't, I'd be in hospital meself.

"He isn't well this week, I must admit. A cold. And I do feel for him. But not when he had to go to hospital. He hadn't been eating. I took him back up the pub, and there was a dinner in the oven. I don't mind him going out. But that was bang out of order."

I'd only meant to ask about the heart scare, but I thought you ought to know the rest.

"Ever been to watch Yew Tree play?" I wondered.

"No! I've been to the pub a couple of times."

"Do you go to the presentation evening?"

"I must admit, I do. I enjoyed that last year, even though I don't like football. I'm a little on the big side, self-conscious. So I don't like to go. Jezz likes Gary Glitter, but he got the babby up on the karaoke last year, and they did *We Are the Champions*. I enjoyed that 'cos it was something more than the football."

"Can you imagine yourself watching a match?"

"No," she said. "It's not in my blood. On a Sunday, I've got all my work to do. I've got the little one to look after, I've got to do all me washing, I've got the kids school things for the next day. I ay got time for nothing else. From one o'clock, I stick the ironing board up in front of *EastEnders* and what ay been done ay done."

"And then Jezz comes in from the Yew Tree and you don't talk about football!"

"No."

8   LIGHTING THE FIRE

EVERYONE SHOULD HAVE SOMEONE LIKE ELLIS DAVIS in their lives. Someone who lights the flame. You see, Ellis, a soft-spoken Welshman with sparkling eyes that devoured all around him, taught me how to love the English language. There's funny.

He also gave me a yardstick for measuring what people around you are worth. This is it.

You're in the nosecone of a Saturn 5 rocket, a few hours from the Moon, when something the size of Stan hits a fuel tank. You need someone with you who'll walk in space with a roll of Duct Tape, or someone who'll make you laugh till the oxygen runs out. Ellis didn't suggest this, but it strikes me you could sub Kylie Minogue for the comedian, if you wanted.

I'd resisted putting these distant cousins to the nosecone test until I'd been invited to sup with them that Sunday lunchtime. By the second post-match pint, it seemed reasonable to tell Maggie I'd be late for dinner every other week.

Then Jezz sent an e-mail that took my mind back to the early days of the season, when I'd rolled the years away and begun to decide which of these blokes I'd have been happy to play football with, and which against. The e-mail contained his and Paul's man-of-the-match scores. I ran my eye down the list, to measure my thoughts (which didn't count) against theirs (which did). I only recognised half the men listed. He'd only gone and used proper names, hadn't he?

Edson Arantes do Nascimento wasn't among them, but Dave Hall, Andy Taylor and Matthew Taylor were. That's to say that, while it was unlikely Pele would pull on a Yew Tree shirt against Khalsa Warriors, Yode, Opple and Tigs probably would. It had taken me 14 weeks to discover some legal identities, not that it mattered.

The day before, Paul had told me about the target he'd set, 10 points from the next 12. God knows how he reckoned it would happen. It meant they could only afford to draw one of the next four, starting with the back-to-back games vs Khalsa.

"Who's the danger?" I asked of our next opponents.

"They've got three players from Smethwick, one in the back four, one midfield, one up front. They've got ball-players, so we've got to battle for it."

"How's Mitch coming on?"

"It ay as bad as what was first feared. He's got some floating cartilage. But he's still got to have keyhole. They'll trim it off and he could be back two weeks after that."

Then, after a pause, he added: "I've been looking for a keeper. Chubbs, another couple of years on him… on Sunday, he lost that ball to make it one-all, then made a great save." He paused again. I half expected him to sigh.

Ten points from four games? From the safety of the touchline, for me, the name Khalsa Warriors alone suggested they'd be lucky to come away with six.

I scanned Jezz's man-of-the-match list, worked out who was who, and compiled a list of averages, a yardstick to measure my eyes against his, and a guide – unreliable, but a guide nonetheless – as to who might be expected to do what in the three-week search for 10 points. Using the line-up that had won the Warley Sunday League Cup First Round tie against Tap House 3-6, the week before, this is what it said:

C Cartwright (Chubbs) Average 5.7 per match played; Paul Bowen 6.2; Matthew Taylor (Tigs) 7.27; Anthony Brannon (Bran) 6.7; Gavin Skidmore 7.25; Mark Horton, 7.1; Steven Meese, 6.8; Chris Bassford (Bass), 5.7; Andy Taylor (Opple), 6.5; Craig Horton (Stan) 6.7; Craig Skidmore, 7. Rob Wall came in with an average of 6.9, Justin Hughes (Yosser) 6.6 and, over his five games before injury, Dave Hall (Yode) scored 7. That left Clark Williams (Ginger) on 5.8 from six games before suspension, and Tuck, averaging six from three until brothers-in-law Gav and Craig had sent his shoulder towards the ceiling. I'd have disputed a couple, but there was little in it, from where I'd watched.

One other thing the list told me was this. Opple wasn't Opple. He was Apple.

The last 22 minutes against Tap House at Lion Farm had produced six goals and as many inches of rain. At the final whistle, I'd sprinted for cover faster than I'd run since my brother ankle-tapped me on the way home from school one day in 1974, and a right hook from nowhere had fattened his lip. I hope I never have to run that fast again.

"You're going to be out in this tomorrow!" I yelled to Rob through the deluge.

"Ah," he said. "Digging for England!"

Maggie shook her head when I returned, bemused by the soggy husband who'd managed to make it back in time for her birthday lunch. She'd grown accustomed to me disappearing for a couple of days at a time while I was researching *Through Fire and Water*, and returning with tales of young men fighting the Falklands War. She'd understood my deepening attachment to them and their stories from the Grantham Sound gunline, but couldn't begin to fathom why I'd patrol a touchline in Oldbury on a pig of a Sunday morning.

She was shaking her head again as I set off north for the Khalsa match. As I passed an Escort on the M5 with ice on the inside of its windows, I began to wonder myself.

It was so cold at Hillcrest the players were huddled in a circle by the dressing room, hot breath and cigarette smoke rising rings of fire. Even Stan had a Parka on.

A few weeks before, a white Mercedes minibus had screamed into the car park. It had three crowns and the name Sweet Turf Christian Centre Shuttle Bus on its flanks, and a woman and child were inside. I'd have seen why, if they were praying. It did a rapid three-point turn and was nearly hit by an Astra. Now it hurtled into sight again.

"Always the same time" Tuck said.

"Always the same two passengers," someone else added.

"They've got permission to build a church by the pitch," Tuck went on, in a considerably better mood than at Tap House, when he was happy until I asked if he was back at work and I discovered he'd had his money cut from £6.20 to £4.10 an hour, because he was on light duties. Now he described the patch of waste ground, a throw-in from the touchline by the bottom pitch, the bramble land Jezz spent half of every game in.

"They're going to love us. How they gonna to cope with balls hitting the windows?"

"Never mind the windows," Jezz chuckled. "Imagine the vicar, 'and Jesus said….' and then one of you lot shouting 'Fucking hell, ref. That were a foul!' It don't bear thinking about." Yes it did, and it was good to hear him laugh.

There was nothing sweet about the morning, but lots of turf. Opple warmed up by running the length of the pitch, then walked back like John Wayne. He'd almost lost a boot in the top penalty area. Stan kicked a ball and his feet disappeared beneath the icing sugar topping. Dudley Metropolitan Borough Council had charged Jezz £110 deposit for the season, and £16 a match. They could still be done for fraud.

The rest of them wandered out, in twos and threes, with all that's necessary to put the nets up, apart from willingness. After a minute or two, Jezz broke the silence.

"Come on!" he yelled. "Everyone does this together."

If the regular stragglers increased the length of their stride, I didn't notice. My money was on Meesey being last to appear, and I was right. He jogged down the hill, the trademark denim jacket over his shirt, and arrived in time to watch the others hammering the last net pegs in.

"Oh," he said, "I told you to wait for me!" No one laughed.

Tree were behind after 10 minutes, a header from a corner. It marked the twelfth set-piece goal since September, and the end of Paul's tactical plan. In the search for composure, concentration and commitment, the defence was flat-footed, the midfield a still-life, and Stan and a shaven-headed Rob – the scalping seemed a little excessive to me – were isolated in attack.

The last time we'd played at Hillcrest, Yode and I had spent the first part of the game talking about the recurrence of his groin injury and watching Tuck trying to retrieve a ball from the tree Bran had hit during the kick-in. To be accurate, we didn't watch him. He and his dodgy shoulder were in the brambles, beyond the drop from the top goal. All we could see was the odd branch flying into the air. This went on for about 15 minutes before he gave up.

"Folk have been known to go in there and never be seen again," Jezz had warned me once, so we breathed a sigh of relief as he reappeared.

Yode was on the line again this day, but now in a sub's shirt. How Tree needed him mixing it where it counted. Paul Bowen was at right-back, playing like an old-time centre-half, operating in such a small parcel of pitch that even the familiar "Go on, Bowe, use your pace" jibe was obsolete.

It must have been bad. Ginger and Carl had rubbished Fabien Bartez and Seba Veron's pitiful displays for Man U, the day before. Otherwise, things were strangely quiet on the line.

Heaven knows what a Sweet Turf Bible-basher would have made of the silence from beyond the stained-glass. Tree's usual Black Country Sunday communion took inspiration from *The Sun*. Their 10 Commandments began with 'Thou shalt not stay in on a Saturday' and ended with 'Thou shalt not listen to a blind word Paul Gennard says'. Happy wasn't clappy, it was a ritual piss-take. But this morning had none of the usual joy and precious little passion. Then it changed.

They'd faced a few black players so far. One was Errol, Barrel's midfielder. Until now, I've not mentioned it because his skin had nothing to do with the effect his skills had on those games. If racism was an issue in the homes running north, south, east and west from Baptist End, the matches I'd seen seemed to be a sanctuary from it.

In my search for Yew Tree, the season before, I'd even seen one match when two players tussled the length of the pitch for possession. When the ball was won, one team manager turned to the other and said "Our black's faster than your black!"

I remember a pause in a John Arlott commentary once being filled by the effects mike picking up a spectator confiding to a bloke that "I could shag your missus". I mention it because it was similar split-second timing that saw Khalsa's Number 4 shout "That's a foul, ref, you fucking racist!" as Meesey – predictably – swung handbags with his marker, after 25 minutes, and the ref waved Khalsa's protests away.

Again, I haven't mentioned it until now – because it wasn't relevant – but most of Khalsa's players were of Asian origin, albeit fluent in Brummie. Ironically, the accuser was white.

It was one to test the sternest of Christian values, let alone *The Laws of Association Football*. His team-mates looked at the guilty party. The Yew Tree contingent looked at him. Ted, shaven-headed like Rob, looked at him. Ted's dog looked at him. We all looked at him. He was the only one not looking at himself. The ref strode, had a word, wagged a finger, then back-pedalled. No card. "And be ye kind one to another, tender-hearted, forgiving one another…." (*Ephesians 4, 32*)

Tree didn't look like scoring before Khalsa doubled their lead on 29, a chip from 18 yards after Bowe had left his man unmarked, and they didn't look like scoring for a long while afterwards. The advice they needed at half-time was "Commit thy way unto the Lord; trust also in Him; and he shall bring it to pass" (*Psalms 37,5*)

Instead, they had "No challenges. Rubbish. Playing like a side that's just come together. Can't keep relying on Rob. Mark's running his bollocks off. They want to win it more than us" (*Gospel according to Jezz Dingley, 11.17am*).

On 47, it appeared to have worked. Stan headed against the post and the rebound went over the line. The ref, 30 yards away, waved play on. "How can you see from back there, you dozy prat?" (*The Paula Tucker Book of Quotes, 11.22am*)

It was another 17 minutes before they saw reward for the digging-in mentality Paul had pleaded for, when Rob nicked possession and squared for Opple. One-two.

I glanced up the line at the Khalsa followers and caught the eye of one, a buck-toothed man six feet away with a four-inch scar down his left cheek. It's wrong to make snap judgements, but also unavoidable. I waited for the 'Who you looking at?' stare back, but he smiled and the scar turned into a crease, and made me feel guilty.

"We ain't good enough to be at the top of the league," he shrugged his shoulders and pointed at Yode, who'd been running the line during the second-half.

"He needs to learn to cheat better," he told Jezz. "He's being too fair."

In the minutes that followed, Craig hit the bar, and Paul told me: "We'm short of three players, a keeper and two others."

Tree equalised close to time, Meesey finishing a loping Mark Horton run from 12 yards. It was just as well Mark passed. Another solo effort ending with mud up his nostrils would have been too much. Two-two. Their joy – "Rejoice in the Lord always; and again I say, Rejoice" (*Philippians, 4, 4*) – was short-lived, however.

Four minutes from time, Mark lost possession on the edge of his area. A snap-shot deflected past the turning Chubbs, but only his eyes followed it. His feet were dead, frozen by the need to move in two directions at once and glued by the mud. As helpless as a man watching a winning Lottery ticket disappear down the drain – "It could be you!" (*Camelot, 2001*) – he saw Khalsa's sub tap the third.

There were chances to equalise, but it didn't happen.

Trembling with cold, I quizzed the ref on the "racist" outburst, afterwards, coming down slowly from incensed to merely disturbed.

"I couldn't book him 'cos his voice was different to the one I heard," he said, though I wasn't sure he believed it any more than I did. I was tempted to ask if Alastair McGowan had been named on either team-sheet but, knowing my luck, he'd have taken my name for resorting to the lowest form of wit.

The pub wasn't subdued, not like after the Hillcrest local derby. But it was quiet, maybe on account of them working out how far their match averages had dipped.

To make it worse, Carlton weren't showing Wolves-Albion. I'd been surprised how little open rivalry there'd been between the handful of Wolves fans and the sole Baggie, Tuck. Perhaps, after years banished from their top-flight ancestral home, the tension was starting to show. They looked at the TV and tutted, and that was about it.

On the drive home, I bounced around the frequencies, trying to find the match. Almost every station was playing a Beatles track. George Harrison had died three days before. It was four before I thawed out. *Here Comes the Sun* (Beatles, 1969).

I couldn't resist it. I closed the study door quietly, pulled the curtains, flicked the computer on and keyed sweetturf.org.uk What kind of religion would compete for souls one side of the railings, in years to come, while another calling was being observed the other? In seconds, Pastor Mark and Gillian Burchell were smiling at me.

It was routine stuff. "We offer two main Sunday meetings", it said, and "Everyone's special to God and we look forward to seeing you soon". Then came a little history, "Sweet Turf Baptist Church was built in 1810. The name Sweet Turf was so called as the church was built on farm pasture land which was known for its succulent grass". Something told me Dudley Metropolitan Borough Council hadn't held the maintenance contract back then, but it was only a guess.

There were sections on *How to Get There*, including "Giving people the ride of their lives on the STCC Mercedes Shuttle bus". It didn't mention the final lap of the car park. *What We Believe In* kicked off with "The unity of the Father, Son and the Holy Spirit in the Godhead" and ended with "the expectation of the return of Jesus Christ". Jesus Christ? They'll hear His apparent arrival a dozen times a match at the pitch next door, when the church is built.

In between, there was the "Dec 16th 'Magic & Sparkle' Christmas special for all the family with Peter McCahon – magician, comedian & escapologist" and the "Dec 24th Christmas Eve by candlelight at 8pm-9.15pm, Speaker: Pastor Phil Collins Featuring the 100 voices of the Dream Choir". There was a *Prayer Request* section too – I made a note, in case Paul Gennard ever felt the need – and the *Pastor's Message for the Month*, which offered the advice that "Whatever shape or size your box is, never lie down in it, because whatever your box is called, it really is a coffin in disguise". That one would have started a debate in the dressing room, I can tell you.

There were pictures, too, of the church they planned to build alongside Tree's home ground, where Dingley's Brambles prevailed. Prayer had already played a big part in securing the two-acre site for £150,000 cash. Not quite your Hundred Club. Sweet Turf hoped the £4.5m project, with its 1,000-seat auditorium, restaurant, TV suite and parking "for everyone" would be open by March. God would have to move in a mysterious way, indeed, for that to happen.

I worked my way back to the Home page. Pastor Mark and Gillian were still there, smiling. Nowhere did it mention a church football team. So, some old Black Country traditions hadn't entirely survived the passing of the years. Still, at least they'd only be a throw-in away from one they could adopt.

Between the Khalsa matches, I kept a date in the pub with club chairman Ted Terry. The thermometer had already gone through the floor as I ran from the car to the Bar behind the women's darts team. When I'd met Jezz there, a month before, fireworks were filling the sky. Now it was Christmas lights.

Twice divorced, Ted couldn't remember the moment the little voice in his head told him to support the fledgling football team, but he recalled the feeling with a smile.

"The hub of the community, it is, round here," he said, and ran a hand over the shaven head that had appeared the previous Sunday. "It was talking to Jezz. He used to come up here after a match, and I'd ask 'em how they'd got on. He said they could start it up here. So we had a meeting. This place was packed. There was about 30 blokes. I sat down and said 'I'll start you off'."

He'd put his hand in his pocket and produced a £300 cheque for kit. Another Tree regular, called Bryn, paid £250 more to put Premier Thermal Insulations on their shirts. Landlady Lin Sanders agreed to pay the league fees and insurance, and they were on their way.

"I'd moved up from Droitwich," Ted leaned forward. "I come here, I was accepted. They're the salt of the earth. That's why I'm reluctant to go back to me roots."

He smiled, and I already knew why. My roots, like his, were in south Worcestershire. But not my genes. They came from Oldbury, the other side of Rowley Ridge, and they had magnetic properties. In my 44th year, something had attracted me to this landscape of iron and steel. I had no scientific proof – as Rob had none that there was a football gene -- just a feeling. But that was good enough.

"I support them. I always will support 'em," he interrupted my thoughts. "The same as the youngsters nowadays. That's why I had this lot done" – he brushed a hand across his shaven head again – "for a kid that's not as fortunate as me."

"So that was for charity then?" I asked.

Landlady Lin had joined us: "They had a charity night here Thursday," she lit a cigarette, "for this lad."

"The junior football team. I did the same for them," Ted added. "They wanted a strip. So I thought 'Go on!' Well, I can't take it with me, so…." Once a copper, always a copper.

"The head-shave?" I asked again.

"One of the lads has leukaemia. Smashing kid," he said. "He was a player. They come up with this idea of playing on a Friday night, down the ballpark. They was all in rag-tag shirts. So I doled out £3 a time, bought eight or nine shirts and said 'Here, put these on, all the same'. Jezz did the motifs and his missus ironed 'em on.

"Little Greeny, Dave Green, he used to come up. Well, he ain't above this high," he lifted his hand, then tugged the collar of his polo shirt. "He was playing for 'em. Great little keeper. Threw himself at everything. Suddenly, he went home one Friday night and his mother spotted some unusual bruising on him, and she knew what it was."

"Who else had the old…," I ran a hand over my head.

"Out of the team, me and Robin. But some of the youngsters too. There were three out of the school that had permission to have it done. James and a couple of the other lads," he nodded towards the Bar in reference to Rob's eldest lad and his mates. "About six had it done, in the end. They got a roasting, apparently, when they went to school. There were that many kids in there, on the Thursday night."

"There weren't much in the *Dudley News* about it," Lin said.

"They didn't want to send a photographer up or nothing. They said 'You can take your own photographs and send them in to us'. I was disappointed at that. They're quick enough to ring up and ask me if I want to advertise."

I knew how weekly newspapers were staffed and how they operated, but this wasn't the time to explain or justify why a community newspaper might not have a snapper on duty.

"Was David here?" I asked, instead.

"Yes," Ted nodded. "I don't know whether he knows it was for him, does he?"

"He doesn't," Lin answered. "He doesn't like a fuss."

Little Greeny was being treated at Brum's Princess of Wales Hospital for Children. No football for a while. The only match he was waiting for was the one that might lead to a marrow transplant. He was just 14.

"Is he aware how ill he is?"

"I think so," Ted nodded again. "He's quieter than what he was. A lot quieter."

I knew enough about leukaemia to realise that transplants weren't the first things they tried. His was coming from his mother, or his sister.

"Shame," Ted said. "Hell of a shame. He's a smashing kid."

Over the coming months, Little Greeny's name would echo round this place until most of the pieces dropped into place. There'd be times when fate dragged me towards the pub while his family was there, then something would delay me until they'd gone. It would be a long time before our paths crossed but, for now, all I knew was that they'd raised £400 for his family. The head-shave had made £200 of it.

In the me-me-me, disposable age of mediocrity called the early 21st Century, the Yew Tree pub was reaching into homes built in Victorian, Edwardian and post-war times and helping to keep the community ticking. For donkeys years, the farmhouse it once was had sat beside a cart track overlooking an open-cast colliery. It had become a pub in 1952, not a large chunk of Black Country history, compared with other places I'd seen, but heritage here wasn't the age of a building. It was the people who'd lived and died in it, and the essence they'd passed on.

Anyone looking for one of Paul Gennard's team wouldn't have to stray far off this beaten path between August and June to find them. Their schedule went like this: "Tuesday nights we sometimes see them, because they play down the ballpark, down in Cradley Heath. They come up for the last hour, then they come up here after training on a Thursday, a few of them, not all. And then, sometimes, I see 'em on a Friday night. Then Saturday afternoon after golf."

Then there were Sundays. Lin paused and sipped a Coke.

"Jezz said to me 'Why does your face always go like that when they go in the Lounge?' I says 'The language'.

"It's mainly Ginger and Scurve," she looked at Ted and lit another cigarette. "When they're watching a match, especially Wolves, they just get a bit excited, don't they? I can hear them upstairs. I grit me teeth."

Ted haunted the Tree most nights, but looked forward to Fridays above all. Friday nights meant racing home from work, "shite, shave and shampoo, take the kids down the ballpark, come back. I come up here and I have me beer and mixed grill. Then I look forward to Sunday morning".

"The kids stick up for you. I find that. Comradeship. I had it in the police but, at the end of the day, you're only a number. I've found that out since retirement. So, I prefer to come up here and mix with the lads."

"What does the football give you?" I asked.

"What does it give me? Seeing a bunch of kids enjoying themselves. All right, they get cussed and shouted at by Jezz. They come in here and enjoy theirselves. As long as they enjoy theirselves, I like to sit back and watch."

Watching a couple of nights before had included Carl calling Ginger's mobile, and handing it to Lin so she could text him, pretending to be Stacy, a girl he was planning to meet at a club later. Ginger took the bait. A minute later, he appeared at the bar, asking Lin how to spell 'gorgeous'. He hadn't struck me as the romantic sort but, then again, I didn't know what he'd been trying to describe, or what he'd already written.

A few weeks earlier, I'd sat here and listened to Jezz reluctantly admit he dreamed of better things for the team. It wasn't long before Ted was doing the same. He was surprised how well they were faring, third in the table when survival would have done, given that they were a law unto themselves.

"They do their own thing," he said. "They never do anything he says!

"But, to go and play somewhere like Dudley Town, and come back with a cup, that's what I'd love to see. Not second. Something in their hand. To be part of that."

"You're still in the West Brom Cup," I reminded him.

"Yes," he nodded. "To be part of that day, with them kids. 'Cos I class 'em as kids. To sit in the corner and buy 'em a beer. As chairman, you've got to, I suppose."

"And what would you cook them?" I looked at Lin, almost smelling the trays of sausage and chips she usually passed around the bar on a Sunday afternoon.

"Scampi," she said. "Even steak, perhaps. Small steaks."

It was a warming thought. But, for every Lowes performance there'd been a couple of George Celtics. Even with two-thirds of the season still to unfold, somehow I doubted it would happen. How little I knew.

9   ONE DAY WE'M BRILLIANT....

ANYONE WHO EVER KICKED A BAG OF WIND and dreamed is in a treasured book of mine. Paul Gennard, for one, even if he doesn't know it. *How Steeple Sinderby Wanderers Won the FA Cup* is about a village team that wins the FA Cup – but you've probably guessed that. Its hero, Alex Slingsby, believes that, by following these five principles, it's possible for any team to win:

- Postulation 1: It is possible to move a ball without staring down at your feet. Women don't watch their hands when knitting.
- Postulation 2: A very good goalkeeper is a team's most valuable asset. Almost alone he can thwart superior opponents.
- Postulation 3: A goalkeeper does not need to be an accomplished footballer. He needs qualifications similar to a good cabinet-maker or bus driver – distinguishing instantly what will or will not fill the space. To this must be applied outstanding agility and courage.
- Postulation 4: The only truly striking difference between the technical skills in amateur and professional players is the latter's control of a ball's movement when struck by his head. (Recommendation: (1) Whenever possible, keep the ball close to the ground and (2) select terrain disadvantageous to flighted passage of balls).
- Postulation 5: Every player except the centre forward must defend his own goal, and every player except the goalkeeper must assault his opponent's goal.

Since the 5-0 defeat at Harborne, I'd gradually learnt what principles Paul craved seeing made flesh on the pitch. Just one Sunday would have done. So, three weeks before Christmas, on the top of a Black Country hill, stars twinkling like fairylights on a dark sky, wind-chill knifing deep into minus territory, I watched his team train at Hillcrest.

I already knew he believed the key to defeating Khalsa would be supporting Rob and Stan from midfield. So, after they'd finished shuttles, he put them in two lines and told one man from each side to lay the ball back to a team-mate. He'd shoot. A miss would cost five press-ups. Within seconds, players were grunting, nose-down, all over the all-weather.

After 15 minutes shooting/missing, Mark, Stan and Rob picked sides. It took me back to Inky Insole, a small, bookish boy who enjoyed kicking a ball around. He was always last pick at dinner time, yet he somehow contrived to score the greatest volleyed goal I ever saw, a blessed, unmatched moment that, had it come in a Galilee Hotspurs match, would have rivalled the fishes and loaves story.

As Stan and Mark argued over first pick, the rules became clear. Two-touch, the scorers stayed on, the losers sat on the cold wall. Unless they'd stocked up on haemorrhoid cream at the pub, it sounded like an incentive.

I leaned against the mesh fencing and watched the sides picked, Tigs first – predictably – then Yoss, Bass, Opple and on through Bowe, Yode, Ginger, Craig and the rest. Rob picked his lad James and, for the next 15 minutes, only the Old Mon and Tigs found the space and angles required. Two-touch? The effing and blinding drifted most loudly over Netherton whenever players realised two plus one was three.

"What's been said about putting things right after Sunday?" I asked Paul through lips swollen with frostbite, sounding like Roy Hattersley. I wiped spittle from my chin and repeated myself, slowly. He buried his hands deep in his donkey-jacket pockets and drew breath. It went something like this:

- Postulation 1: "You cor play football unless you concentrate…"
- Postulation 2: "… and you cor concentrate unless you'm fit."
- Postulation 3: "They cor play 35 minutes, and go to sleep the rest of the game…"
- Postulation 4: "… and they've got to support from midfield. Stan and Rob was left on their own on Sunday. No one supported, no one supported."
- Postulation 5: "And someone's got to look up and see what's going wrong. It's no good telling 'em before and after. Someone's got to 'ave the vision on the pitch."

I nodded in understanding and agreement as he returned to the five-a-side pitch. I watched him go and listened to him try to make a point to his players.

Where I'd always read Alex Slingsby's lines with a note of confidence in my head, Paul's voice carried none. He needed his players to spend 90 minutes bringing his beliefs to life, proving he was right. Until then, he'd sound like a man for whom it was hopeless to even consider hope.

It was nearly 9pm as I pulled off the car park, wishing someone had asked me to step into a game, even for five minutes, but knowing I'd have been crippled if they had.

Christmas had come earlier in Netherton than elsewhere on the drive home. The best lights were in a mid-terrace, a remnant of Old Hill's industrial past, a white tree decked with white lights behind a window framed by even more twinklings of white, as if someone had nicked a small galaxy from the winter night sky.

In my mellowness, I mused about how many Christmases the house had seen in its time. For the rest of the 30 miles, though, I thought about Paul. Would he ever see the football he wanted, not by chance, but by design? You know the answer as well as me, by now.

It was half-nine before I was home and – to maintain the flow of condition checks – midnight before I could feel the tips of my fingers.

A crowd of pigeons was huddling for warmth in the centre-circle when I pulled up at West Smethwick Park for the Khalsa game, and a row of gulls was strung along the crossbar of the nearest goal. On Thursday night's evidence, every last one was safe.

The radio chat had been about Man U's 0-1 loss to West Ham, and their slide to 13th in the Premiership. Sad, but not as sad, as the mist lifted and the frost became dew, as Sir Alex explaining that Sebastian Veron and Ruud van Nistelrooy – £42m worth – hadn't even been subs because they were "tired". Poor souls. What luck they weren't digging roads for a living as well. If, by chance, he passed Manchester's version of West Smethwick Park that dank morning, he'd have seen real theatres of dreams.

The poached eggs on Marmite toast had slid down well enough, but I had no appetite for what was to come, I confess. It had been a late, sleepless night because of the kind of problems families have. To start with, Dad's recovery from a summer cancer op had taken a sharp turn down a dark road, and he was facing another op before Christmas.

If that wasn't enough, my 16-year-old daughter had been the target of a false and nasty accusation from an apparent friend. I say 'apparent' because, years before, the girl had bullied her into retreating beneath her duvet with playground threats like 'If you don't have me as your friend, I'll tell the teacher that….'

Maggie had been concerned when the girl worked her way back into the social circle. Naively, I was prepared to believe in the power of redemption. I should have trusted Maggie's instinct. It would take months of anger and anguish to drag an apology and retraction from the family but, here and now, waiting for the teams, I felt damaged and hollow. I even thought about jacking it all in, thanking Jezz for the season so far, and quietly disappearing to find a duvet of my own.

The way Tree had played seven days before had hardly made the prospect of a freezing touchline appealing anyway, and I wasn't alone. Outside the dressing rooms, Lin said Paul had picked Ginger. Tigs had a knee injury, not that it mattered to Stan.

"I can't believe Ginger's playing," he emerged with his kit, on cue, muttering. It wasn't his morning. Farts in a confined space, or water on the floor, normally sent men scurrying to cars to change. This time, he'd been driven out by cigarette smoke.

Then Flapper appeared, Netherton Hillcrest's buck-toothed keeper, a man of indeterminate years who worked with Gavin Skidmore. He'd produced some decent saves in the first match at Baptist End and, for 45 minutes, I'd wondered how close a nickname could come to slander. But he'd asked to come off at half-time in the return because his nerves were shot. Now he was sniffing after a game with Tree. That's all they needed, I thought, an insecure keeper. Stan wasn't happy about that, either.

Jezz appeared after Flapper, and I asked the obvious about what was to come.

"They know what they've got to do," he said.

Then Paul appeared and said Yoss had been dropped. Bass was in midfield, behind the front two. (Postulation 4: They've got to support from midfield). It was up to him.

It was up to all of them. Postulations 1-5 sat between them and another six-pointer for the league leaders that would roger the '10 points from 12' plan as surely as Jezz spent most Hillcrest Sundays up to his ears in brambles. This was the moment of the season when teams put themselves in with a shout, or stuttered towards the murky depths alongside Walsall Bengals, the time when winter and the Warley & District Sunday League fixture pencil began building backlogs that would leave players shagged in May.

Postulation 1 – "you can't play football unless you concentrate…" – took the biggest test, most frustratingly in the first 20 minutes, as Khalsa stretched Tree's midfield and defence, drawing lunging tackles where patience was called for, opening gaps through which even Veron might have probed, if he'd had the strength to lace his boots, poor lamb.

Postulation 2 – "… and you can't concentrate unless you're fit" – was next on my tick-list. You know already which legs gave second best to the conditions after half-an-hour, which started in third gear and stayed there, and which never gave up. Postulation 2 was responsible for Postulation 1. The answer to that lay at the bottom of a beer glass.

Postulation 3 – "They cor play for 35 minutes, and go to sleep the rest of the game…" – was where the game hinged, though. But Tree didn't play for 35 minutes, then fall asleep. The opposite, in fact. And I imagine you're as surprised at that as me.

They didn't wake up for 19 minutes. But, when they did, they ripped Khalsa apart, even though none of the four goals they scored between the 20th and 65th minutes owed anything to Postulation 4 – "… and they've got to support from midfield…." – or Postulation 5, "someone's got to look up and see what's going wrong… Someone's got to 'ave the vision out on the pitch".

To begin with, apart from one rising shot, Meesey was drifting. Bass wasn't reading the game, Rob lacked support and Stan just looked frustrated. So did Paul.

It's hard to say which of the goals was the pick, either from my point of view or Paul's. The first came when Mark collected the ball five yards in front of his back four, played a one-two, then hared off through the middle before drawing the keeper and driving a low shot into the bottom left corner.

"When was the last time you saw him score a goal?" I asked his mum.

"Fuck knows," Lin said.

If the second was ridiculous -- Bass' shot going through the keeper's legs – the third was sublime. Rob picked up Ginger's hopeful pass with his back to goal, 40 yards out. He held off a challenge, turned and looped a left-foot shot past the flailing keeper. I don't remember even Georgie scoring one like it.

"Oi! Listen up!" Jezz did most of the half-time talking. "Remember Hillcrest? For fuck's sake don't let it happen today. We got away with murder. You've got to work hard. Get the ball to feet and pass…." Then the rest started.

Bran: "We'm playing fucking all right boys…." Rob: "Loads of confidence…." Paul: "You got to be 100 per cent lads…." Mark: "I'm Stevie Gerrard." Jezz: "No, no, no, no, no! Another 45. Then we'll talk about Stevie Gerrard."

Khalsa pulled one back, a header from a corner a minute before Rob restored the three-goal cushion with a run from half-way. The home side had the last say, but not the last laugh, when Meesey was robbed trying to run the ball out of defence, and upended the thief. Pen. Chubbs went the wrong way. Game over.

I jogged to Paul, smiling, unable to believe I'd been watching the same teams as the previous week. He had a bewildered look on his face. It took me a while to realise who it resembled. Half-way home, it came to me. Stan Laurel. If he'd had a bowler on, and taken

Principles and Postulations: Paul Gennard, the man who fought a fruitless fight to persuade the Trees that they could do great things... for more than a couple of minutes in a row. Picture by Aaron Manning

it

off, I'd have expected him to start tugging at his hair.

From: Jeremy Dingley
To: Mark Higgitt
Subject: Re: I tell you what...
Date: December 11, 2001 06:45

Mark – You should know us by now. We have got to be the most frustrating team you have ever seen. Never mind top managers having heart by-pass operations, they would be dead if they were with us. Maybe last weeks result could tell you how Khalsa are at the top. We were up for that game on Sunday, we rode our luck for the first 20 minutes, then they say, "The rest is history". I haven't stopped smiling yet. We are at home on Sunday against George Celtic. League table attached. Jezz.

The top of the league table looked like this:

TEAMS	P	W	D	L	F	A	P	GD
Harborne	12	9	0	3	65	20	27	45
Khalsa	9	7	1	1	33	16	22	17
Yew Tree	9	6	0	3	30	20	18	10
New Fullbrook	6	5	0	1	19	8	15	11

I rang Rob on the Wednesday and we talked about Khalsa.

"That's us, " he said. "One day we'm brilliant, the next we'm rubbish!"

One day we'm brilliant, the next we'm rubbish.

Mark Horton drifted to the touchline as a ball sailed past the bus shelter during the Sunday kick-in. As the traffic stopped and a man, hands in pockets, brought it under control with one touch and chipped it back with the other, someone asked the crew-cut 20-year-old why he wasn't in the back four.

"I'm Stevie Gerrard," he answered, and described his goal against Khalsa, stride by stride. "No word of a lie". He didn't exaggerate. But he will.

"Right, everyone who's on the dole, stand here!" Brian, his dad, interrupted.

Stan walked up, not laughing.

"Don't worry me," he said. "Mind you, I gotta get a job tomorrow. Gotta pay mum."

"You need to get a job for yourself, son, not me," Lin said.

His walkout had been coming for about 10 months. He hadn't been happy rising at some ungodly hour and driving to Leicester since Southern Syringes, a medical supply firm, moved from nearby a few years ago. But it wasn't just Stan who'd lost his job. Yoss, Carl, a mate called Naylor and Lin's eldest son, Robert, had lost theirs too. They'd had to leave on Thursday because they couldn't make it home without Stan. They'd gone back in on the Friday, but the boss sacked them.

On the pitch, the George Celtic captain sucked on an inhaler and called his side together into a huddle. They'd won the first meeting in the dying minutes, with Ginger red-carded. The seriously-tight huddle suggested they meant business again.

Barely a minute had gone when Bass failed to close his man down quickly enough. Paul Gennard watched and muttered "It's terrible". It seemed a little hasty, given even Paul's frail spirit. But he hadn't finished. "It's fucking terrible," he added.

It was. I headed up the hill, slowly enough to keep an eye on the game, but fast enough to avoid exposure, despite the three pairs of socks, boots, shirt, jersey, fleece, waterproof, hat and gloves, waddling like an Eskimo with a bowel problem.

There are a handful of unwritten rules about Sunday football. One is that, at some point, a man appears with a dog. Another is that it's compulsory to speak to him. There are sub-clauses that dictate what your opening question can be, though convention says it comes in the form of a statement, and you amble as you converse.

There was an old fella by the corner flag, in a grey anorak and trousers, wearing wellingtons and a blue woolly hat. He was rubbing his eye. The dog wasn't.

"It's cold," I said, taking the tear as a response to the icy Ural wind spinning off Rowley Bonk, rather than what he was witnessing.

"Ah," he replied.

"I remember Dad telling me how cold it was over here."

"It used to get colder than this," he said, then nodded towards Stan. "He's bloody good, but he's a yard too slow, mate. He's got everything else."

"I think he'd acknowledge he's a couple of stone overweight," I lied. He could actually have done with shifting more than the media-yardstick 14 bags of sugar.

"They're one-nil up," I mentioned the goal Tigs had poached on 23 minutes.

"I saw the goal, ah. Warley League, is it?"

"Yeah." Another pause.

"Having a walk out?" I asked. Ridiculous. Who'd walk for walking's sake in this?

"No, I like to come over and watch a match, Saturday and Sunday, if I can."

Rob spotted a loose ball and chased the defender down, eating up the ground.

"Thirty-seven, would you believe?" I pointed at him.

"Thirty-seven?" he chuckled. "Bloody hell!"

We watched in silence a few more seconds. The wind blew.

"Bet you've seen a bit of football," I said. "What's the standard like these days?"

"It's improved tremendously. Only problem is there's too much effing and blinding. This fella," he jabbed at a loud man on the George Celtic line, "he says 'We ain't talking enough'. You don't want to talk, you want to think."

He laughed, pulled his left hand from the depth of his anorak pocket and pointed to his head.

"Football's played from up here. Talk to your team-mates, don't get me wrong. But listen to him," he went on. "He ay shut up all mornin'. Now look at him. He's talking drivel."

"This little number 11, you know," I nodded at Tigs as the ball broke to him, something positive to talk about. "He can judge when to drop off, when to start making his run. He's fast, but he gives himself. That's the difference," as if this fella needed me to tell him. Another pause. "Did you used to play?"

"Only as a boy. I never played once I left school," his voice dropped a note. "I was mad, really, 'cos I loved the game."

"You local?"

"Yeah, on Hockley Lane. The Yew Tree's my pub. I used to live in there at one time. I don't drink now. I day know they'd got a football side."

"Couple of years now," I said, and explained how they'd come together, Albron, fallings out, Lin, Ted's £300, the kit. He nodded and Tigs threaded the needle with his left foot, a ball straight into Rob's path that sent the Celtic lino's flag up.

"I think he's biased," the old fella waved an arm. "He's done that a couple of times. That's the trouble when you've got to rely upon club linesmen."

And so it went, until my left foot began to throb and I knew that, in the interest of fending off frostbite, I should move. We exchanged a final word, and I shuffled on. A few minutes later, the half-time whistle went and I looked across to the top of the pitch. The old chap was kicking an empty plastic bottle towards the bank of bushes.

"He loved his job," Lin told me about Stan, a few minutes later, as the Trees ignored Paul's latest half-time talk, believing they'd wrapped three points up already. "Been there since he was 16, now he's 23. Robert's got a family to look after, so I'm in the doghouse with him. He's got to go up Friday and get his pay," she paused between thoughts. "He's been assured of a good reference. His manager told him 'I know you walked out, but you've been good' He very rarely had a day off."

"At least he has his football."

"They'm either brilliant or they'm crap," she nodded at the pitch, but Carl Evans interrupted her.

"Ginge got off with this wench last night," he turned to the bunch huddled near half-way. "From Willenhall."

Sam, Mark's girlfriend, looked at him.

"Willenhall!"

"It's like training," Lin went on, before I could ask what was wrong with Willenhall. "He had no social life. I know his work had to come before training, like. It's only Saturday nights he could go out. Then he's got football the morning. He come down my work to tell me, 'cos he knew I wouldn't go mad at him there…. Our Mark's said he'll help him out. That's what they're like." She let me fill the gap, then added, "I shall miss all me plasters."

I walked past Paul soon after. Celtic had just equalised, and then nearly gone ahead.

"Come on, Yew Tree!" he called. "You've got to wake up! It's… it's…." but his plea died on the wind.

I'd noticed the big red sign at the bottom of the wasteland beside the pitch, facing the Halesowen Road. It read: 'This site acquired by the Sweet Turf Christian Centre, Netherton, to build a multipurpose church for the new millennium'. Fine, but where was God when you needed him, I thought.

I didn't see Celtic go ahead, seven minutes from time. I was still watching Paul. But I did see them add a third five minutes later. Long ball. Chubbs missed, hit divot, knocked back into the six-yard box, Number 11, unmarked. Goal. Another that took less time to happen than it took to write. And that was it.

I was glad Jezz hadn't been there. Someone's wiring had gone 'buff!' and he'd had to try and sort it out. The risk of electrocution or a slow death at Baptist End. Not a hard choice. I collected the step-ladders and balls while Paul bagged the nets.

"This is as good as we'm going to get," he sighed as we crossed the red-gra pitch.

"Eleven chances" he shook his head. "Eleven chances… eleven chances…."

I couldn't begin to imagine how he'd trawl the depths of his love for this game to find a reason to come back, and risk seeing the same again. But I suspected he would.

The players were 10 yards ahead, saying the right things 90 minutes too late, things like "We don't talk" and "We don't pass".

We don't do this. We don't want that. We don't want the other.

"If we want this that bad, we'd say these things out on the pitch," Bran grumbled, finally. I looked round for Stan. I couldn't see him. Just as well.

The signs outside the Yew Tree said 'Tuesday Karoake, Wednesday Quiz, Thursday Karoake, Sunday roast starting this Sunday, Entertainment here every Saturday'. In ones and twos, they arrived, bought their drinks, sat down and stared at the TV. Wolves were playing Blues at Molineux. Wolves took the lead, and there was a muted cheer from Rob and the other Old Golds. Then Blues equalised from the kick-off and Rob stood and walked through to the Lounge. A couple of the others followed him. At least it was comfy there.

Landlady Lin Sanders carried two plates of chips and fish-shaped potato nibbles in, with a pile of bread and butter.

"Where is everyone?"

"Lounge," someone muttered, but it was 20 minutes before anyone else said a word.

"Lads, that was dire," Opple sighed into his pint, finally. The rest looked up, then down again. I swigged the last mouthful of apple juice, folded the empty peanut wrapper, put it quietly in the ashtray, and left. It's wrong to intrude on private grief.

I sat in the car and jabbed buttons to avoid Five Live's Wolves coverage. I'd had my fill of football. I landed on Classic FM, and Sibelius conjured visions of snowy, Christmas landscapes. My feet were frozen, my fingers only now beginning to tingle. When *Finlandia* ended, David Mellor began prattling on. I put Five Live back on. I'd had enough of football, but not that much.

10 MEN LIKE ROGER HANCOX

MEN LIKE ROGER HANCOX were living anonymously behind the curtains of unremarkable Netherton semis, but I hadn't stopped to think that I might have passed their front doors a hundred times until I met John Acock.

Rob Wall had suggested that, if I wanted to talk about football back in the 60s, I should call John. So I did. It didn't take him long to hit his stride. Within seconds, he'd mentioned Hancox and his kind.

"If professionals today are worth £50,000 a week, you should have seen the lads who played around Netherton 35 years ago, the likes of Roger Hancox."

Within minutes of meeting in the Yew Tree the next night, he'd supped the head off his Banks's and taken up where he'd left off, as if he wanted to get something off his chest, and didn't have much time to do it.

He was 56, five-six, maybe, the chiselled side of craggy, broad-chested, narrow of hip, with the hint above the belt of his crisp blue jeans that, however he'd earned his crust over the years, he'd enjoyed some of the comforts it had brought.

"When I played round here," we walked to the Smoke Room, "there was blokes who would, today, no doubt about it, have earned money playing. There's people earning lots who have no more talent than Roger. He went to Liverpool with Shankly. He's down Baptist End Lane now. Comes in sometimes. The things he used to do… mesmerising. Today, you'll only ever have three or four who know exactly what they'm doing. The others are the humpers."

My mind went to the dank dressing rooms at West Smethwick Park, and I tried to imagine the conditions that jobbing pros like Hancox would have regarded as the norm, 40 years before. Closer to a DSS hotel than the Raffles accommodation his kind probably expected now, I shouldn't wonder. I didn't have time to dwell on it before it became clear that John feared for the generations to come, too, not for the quality of shower or clothes peg, more the problem of interesting them in a ball in the first place.

"You've got computers, you've got the dangers of loosing a kid out. If they put a piece of grass down, they put a sign up, 'No Ball Games'. They don't encourage kids to play. Do they? You'm out and about. How many times have you seen a kid kick a ball about in the street?" He didn't pause for an answer. "That's where they used to hone their talent. If they can do it with a tennis ball, they can do it with a bigger ball."

He was steeped in Netherton football, I already knew. Any ambitious lad raised in Netherton had wanted to play for his schoolboy teams, like the Stute – Netherton St Andrew's Institute, in their "rag-tag and bobtail stuff" – and Parkdale Rovers. He used to watch Ken Wall wheel Rob in a pram round the old LMS pitch, between the Dudley Canal and the old railway goods yard, off the Cradley Road, and the Yew Tree link hadn't ended there. His daughter, Julie, was Bran's girlfriend.

With a sweep of his arm, he listed other places where men like Roger Hancox had honed their skills. Like Netherton Park, where schoolboy games were often 32 a side, "cos, if you turned up, you played". Or the Marl Hole, after they filled it in. Then he said "Netherton's a shit-hole now, a proper shit-hole", and football left the conversation. It caught me off-balance.

"I mean," he contradicted himself, "I like Netherton, but it isn't such a nice place to be. You know in front of the Arts Centre?" I did. "That piece of grass there. How they let that go down. They closed the toilets. It used to be Ernie Baker's Stores. You know Arkwright, *Open All Hours*? Well, Ernie Baker was the original Arkwright. If you wanted a cigarette and two matches as a kid, you could have 'em.

"The majority of Netherton people knew one another. You know what I mean?" I didn't. I'd never lived in a place like it. "You knew people in virtually every street.

"When I left school, I worked at Grovewoods, down Northfield Road. Fencings and ladders. Fell out with the foreman, Ronnie Fellows. 'Stick yer job up yer arse!' I walked down to Simms Lane, into Park Road, to the Hamptons factory. It's flats now. 'Can I have a job?' 'When can you start?' 'Tomorrow.' Everywhere was different trades. You could pack a job in 'cos you didn't like it." I thought of Stan.

Industry started to move out in the 70s, and it had been going ever since. He recalled the landmark names of his youth and his early married life to prove it. My mind's eye recalled the bombsites and the dereliction of every drive up here.

Danks's. "No longer exists." Grazebrook's. "No longer exists." Thompson's. "No longer exists." The list went on.

He named the massive Merry Hill shopping centre that sprawled where Round Oak Iron & Steel Works once gave life and a living to the western edge of the Black Country, and then choked it again. Merry Hell, some dubbed it, including me.

"It's great – for the people who own it. It ay particularly great for the people who've had to live round it, you know."

"You've seen Netherton slowly dying?" I hoped he'd offer a little evidence, something based on calm reflection of the social and economic life of the past 20 years, rather than what came from the pit of his stomach or the bottom of his heart.

"If you go through Netherton, there's fish and chip papers everywhere. They put a statue of Joe Darby, 'cos he came from Darby End," he mentioned the former all-round champion spring-jumper of the world. "He was a mate of my grandad's.

"Have you seen it, that statue?" I had. Wasn't impressed. "Dudley Council spent a fortune on it. It's like a bloke using the toilet, not someone you should be proud of."

He hardly paused to sup or take breath. It was as if, outside of his close circle, he'd harboured these thoughts for years and feared never having the chance to tell a stranger, someone who couldn't argue, only ask.

"Dudley town is a forgotten place. I don't know whether it's the people what we elect. They don't seem to have a lot of pride in what we got. That seems to be this country as a nation now, don't it?"

I sat back.

"The Black Country's been allowed to go down and down and nobody's give a shit. Nobody. The heart of this country was here. If you stop the heart beating, the body will die. And not just the Government now, governments before – Labour or Tory."

The photographs around the Smoke Room were a window on some of those years. Like the gang working on Titanic's chain at Noah Hingley's, the canalside works that once dominated the landscape a mile from where we were sitting. The horizons of Dad's youth must have been filled with places like it. Except, on the Oldbury side of Rowley Bonk, it was Pratt's Brickyard, Birchley Rolling Mills, the Blue Billy – the mountainous, luminous chemical dump started by Chance & Hunt's and grown by Albright & Wilson's – and Charlie Spalding's factory, where horses who'd already worked themselves into the ground were exploited, after breathing their last, in the interests of glue.

And, in case you think this vision of greys and browns is rose-tinted too, there was the Labour Exchange. My Grandad had waited in a long queue there every week, during the 30s, for the pittance we now call dole. Every week for four years.

"The steel industry, platers, welders, stampers," John went on, "at least two-thirds of these people gone. Brickyards, like your dad worked at. Gone. Now they'm talking about Dreadnought. It's been belted and belted. It cor take no more."

It was puzzling how a man who'd done this and that, and moved to posh Kingswinford 10 years before, could say his town was a shit-hole, yet come back with his wife Iris every Monday for a meal at the Yew Tree. I'd driven through the lashing rain anticipating that, by the time I left, I'd have proved football was the thing that linked the years in his life and, thus, in the lives of most of the others passing through this snapshot. I'd made the same mistake at Lin Horton's, in October. The constant wasn't what the people did. It was the people themselves.

"I lived on this estate" – he did the maths – "45 years. Solid houses. I remember it being lovely. But, today… they seem to have this thing about putting people in houses and their standard'll be lifted, when the fact is that they don't tend to their gardens, and the other people gi' up and say 'I ay gonna bother now'. But I love Netherton people. There ain't no better people. Black Country folks, if they think you'm a prat, they'll tell yer. And that's the way they am. But they'm warm," he stretched the syllable further than any other in the conversation, "and they're friendly people.

"I've sold insurance. Very few people round here keep you standing on the door. You'll say 'Now, wait, tell me to sod off in a bit, you ay listened to what I've said yet'. And they'd say 'Well, come in then. You may as well have a cup of tea'. Everyone's got an opinion, so they'll listen to people.

"The Black Country is one place where you can go into a pub and, I'll bet you, someone will have a conversation with you. They'm the friendliest people. They say Liverpool people are the same."

Then he came up with a theory to match Rob's football gene.

"They've never had a fortune, have they, the majority? So they coped with what they'd got. And it's bred down. They got more today, but they'm still laughing with one another. You hear the old 'uns talking about when 'We used to 'ave to scrape....' When they talk about the good old days, the young 'uns sit and listen."

After John left, I poked my head in the Bar, for a word with Rob and Ginger, and was introduced to Rob's wife, Tracey. Ted was there too. We talked about the Celtic game. Rob was philosophical. You needed bad days to enjoy the good.

They'd just taken more than £600 to Little Greeny's house, they said, and I was suddenly reminded of the difference between bad days and really bad days. The 15-year-old had been venting his frustration by hurling things across the kitchen. But James and his mates had been able to talk to him about the leukaemia. He'd had three rounds of chemo and was praying the new year would bring a marrow transplant, if his sister or mother were a match. He was evidently about to face his greatest battle.

"You'd never wish it on anyone, but the last person you'd want it to happen to is someone like David," Tracey said. Then Rob invited me up on Christmas Eve.

Minutes later, I stopped to use the hole-in-the-wall by the gate to Netherton Park. The image of 32-a-side football was fresh in my mind. But, seven days before Christmas, fresher still was the thought of a bunch of 14-year-olds pulling together for their very sick pal. Seven days before Christmas. Peace on Earth and goodwill to all men.

There was a West Midlands police A-frame on the pavement. It read: 'Mugging / Robbery took place at Netherton Park on Wednesday 12th December. Time: 2240. Four offenders approached two females and demanded money. When they refused, the offenders struck them with a metal bar. The offenders then stole cash and mobile telephones prior to making good their escape. Quote case number J116885/01 Four males, colour Asian, age 19-20, medium build, clothing casual.'

Goodwill to all men? Well, maybe not all.

Who was I to doubt John Acock's blunt view of Netherton? It wasn't my town. The first time I'd driven through was the day I'd met Jezz to find out whether Yew Tree Rangers would have me for the season. I had nothing to measure it by, except the welcome I'd received, and the weekly drive to Hillcrest.

The more I thought about it, though, the more I realised he was right. If you drove from the statue of Joe Darby, bog-crouching champion of the world, towards the pitch, especially on a Sunday, there was something that made the decaying buildings stand out from the merely scruffy. On Cinder Bank, just past the Fish Bar on the right, my eyes were always drawn to Used Storage Systems, seemingly abandoned. Jennings Spares and Service came next. Decaying as well.

Thousands of people must have had reason to make the buildings their destination over the decades, to buy or sell or earn a crust. Maybe a million footsteps. And how many to the buildings that were here before, and before that, and all the way back to when this was farmland, before the Ten Yard coal seam changed it all?

The land was spent, unloved, abandoned, because there was a tax break involved, or because there was cheaper land, or because demand had died for the things created on such spots, or because starvation-wage workers in the Far East could knock out twice as many at half the price.

When he had a job, why did people like Stan have to drive all the way to Leicester, five nights a week? The answer was because he could. Most of the men who'd pulled on orange shirts the day before were sons of sons who'd hawked their brawn from place to place, and ended up in Netherton because the mines or metal-shops in such places as Rugeley or Rotherham didn't need their skills or muscle any more.

Many families had been divided by the call of the New World, one half letting the family tree sink a tap root deeper into the north Worcestershire clay and limestone, the others forging equally hard, equally perilous, equally uncertain lives in America. Did the Walls have distant, rediscovered blood in Troy, New York State, like I had?

The more I became comfortable in the company of these men, their families and friends, the more I wondered what the next big social change would be. This land had been devastated by the 70s and 80s, yet no one beyond its scarred face seemed to know, far less give a toss. John Acock was right. The old A-Z in my glovebox bore recent testimony to that. Its grids had barely changed in 70 years. Names like the Round Oak Steel Works had long since been wiped off the map. Places like Jennings and Used Storage Systems had come and gone. That said more than the industrial estates either side of the Halesowen Road, neatly laid out, part of an imposed suburban scene, rather than the one that it had replaced, the one that had gone through a process of evolution. The old and not-so old. Neither said much about the present. Neither said anything about the future.

I was also starting to ask myself what kind of life I'd be living if Grandad hadn't moved his family's forging skills 30 miles south at the start of the war.

On the way home from my drink with Rob, I'd wondered whether I'd have been content here. I'd needed someone to sift the evidence, in case I'd been fooled by eyes seeing things as a grainy 60s documentary and couldn't tell whether this was real life, or a trick of the light. Yet I still didn't know much beyond the obvious fact that the economy had changed, that Church and chapel no longer fuelled the workers with fear or faith, and that, through it all, there'd been football.

What of the future, though? It would be months before I'd find the first clue to the Netherton the likes of Rob's lads would call home. It appeared in the shape of Dudley Metropolitan Borough Council's plan for putting a smile back on John's face, and dragging Netherton into the late 20th Century before much more of the 21st had gone. It was enshrined in the snappily-titled *Adopted Unitary Development Plan*, a 10-year blueprint that had included ideas for Netherton's redevelopment up to 2001.

That landmark had already passed, but it bears mentioning anyway. It also bears a mention that my heart was sinking before I'd finished the first par, and here's why.

Until *Neighbours* clamped itself to the nasal passages of impressionable British youth, I'd believed the greatest threat to the English language came from those who pen local government reports. The ADUP confirmed it, for me.

I dipped cautiously into a few dark corners and tried to fathom how new life was supposed to have been breathed into a corner that had been forgotten – if John was right – by the Grocer's Daughter, and every government since.

I saw shops first and, to be fair, it wasn't too bad, if stating the obvious is your thing. The *AUDP* sought to *"ENSURE THE LOCAL CENTRES CONTINUE TO PROVIDE A RANGE OF CONVENIENCE SHOPPING SERVICES TO MEET DAILY NEEDS" WITH EMPHASIS ON THE "RANGE OF GOODS AND SERVICES IN THE CENTRE AND THE PROPORTION OF VACANT PREMISES".*

However, Linear Open Space stood as an example of the rapid slide into jargon. I took it to mean what we grew up calling bomb-sites. It aimed to *"PROTECT AND ENHANCE LINKED OPEN AREAS FOR THE RECREATIONAL VALUE AND INTEREST AS WILDLIFE LINKS AND CORRIDORS", AND SOUGHT TO "MAINTAIN OPEN CHARACTER AND LINK OPEN SPACES IN THE URBAN AREAS WITH GREEN WEDGES".*

There was a similar lack of conviction or expectation about housing renewal. *"ENCOURAGEMENT WILL BE GIVEN," IT SAID, "TO INCREASING THE RATE AT WHICH UNFIT HOUSING IS IMPROVED TO ACCEPTABLE STANDARDS OR, WHERE NECESSARY, REDEVELOPED...." ENCOURAGEMENT? THE CHOICE OF THE WORD WASN'T ENCOURAGING.*

I was in no position to say whether it had even begun to scratch the surface of the problems John had described in plain, working man's English. What had been stamped most strongly on my mind were dereliction, chip papers, a tired landscape and a warm community.

The Son of AUDP – the quaintly-named *Revised Deposit UDP* – is no better. It will run until 2011, by which time lads like James Wall will have families of their own. It has a lot to achieve.

Paragraph 2.3 acknowledges that "the Black Country has a long tradition as a manufacturing centre and the decline in some traditional industries has left social and environmental problems". Nothing new there, but worth stating.

Paragraph 2.4 explains that Advantage West Midlands has "designated six Regeneration Zones in the West Midlands. One of these Regeneration Zones, the Arc of Opportunity, stretches from Brierley Hill in the west, through Sandwell and into Birmingham City Centre in the east. The predominantly urban area is the historic heart of invention, innovation and enterprise within the West Midlands Region".

The Arc of Opportunity? That's where I lost interest. Unless Paragraph 2.5 was one of Paul Gennard's Postulations, a move started by Ginger on the half-way line and finished with Rob nodding in at the far post, I'd stick with John Acock.

As I said, I wouldn't happen on the AUDP for a few months after John's shit-hole chat. Maybe it was a good job because, three days later, I walked in to the Dudley Historical

Archive, at Coseley, and began putting his eye and heart to the test.

The old school building's aroma and round-cornered bricks took me back 35 years. Close my eyes and I can still smell it.

I browsed the shelves and picked up *Chainmaking in the Black Country*, *Joe Darby – Champion All-round Spring Jumper of the World*, *The Black Country Nailers' Riots of 1842*, *Dudley in Old Photographs*, 1901 OS maps of Round Oak and Netherton, and a reproduction map titled *Plan of the Borough of Dudley in the County of Worcester, 1865*. Then I sat between an elderly couple scouring an old marriage certificate and a shrewish woman deciphering a frayed, hand-written will. I unfurled the old OS map to find the colliery that had once spread its tentacles deep beneath the Yew Tree pub. The watering hole wasn't there, but Hingley's Chain & Anchor Works was, alongside the Birmingham Canal.

Then I ran my fingers through the index cards, to follow Netherton's decline for myself. The cross-referenced newspaper cuttings soon painted a picture. The first said "New flats, 1966", the year John and his wife moved in to Swan Street. From there, by and large, it was downhill – 'Rubbish is ruining town's image, 1970', 'New shopping centre not needed', 'Netherton dying on its feet', 'Netherton bottom of health league', 'Netherton will be pleasant for shopping when bypass is built', 'Disused shops a danger and an eyesore', 'Plans for new shopping centre', 'Vandalism rife, 1974' and 'Councillor calls for vigilantes'....

The list was relentless: 'Planning gone mad – shops being built but old ones derelict, 1974', 'Clean-up campaign going well, 1974', 'Open-cast mining plan, 1974', 'Council to build homes in Baptist End, old mining area, 1975' and, finally, 'Clay pit to be soccer pitch'.

On my way out, I saw a poster on a door. It announced the 50th anniversary reunion of Parkdale Rovers and listed phone numbers where you could buy tickets. One was for a man called John Hingley. I made a note, little realising where it would lead, then headed home, counting the chip shops and takeaways between Baptist End and the old Labour Club. There were five, all with chip papers blowing in the wind. Then I took a detour to see Mum and Dad.

He was in good spirits, recuperating from his second cancer op in six short months. I explained where I'd been, and why. I mentioned the name Joe Darby, and then sat back and listened.

"I used to work with his nephew at Pratt's Brickyard," he said. "When you were a boy, you never believed me when I told you he could jump a canal in two leaps."

He was right. And I still didn't, though I'd reached the age where that didn't necessarily mean an argument would follow.

There were no games on December 23 or December 30, or, with deep snow turning this corner of England into the White Country, on January 6. Sandwell Borough Council wouldn't let Walsall Bengals play at West Smethwick Park. I did ring Rob, though, and the chat eventually drifted to his grandad, the one who'd helped to strike Titanic's anchor chain.

A copy of the *Dudley News* of Friday, December 14, caught my eye a few days later. Under the headline *Close shave helps mate*, it read:

THREE lads from a Netherton school lost their locks in a show of solidarity for a fellow classmate suffering from leukaemia.

James Wall, Matthew Rogers and Stephen Cartwright, of Hillcrest School, are now sporting shaved heads.

The trio had their hair sheared as a show of support for popular Year 10 youngster David Green, who also plays with the lads for Yew Tree youth football team.

Principal Mo Brennan said the school had a strict code on hairstyles, but she was happy to make an exception.

She said: "The school would not usually condone pupils having shaved heads, other than for medical reasons. But the boys approached me with the idea in a very mature way and they are a shining example of positive citizenship in action."

The boys have raised £200 for David.

11 THE KING IS DEAD

'ASTLE IS KING' was daubed in dull white paint on the dark brown Dudley Canal Bridge, on Cradley Road, near to where John Acock and his pals once played on the old LMS pitch, not far from Noah Hingley's, the foundry to which many so many families had once owed the bread on their table. There were toolmaking firms there now, and aerospace firms. But nothing of the scale that once dominated the landscape.

I've meant to mention something I found on the internet, and here's as good a place as any. Noah Hingley was born a nailmaker but, by 1857, his chain and cable empire was thriving, and he was trying to save the career of William Perry, the Tipton Slasher. Perry was preparing for his last fight. The 5ft 8ins middleweight Tom Sayers was brave but given no chance against the 6ft 1in 37-year-old Slasher, bareknuckle Champion of England since 1850.

Pride of Netherton: An advertisement for N. Hingley & Sons. Origin unknown

The Slasher was a canal boatman whose job moving night soil – no flush toilets in those days – often involved fists. He had the build and the stamina to escape poverty. He was cool and a good judge. Until the fight night of June 16, 1857.

Sayers would surely be ripped to pieces, many said. So, ignoring Hingley's advice to invest some of his fortune in chains, he spread it all among bookies at 2-1 on.

"Yo bay gettin' no younger," Hingley warned him. "Yo con lose."

Tass Parker and the hideously-disfigured Jack MacDonald were his seconds. He entered the Isle of Grain ring at his peak. He left it half-blind and mentally-impaired.

Early in the fight, Sayers put the Slasher on his back. When he stood, his skill had gone. The contest lasted an hour and 42 minutes. One round was 50 minutes alone. Owen Swift, the Slasher's main backer, was so sickened he stopped the fight.

"Perry's face had long since lost its humanity," a witness said of the Slasher at the end of the fight. "A hideous gash stretched from his lip to beneath his right eye. His right ear was hanging in ribbons. His eyes no longer saw. Where they should have been were two black swellings oozing blood."

Yode was in his kit, 5ft 7ish, more of a Sayers than a Slasher, shin-pads bulging like radiators when I saw him before the Rhodia match at Hillcrest, but walking like Gary Cooper. We swapped New Year greetings on a dank, misty morning and I asked whether they'd trained since Christmas.

They had. On Thursday night. They'd been doing bunny hops, a ridiculous-looking exercise with no obvious benefit that I've ever been able to fathom, apart from splitting cartilage. My legs haven't stopped aching from the last lot I did, and that was 23 years ago as I write. Yode grimaced.

"We'm fucked today," he managed a laugh. "I couldn't walk on Friday morning."

The snow blanketing the pitches a week before had gone, and the ground was firm. Most of the team were out, some doing the nets, others what passed for a warm-up, seeing who could blast the ball widest of Chubbs. Only Yode and Mark bothered to stretch their aching quads. Some were having a final drag before attempting to put the horror of George Celtic behind them. They were walking like Gary Cooper too.

Paul appeared and I asked what he'd said to them about the game.

"I haven't."

I asked him why none of them were trying to ease the bunny-hops out of their limbs.

"They'm grown men," he said curtly. "They should work it out themselves."

Then he told me about Mitch, out for weeks with a duff cartilage. He'd missed his operation because there'd been no parking space at the hospital. He found one a mile away and ran, and his blood pressure was too high at his pre-op check. The op would probably be in June now. That was him done for the season. With him went , and the only Tree playmaker who combined vision, aggression and poise with the ability to accelerate from 0-10 in fewer than five seconds.

The Rhodia players appeared in a ragged line, an insignificant-looking bunch of men of insignificant height, wearing dull red shirts, black shorts and red socks. They were three or four places behind Tree in the league, and on a decent run. They lined up and began a slow, gentle jog across the pitch. Then they ran back, jumping, stretching their arms and heading imaginary crosses. The next shuttle was running sideways, using those dinky little skips that can end with your ankle bones clacking together. Paul shouted across to his players and pointed down the pitch at the warm-up display.

"See that?" They could. And they were laughing.

Bran, Ginger and Gavin jogged towards Chubbs' goal. One ball was at the top of a hawthorn tree, another over the railings and a third was flat so, for now, there was nothing to hold a kick-in with. As I watched, Bran jinked to the right and jumped in the air, his left leg cocked, as if to mimic Eric and Ernie. He didn't. Instead, he farted.

The flashback was instantaneous. The wet rasp echoed in my ears, a loud, wet, fuzzy fart. Then a blurred shape in blue moved into my peripheral, flashback vision. Then another wet fart, clearer this time, gave way to the figure once more, in sharper focus, quickly followed by another rasper, and on like that till sound and vision merged and I heard a woman's voice again, off-camera, demanding to know "Have you finished?"

Then it dawned on me. The wet touchline fart as Yew Tree kicked off the season, the morning after England's joyous 5-1, Germany's humiliating 1-5. My first contact with these people. Wet fart. "Have you finished?" "Not yet."

Bran! I'd have put my signed Kevin Keegan birthday card on it. I'm not sure of the science. The length of the alimentary canal, or sphincter bore? The trombone principle? Maybe, one day, it'll take over from DNA profiling. The E-fart picture.

By the time the old fella with the dog turned up, Tree had gone a goal ahead through Meesey and they'd been pegged back to 1-1. By the time Rhodia went ahead, nine minutes on, Lin had told me about Stan's new forklift job, starting on Monday, down Saltwells Road. I asked if it was a weight off his mind, and what kind of a Christmas they'd had.

"Quiet," she said. "He was miserable most of it."

Other jobs news: Yoss was due to start work the same day, but not Carl.

Tigs made it 2-2, a minute later, by which time I was mulling over John Acock's view that this was a simple game – you played in units, you linked them, back to front, and you talked. But this wasn't going to change for the rest of the season. I wasn't going to hear them talking, or moving as a fluid team, for more than 10 or 15 minutes at a time, let alone 90. The closest we'd come so far were the games against Lowes and Khalsa. I looked at Paul and my heart sank for him.

It was 3-2 at half-time – another poach by Rob – and only a few minutes into the second-half before they ignored Jezz's umpteenth plea to "Get it sorted…." I looked at him and wondered if he'd make it through the season without troubling the cardiac unit at Russell's Hall Hospital again.

If Yode – or Stan or Gav, let's face it – was the closest thing Tree had to the Tipton Slasher, Tigs was Joe Darby. Among other feats, from a standing start, whatever the Netherton bog-crouching statue suggested, the Champion All-Round Spring Jumper of the World could leap two chairs placed 28 feet apart. He could also jump over 20 chairs placed 11 feet apart in 20 jumps. Then clear a 15-hand horse with his 21st.

Tigs often rode tackles as if he'd bounced off an invisible mid-air springboard. Thus he also reached a loose ball on the edge of the visitors' penalty area before Rhodia's Number 7. They were two mismatched jousters. Except Tigs was faster.

I couldn't see where the ball was as he cartwheeled through the air before hitting the ground with a sickening smack. People with a better view winced.

"Jesus, he's got to go to work in the morning," someone yelled. The Rhodia lot were conspicuous by their silence. Tigs sprang to his feet and angrily confronted the player, four or five inches above him. The whistle blew but only, it seemed, when the Rhodia player dropped the nut. The ref booked Tigs first, then waved red at the true villain – and the Rhodia manager lost it.

"Fucking hell, ref!" he shouted. "He tried to nut him."

"Oh shut up!" The livid voice belonged to Lin Horton. "He day be tall enough to headbutt anyone!" It was the first time I'd heard her voice raised since Mark had laughed at Stan falling in the away match at George Celtic.

"That's going in the report, that is!" the Rhodia man pointed to the ref.

Craig put Tree 4-2 up from the spot, 10 minutes later, and it deteriorated. Gavin floored Rhodia's Number 6, who jumped up, seething. Slap, slap. Then three Rhodia players rushed in. So did four Trees. Yode was the last there, anxious to prevent a mate saying something he may later not wish to rely upon in court. As he stretched to pull an orange shirt away, someone drew an arm back, ready to thump. From moving forward at a rate of knots, Yode's jaw came to a halt against the elbow. But his legs carried on. They eventually lost touch with the mud and swung like a pendulum until he was horizontal, three or four feet off the ground, hovering in his own cartoon frame, before gravity took over. He crawled from the forest of legs, rubbing his chin, as common sense returned and Bass and Yoss wet themselves laughing on the line.

The Rhodia player saw yellow first this time, then Gav followed him into the book.

"That's a disgrace," the manager ignited. "The report's being written already!"

I looked down the line. It wasn't. He didn't have a pencil, let alone paper.

At such points, on top and believing they could choose their moment to walk the ball into the opposition net, Tree often conceded a goal, then panicked. Barrel? Hillcrest, home and away? Tap House? Khalsa? So, when Rhodia's centre-forward volleyed a sweet right-foot, the moment turned slow-motion again. It looped up and down, radio-controlled, until Chubbs arced up from a back-pedalling run, stretched his finger tips beneath the bar and tipped it over. I'll run through that again. It looped up and down, until Chubbs arced up from a back-pedalling run, stretched his fingertips beneath the bar and tipped it over. Disappointingly, no one rushed to tussle his hair.

Yoss came on for Meesey with 13 minutes left. Craig could drive you bonkers with his stop-start concentration and contribution. But Meesey? He was blessed with fast feet and pin-head precision when he wanted. But he didn't want often enough. He was one-paced. He rarely looked up. A team with him in midfield and Rob up front should win by six every week. Meesey. For me, the enigma of Yew Tree Rangers.

"Why can't we head like that when we're defending?" Paul said as Gavin rose like a salmon at the back post to crash the sixth home from a corner. He might as well have asked where the wind went when it wasn't blowing.

My mother-in-law's birthday would draw me home before they hit the Yew Tree. But I had time to give Rob the Coseley archive maps and books before I left.

I was hoping he'd be as engaged by them as I was. Finding a link from this lot to the men who made Titanic's anchor chain was enticing, one slice of Netherton's rich heritage, now at the bottom of the deep North Atlantic, attached to another with the name of its birthplace on its side. Titanic's anchor.

Jezz e-mailed me the next day with some other results, the league table and an A-Z reference for New Fullbrook's ground in Walsall. Tree were nine points behind Harborne, four behind Khalsa and three ahead of Lowes. Goal difference kept Hangman's Tree one above Walsall Bengals on a measly three points in the basement.

On the Wednesday, I rang Rob Wall about the maps.

"Wonderful, ah," he said. "I've lived in Netherton all me life, like. There's that much difference then to now. I must have had a good couple of hours with 'em last night. Brilliant. Brilliant."

The *Dudley News*, a couple of days later, cast fresh light on the image John Acock had planted in my mind, something more up to date than the one Rob and I were susceptible to, one laced with nostalgia for something neither of us had seen. It reported:

PLANS are in the pipeline for a much-needed community centre in Netherton.

Support for the idea has been shown by residents and ward councillors, who say the town is crying out for a place where all age groups can meet.

Cllr Mahbubur Rahman said Netherton needed a community centre focal point.

He said: "There is no youth club to help keep youngsters off the street and with a growing population of elderly people it would be good to have more facilities for them in addition to Age Concern which does an excellent job."

It seemed John had it right.

The Sunday morning that Tree faced New Fullbrook was a morning to stay tucked up. Every gust against the window brought the blanket an inch higher. But I swung my legs out of bed, creaked down to put the eggs on, then grabbed the TV control to see what was happening in the world. That was when I read it. The King was dead.

An hour later, I was on the M5, low clouds scudding, the Hawthorns floodlights just about visible, listening to a phone-in tribute to Jeff Astle on Radio WM.

He was the man who scored in every round of the 1969 FA Cup and went on to sing karaoke on *Fantasy Football*, one fan remembered.

"He left in 1974, but years after you could hear his name come tumbling down the Brummie Road terraces, 'Jeff Astle! Jeff Astle!'" a second added.

"His heading ability was second-to-none," another said. "He was taught by Tommy Lawton. The thing is with football, it's such a central part of people's lives, when something like this happens, it's like you've lost something personal."

A very sad Bobby Hope, his old inside right, told a story: "He was one of Jimmy Hagan's first signings. When he came he got a bit of stick because he was a yokel. On his first day, he had a green blazer on. We thought it was the coach driver. Needless to say, he never wore it again…. He was a very humble man."

You thought about footballers today, and the amount of money they earned. When Astle finished, he had run a window-cleaning business in Burton. His sales slogan was 'Jeff Astle, never misses corners!'

There was an awkward eloquence in the listeners' determination to express themselves about an ordinary man who became a star, then an ordinary man again.

The King is dead: Phil Tucker alongside the Primrose Hill bridge that's cherished by some football fans, but clearly not by others. Picture by Aaron Manning

I listened to them on the car park in Walsall while I watched four blokes trying to put nets up in the wind. When the net bag blew away, inevitably, it was the one who could have done with losing three stone who gave chase. Whenever he caught up, it flew off again. So, even on a grim morning like this, God had a sense of humour.

Tuck had his Baggies away shirt on when the Trees turned up, kitbag under arm. They headed straight for the dressing room block, a filthy, red-bricked thing with moss descending from the north face of its flat roof, and timber missing from the fence around the heating oil tank. Firewood, I guessed.

A lad of eight or nine was on the pitch, conjuring little feints and turns, flicks, back-heels and dummies in the face of an imaginary opponent. He didn't have to look at the ball to know where it was. He curled a cross into the net from wide out near the left-wing corner flag. Then he went and ruined it all by unzipping his anorak and revealing a Manchester United top. I wondered if there was a young lad in Salford who'd done the same, this morning, and revealed blue and white stripes.

New Fullbrook emerged first and began the warm-up, stretching quads, scratching bits, executing deft, confident first-time lay-offs to the feet of a team-mate. They looked lithe and beer-free. Their hamstrings hummed like harps.

Tree followed. Stan handed his mum an ear-ring and I asked how the new job was going. Great, he said, before walking to join one of a cluster of tangerine-shirted visitors. They didn't look like condemned men, but several still took long, final drags on their fags before attempting to become the first team to beat Fullbrook on their own territory this season. I didn't hold much hope.

The Fullbrook players came together. Everyone knew their place in the tight huddle. One man did the talking. Eighty yards away, Jezz and Paul drew their men in to a loose circle. Yoss was back in midfield, for Meesey. Otherwise, the men facing an uphill task were the ones who'd walloped Rhodia. The talk was short. All I heard was Rob saying "Let's not let them play football".

Paul walked to the line and I asked where Meesey was.

"Day turn up," he shrugged his shoulders. I didn't need him to say any more, but he did anyway. "We told 'em on Thursday night to be there at 9.20."

As the teams swapped ends – Tree kicking up the slope against a stiff westerly – I asked Tuck if he'd had the all-clear. He had. I asked him how his dad was. He was fine too. The ref blew and Tuck yelled "Come on, boys!", like he always yelled, a battle-cry in the first minute, if occasionally a lament later in a game. But not this day. There were massive contributions across the park, but the fourth minute acts as a memorial to what would follow.

From the moment Chubbs had dropped a shot in his first Yew Tree pre-match kick-in, then tripped over his own feet, I'd worried for him. I'd seen days when he'd looked like he was keeping in oven gloves. I'd seen him save a threadbare defence and not receive the pat on the back he deserved. I'd watched him and remembered my first open-age game as a 16-year-old.

So, when the first high ball floated over, and a Fullbrook forward zeroed in on it, and Chubbs came out, we held our breath. But he punched it clear under pressure. Within a minute, he met a shot with his feet after Ginger had played an air-shot. The noise the 17-year-old keeper heard from the line was applause. Bran ruffled his hair. Almost a sign of affection. From that moment, this was Chubbs' day.

The only low spot in a first-half of dogged defence came in the 19th minute, when a throw bounced from leg to leg and fell to Fullbrook's Number 7, who fired through a crowd. Chubbs tipped the ball on to the post, but it rebounded against his body… and in.

Tree simply dug deeper. They made the Prize Guys turn to play their short passes backwards, or harried them in to long passes that sailed beyond their target. They matched Fullbrook in passing to feet, too. But Rob always seemed too distant, on lone patrol just in front of Fullbrook's back four, to make the possession count.

Fullbrook should have been four up as the half-time orange-box beckoned. But Tree didn't panic, and they didn't moan. Chubbs had followed his opening saves with a string of others. The body language of the Yew Tree players said they'd regard 1-0 at half-time as some kind of a moral victory, and that's how the 45 minutes ended.

"Let's not be complacent," Paul told his troops at half-time, sucking citrus, huddling against the wind while the home side had tea indoors.

"Just 'cos we'm kicking downhill next half doesn't mean shag-all," Jezz told them, walking small semi-circles and looking at his feet, as he always did at such moments.

"Let's get more than one person in the box," Mark Horton added, then slipped into broad Netherton which, even after this long listening to half-time talks, I couldn't translate. Stan's eyes were bulging. Jezz clocked them.

"A saft yellow card and we'm under pressure," he told him. Thirteen weeks later, on a grey Thursday night, on this very ground, I'd have cause to recall the warning.

A minute in to the second-half, Jezz resolved never to worry about the Hillcrest hawthorns again. Every time the ball sailed beyond the top goal, the Fullbrook sub squeezed through a gap in the hedge on to a railway line. Never mind what it might have done to a train driver, it was a cheap incentive to keep your place in the side.

Hindsight's a powerful thing, so let's pause. I'd first met Jezz Dingley, by chance, in the Arctic wastes of Lion Farm. I'd met him again in a Black Country pub. I'd begun to follow his team. I'd run a dispassionate eye over them and feared the worst. I'd stuck with them and seen that fear come true, then the opposite. I'd lifted a couple of corners of Netherton life, unexpected ones, and discovered that the constants in its history of industrial revolution and ruination were people and community. And I'd started regarding Dad's formative years with eyes that also watched from behind Chubbs' goal as Yode was skinned by Fullbrook's man-mountain Number 9.

The young forward raced goalwards, but nudged the ball too far ahead. If he hadn't, Chubbs might have remained at his near-post. Instead, the keeper left his goal. The Fullbrook player launched himself with both feet and his considerable weight sledge-hammered Chubbs' right ankle. The crack was sickening. Even before the ball spun still in the net, Chubbs was beating the ground with his fists, yelping, gasping. The ref pointed to the centre-circle. Two-nil. Two-nil?

I was four or five yards away, the back of my knees drained, my head swimming at what I'd just seen and heard. The culprit had vanished, but Gavin and Stan were about to make the ref wish he'd gone train-spotting. I took four strides and planted a foot right in front of him. On the pitch. I was never booked or sent-off in my career, I'm proud to say, but now I'd stepped beyond the line I'd tried to draw all season.

"Gavin, Stan, I'll say what you're about to say," I interfered. "Go away."

They stepped back and I turned to the man in black.

"Ref, that's the worst tackle I've seen in 25 years." I was lying. I'd seen worse and, anyway, I began playing open-age at 16, so it was more like 27. "It was a disgrace and you know it. That lad's supposed to go to work tomorrow and you've given a goal?" The family can probably imagine the scene.

As soon as I said it, I realised it had nothing to do with me and took a step back. As Jezz and Paul lifted Chubbs from the mud, and Tuck prepared to make a quicker return than expected, I looked down the pitch. The Fullbrook players were ready for the restart, but the ref pointed to the six-yard box. A foul. Still 1-0. No one said a thing.

Nine minutes after the whole sickening episode, Mark found Tigs wide on the left. He found Rob through the rain, but the striker's shot was blocked. It rebounded to Mark. This time, it was Stevie Gerrard. His low shot skidded past the keeper's despairing dive from 18 yards. Germany 1 England 2, New Fullbrook 1 Yew Tree 1.

Fullbrook were rocked. They laid siege. But Tree hadn't caved in yet, and they weren't about to. Stan dropped further off Rob, playing deeper in the quagmire to stifle the Fullbrook midfield. I was on tip-toes almost constantly from then on. It was the first game I'd craved playing in, just to feel the satisfaction that would have washed over my weary body as I walked off with a draw.

Then, on 72 minutes, Yoss won possession in midfield and, after finding his feet, tuned his radar to Rob's run. The defenders gawped, assuming the ball was heading for the keeper. It wasn't. Rob caught it, jinked right to beat him, then steadied himself for a second that lasted an hour, and tapped the ball into an empty net. One-two. 'They call him the Belfast boy,' I sang to myself and – "Hah!" – laughed aloud.

Fullbrook pummelled the Tree goal, hunting the equaliser. They hit a post, and Tuck pulled off a double save moments later. But they shall not pass, and they did not.

It was Bran's birthday. So his team-mates jumped on their captain and rubbed his face in the mud as the whistle went. He disappeared as body after body piled on. When he climbed up, caked, the only player left in the mud was Yode.

Then Jezz hugged Stan, and Stan wiped his muddy paws all over Jezz while Paul quietly packed the balls into a bag. He put the lid back on the orange-box. He slipped the first-aid kit away. And he smiled.

The sight of a Fullbrook player marching to the dressing room, ignoring a team-mate's four-letter reminder that the nets needed taking down, made me laugh again. There was silence from Fullbrook, yelling from Tree. Stan's voice echoed above everyone else's, as always. Chubbs hopped past and I asked if he was all right. He said he was, but I wasn't so sure.

I was in the car, half-way home, before I realised that I hadn't heard anyone mention The King. Not even Tuck.

From: Jeremy Dingley
To: Mark Higgitt
Sent: Monday, January 21, 2002 1:57 PM

Hi Mark – A good battling performance yesterday. We rode our luck, but I'll take that. (Got voice back nearly). On a sad note, found out 10 O'clock last night, Chubbs is in hospital with a broken ankle. Should be having a pin put in today. This is when the other side of my job makes you feel responsible. I should have taken him to the hospital myself, there and then, instead I go down the pub and have a few beers. (Not the way to run a club and look after your players), I think you would agree. Look forward to seeing you on Sunday (at Home). Jezz

12 SAME LIFE, DIFFERENT BRICK

THERE WAS TITANIC IRON IN ROB'S HANDS, and it took just a couple of minutes with Greta, his mum, to trace it. Sidney Lawson Willetts, her dad, had struck chain at Hingley's. He was Rob's link to Titanic, and ours.

I'd looked at the maps, run my fingers across the streets, mines and foundries, and hoped a whiff of sweat would rise from them. It hadn't happened, of course, but the tone in her voice brought enough back for now, and the brief pauses that peppered her conversation suggested there was more within than I'd hear in a couple of hours. And I did.

Soon, it dawned on me that this wasn't just her story. How many Netherton families could have been here, rolling back the years to the White Star liner? My Coseley archive visit had unearthed the fact that, in 1928, 6,000 people worked in the district's chain trade. Multiply the size of families over the four generations since, and how many people were connected to the lump of iron that hit the bottom of the Atlantic on April 14, 1912? How many Netherton folk had its molecules in their blood? Bran? Ginger? Stan and Mark? I didn't even start the maths.

"I was born in the Boat Inn," Greta looked at her husband, Ken, and unfurled a family tree that took in the Bumble Hole – Dingley Dell with poverty and furnace smoke – The High Side, the New Inn, the Fox and Goose, and the Queen's Head.

Sidney Lawson Willetts would have been about 14 when Titanic's anchor chain was struck, the same age as Rob's eldest lad, James. Young Sidney was bright, but poor families didn't send their children to grammar school, so he grafted at Hingley's and stayed there, even when he worked as a Pearl Assurance agent, even when they were running the pub. It was the only way he could make serious money.

"He used to get up at four in the morning to strike chain, in for five, and back home at 11," Greta pointed at the map spread across the table in the Yew Tree's Smoke Room. "They called at The Washington first, on the corner by Hingley's, to put back some of the fluid he'd lost in the foundry. Then he used to walk up this big hill here, up Marriott Road, until he got to the Queen's Head, and have a wash and brush-up. We didn't have a bathroom. Me mother used to open the pub at 10. He used to be in the pub till two. He'd have his lunch, then get his head down for three hours, then up at five. They opened again at six until 10. Then back up at four in the morning.

"All as I know is that they worked in gangs. One fired it and the other shaped it. I never used to see him go, but he used to come home with a big coat on, and a muffler round and a cap, to keep the heat in, because they'd sweat so much it was freezing when they come out. You know what I mean?

"It was a hard life. When he was 52, he died. I was barely 16. He had a burst blood vessel. In them days it was a case of lying and it would heal. But, instead of healing properly, tuberculosis set in. All to keep us, that was. He was wore out."

I thought of the 40 years in a fiery forge that had turned Dad's hands to leather and was grateful, and surprised, that he'd made it to 77, now on the mend again.

Rob nudged a pack of pork scratchings towards me. Greta smoothed a crease in the map, then she and Ken drifted off on a random walk around the streets and decades.

Chapel Street was close to Hingley's. It was where one of Greta's grandmothers had lived, though the houses had long gone. The other gran came from Marriott Road. A grandson still lived in the same house.

"How old's Eric?" she asked Ken, and didn't wait for answer. "Sixty-seven. So three generations have lived in that one house."

Her own parents had also lived in Griffin Street, a cut-through I'd already discovered to the Yew Tree. "They were new houses then," she said. "They could have bought it for £400, but they hadn't got the 25 quid deposit. My dad kept a family of six on about three pounds 10 shillings a week."

Ken and Greta started married life with her parents in a house the Willettses finally did buy, for £800. Then they bought their own in Dudley Wood, for £2,400. Ken earned £10/10s a week, Greta £7/10s. The mortgage was £13/10s a month. We're talking mid-60s.

Luxuries? There weren't any.

"Play was youth clubs, tuppence a time on a Friday," she retreated to childhood, "and tuppennyworth of chips when you come out. And a natter on the corner. We used to go dancing every Saturday night, and walk from the Town Hall at half-past one in the morning and, you know, we'd meet a policeman at the top of the hill and he'd walk down to the bottom with you.

"You know the long entry between Noah's Ark and the doctors?" she asked me. I didn't. "Well, when you get to the end of it, on the opposite side, where the surgery is, it used to be an ironmongers, and her used to sell everything."

Then there was Emile Doo's, the chemist.

"You'd go in," Greta moved on, "and all one wall was little drawers. And he'd go and take something out of this, and something out of that."

"While he was serving," Ken sat forward, and they all laughed, "he used to go like this," he whistled through his teeth, and they laughed again, a private joke between them and a few thousand other old Netherton folk. "You could go to him without a prescription and he could treat you better than a doctor. He was amazing."

Doo's shop was at now the Black Country Museum, John Acock had already told me.

"There's a chapel there as well," Greta added. "Just over the bridge in Northfield Road, on the right, just before you come to the fish shop on the corner, there used to be a big chapel, Providence Chapel. They took that brick for brick."

Chapels. I unfolded a 1903 OS map and pointed at them, many still standing, though you'd have had to stand very still in most to hear the faint echo of the prayers, communal and private, that had once been their purpose in life and death.

"Look at the number of them," I said, like a tourist.

"There was Cinder Bank, one at Swan Street, St John's, Noah's Ark, there was a Wesleyan Chapel, Primrose and St Peter's," Greta added, "and they had a football team out of the pub I lived in, the Queen's Head. Well, there worn't a lot to do."

Ken sat forward again.

"A lot of today's children get bored. We didn't. We always found something to do."

"You always did," Greta reminded Rob, though it wasn't news, given how easily he strayed into PlayStation territory, the boxed death of football. Possibly. She was on to winter fogs as the door squeaked and Rob's boys – James, Dan and Aaron – came in.

"But we used to have good summers. When I lived in that pub, I was telling Rob last week, the fellas used to come in, and their wives. Pop bottles then was a big glass bottle with a big screw top, with a rubber round it. They used to fill half-a-dozen and sit on the steps, especially on a Saturday. My brother and me used to stick our heads out of the window and listen to all that was going on. 'Cos there was no television."

She'd been studying the map as she spoke, running an eye down Blackbrook Road, up Netherton Hill, to the churchyard and the canal. She pinpointed the Yew Tree's spot on the map. Cheering from the Bar said goals were being scored in the Spurs-Chelsea Worthington Cup semi-final. We didn't know who'd scored, far less cared.

"That's the claypit at the back of here," she crossed the fold of the map. "Yew Tree Estate, in my day, it was Shepherd's Walk. It was one big field and led on to the reservoir and canal. And the marl hole. There used to be water in it. We used to have Sunday School summer parties on Shepherd's Walk, races and sports and a bag of cakes and a bit of jelly and a bottle of pop. Merry Hill Farm was down there."

She pointed beyond the Smoke Room's door: "My brother lived over the road. He's 72. When he built his house, it was mining all over the back."

At some point, the tape ran out. By the time I noticed, we'd run through discipline, National Service, the phone box that had a glass panel kicked out every day, and taking high-heels off to walk home "so you didn't wake people up". Ken and Rob didn't make much of a contribution to the latter.

"It makes you frightened to let these out of your sight," Greta nodded at the lads.

When I was 12, I was taken into the forge where Dad earned his living, and swore blind I'd never follow him there, like he'd followed his dad.

"You wouldn't want your child to go into a chainshop at 14," I said to Rob. He pointed to the wall, first at the picture of a Titanic anchor being taken by horse and waggon through the town, then one of the Titanic chain gang.

"See them there, the four of 'em," he said to Dan. "Well, that's me and Mark on the left. Imagine you being on the right."

"Imagine working by a big, hot fire," Dan's grandmother added, "chain-striking, sweating your eyeballs out all day. You've got to have a cloth round your head."

"I'd rather play football," James said, then the evening went the same way as every other in this room. I packed to go but, half-an-hour later, we were still there, talking football, why it was important to places whose daily grind had been as unforgiving, like Tyneside,

Liverpool, Sheffield, the metal districts of the Second City, 20 minutes down the road. All kinds of places.

"Same life, different brick," Rob said.

I stood, and still we talked, about the subtle difference in dialect from one Black Country street to another. We burned a few ears too, Chubbs', Jezz's, Stan's. And Thatcher's. Rob wondered how much the Black Country had given the country.

"She doesn't even know it exists," he said, and I heard contempt in his voice for the first time. I didn't argue. Still wouldn't.

He asked the boys what they thought of the things they'd heard their grandparents say and, more strongly than I'd felt it before, I realised this was the life I'd have had, if Dad had stayed in Blackheath when the war started.

"No hammering, no swinging any more," I said to James as he studied the pictures.

"There's still digging, though," his dad laughed. "There'll always be digging."

Always be digging. But not on a day like this. It was wet, and the wind was ripping across West Smethwick Park on the first Sunday in February, the strongest I'd tried to stand in since the middle of the Channel on the way home from the Somme. Within a few minutes, kit was back in cars. Walsall Bengals would have to wait.

I was heading off when Rob called. He handed me a *Dudley News* cutting and pointed to his Uncle Roger in a picture of Parkdale Rovers, taken in 1952.

I bumped into Jezz before I could read it. The wings on Pitch 6 were fine, but the ref wasn't about to risk a player drowning in the lake that separated them. Chubbs hobbled by as he said it. It was like a well-timed moment from a TV drama. Risk. Player. Safety. Crutches. Irony. The teenager had spent five days in hospital. His left ankle had been pinned. Out for a year. Both "circles" – the knobbly malleoli at the end of the tibia and the fibula – were broken, he said. No wonder he'd pounded the ground. The back of my legs turned to jelly again.

In the car, I peeled off the layers of weatherproofing, then read the cutting:

A NETHERTON football club who were formed in 1952 by a gang of pals looking for a kick around are celebrating their 50th anniversary.

Parkdale Rovers – who play in the Kidderminster League – are staging an anniversary reunion and want as many of their old players to come along.

The club's longevity is largely down to a hardcore group of six committee members who between them have notched up a whopping 220 years service. Club president John Hingley and chairman Ron Barnett were both in the line-up when Parkdale played their first match against Upper Gornal and have been with the club ever since.

John Hingley, who until the early 80s was a mainstay of the all-conquering side, said: 'We've always attracted the right sort of players. It's basically down to the tireless efforts of a dedicated band who've kept the club afloat.'

The name John Hingley rang a bell from the poster I'd seen at the Coseley archives. I glanced at the Front Page, afterwards, and saw a picture of a lone floral tribute on the parapet of a bridge, above the legend 'WBA 1968 RIP Astle'.

The caption read: Astle Bridge, or Primrose Bridge as it is properly known, is in Cradley Road, Netherton, and spans the Stourbridge and Dudley canal. It has become a landmark across the Black Country since it was daubed with the words `ASTLE IS KING' on the evening of Albion's 1968 FA Cup win over Everton.

Inside the paper, there was more: Astle Bridge' in Netherton to be officially renamed after the West Brom legend who died at the weekend.

"Jeff mentioned the bridge a few times and it meant a lot to him," it quoted former team-mate Bobby Hope. "It would be great if the powers-that-be could dedicate the bridge to his memory – it could become a shrine to Jeff. I'm sure a lot of fans would make a special journey to the area just to see it."

Five Live presenter and Baggies devotee Adrian Chiles added: 'This bridge is a legend and has stood the test of time. People who know nothing about the club are familiar with Astle Bridge. I think it's a superb idea to change the name."

A spokesman for British Waterways said they'd seriously consider the idea.

On the way home, for old time's sake – Dad's – I drove down Birchfield Lane and glanced left at 567, the house where he grew up. At the bottom, Birchley Island steers you towards Wolverhampton, Oldbury, the M5 or Quinton. I took the second turn, then went left up Park Street, and right by Manchester Stores into the remnants of the old Birchfield Lane, where I turned round outside Good Shepherd School. A few yards on, I stopped at Thurston Avenue, though I knew the house he'd been born in had long gone, then drove slowly past the house where Aunt Lilian had been brought up, the only girl in a family of eight boys. Today was her 80th birthday. I wondered what a young girl in a family of Baggies fans, now a wise, firm-minded old lady, would make of today's young men on a football pitch, the foul-mouths, the aggression, the release after a week of hard graft. How would it sit with her memories of the 30s here, her father and brothers? How would Dad?

I didn't have a clue.

13 DUNCAN AND WILF

DUNCAN EDWARDS AND WILF FOLEY were about to enter my life as I turned into John Hingley's road. John was at the bottom of his Kingswinford drive, on his mobile, speaking to me on mine, a bomber pilot being talked home on a misty night. We said goodbye on our phones, face-to-face, then shook hands and said hello. It must have looked absurd.

My Grandad would have been bemused by the technology. But he'd have known the stock frame in front of me, the firm handshake, and the images conjured by John's first words.

I've been lucky in my working life. Blessed, really. No sweat, no danger, no dole, but the chance to meet more sporting heroes than a man has a right to expect. It would be a name-drop to mention even a handful, and a disappointment to admit that most have left me underwhelmed.

Every journalist has a dozen interviews he'll remember to the day he or she dies. All but a couple of mine are with unknown men in small, suburban kitchens or parlours, reminiscing modestly about the kind of heroics you don't find on football pitches. That night, in John Hingley's lounge, I extended the list by one. I wish you could have been there.

The founder of Parkdale Rovers shared a name with Noah Hingley, but he was on a distant wing of the family, and his only real link to the Chain & Anchor Works was that his grandfather had struck chain there. He told me so as a seamless continuation of the news that Parkdale's first gathering place was, aptly, in his mother's lounge in Meeting Street, Netherton.

"He kept the Netherton Liberal Club," he went on. "He used to come back from the chainmaking to the Liberal Club, for nigh on 30 years. He was also an excellent bass singer, and his chapel was the Darby Hand chapel, which has been restored on the Black Country Museum, you know." I did. Greta Wall had told me.

"He was a real tough guy. Now we're going back to the late 40s. The bars, them days, there was no pulls. There was the brass taps in the barrels. And in the little bar, there was four lovely snooker tables. I've seen him behind the bar there, when one of the members uttered an oath, and I've seen him vault the bar and drag him outside. We all grew up in this sort of environment. Some of us meet there every Thursday evening, 50 years after. It's a roots thing.

"The Stute were our arch rivals. They was connected with a church at Netherton. St Andrew's. It was a remarkable little club. Football, and everything else, in those days, as far as we were concerned, probably originated from the Church of England school in Netherton. There was a guy there called Mr Griffiths. He instructed us in the first arts of football. Then we took the 11-plus. The brainy guys went to Dudley Grammar School, the p'raps-not-so-brainy went to Dudley Intermediate School, and the guys who didn't went to Northfield Road School. But we still all stuck together.

"In 1952, we decided to start a team. I was 15. We were walking, a gang of us, on Netherton Park one late summer night in '52. It was drizzling. We were walking along the rose garden, and we decided to form a club. Someone said 'What shall we call ourselves?' Someone said 'Well, we're on a park'. 'Okay, Park.' The pitch was in a dale. 'So we'll call it Parkdale.'

"I can remember some of 'em. There was a guy called Alan Parsons – Smiler – Ron Barnett, who's the president now, Tony Clift, my old mate, who was treasurer – he lives over in Toronto, he's hoping to come over to the reunion. Ronnie Baker only stayed at the club about 12 months. Ronnie was there," he smiled. "Most all of us lived within a square mile of each other. We joined the Coseley Boys League for a couple of seasons. It was purely on our own. We paid a sub, probably about a shilling a week. I think we won the league and a cup in our second year.

"The first game, we caught the bus from Netherton to Dudley, Stone Street, then the trolley bus from Stone Street to Upper Gornal, and we changed in the Horse & Jockey. It's now The Blood Tub. We galloped on to the pitch in an old green-and-red striped kit with laces" – he touched his collar – "and we got heavily beaten, 7-1. I was inside right those days. We stayed in there for two years in the Coseley League, two years in the Halesowen Youth League, and then we joined the Brierley Hill League.

"It started at that school in Netherton, but we also drew players from the youth clubs belonging to churches. There was one at St John's, Netherton, one called the Messiah Baptist, the other side of Netherton. There was a couple of Methodist churches down at Darby End. We used to meet in Netherton evenings and weekends. There could be as many as 22, 30 of us. We'd go over the park, holidays particularly, after breakfast and you played till dark. It was from this kind of environment that the club started.

"We've played on," he pointed to a list, "… those have been our home pitches. Netherton Park, Buffery Park, Tanfield Gift Ground – in Dudley – the Marl Hole, Netherton, behind the pub. Hingley's stadium we played on for a number of years. That was a lot of money in those days." It cost Yew Tree £16 a game at Hillcrest, I said. "I can beat that. I remember Netherton Park being £11/10s a season.

"Our first pitch was Netherton top pitch. Then we wanted the bottom pitch, but it was always waterlogged. So, we asked permission of the council to drain the ground and we put in pipes. And they turned us off it by the spring!" He laughed.

None of his relatives played much football, but his own love of the game was nurtured by his father and followed a well-trodden path.

"He used to take us to West Brom," he went on. "Most of our lads now are Albion, Villa or Wolves. The first game I remember, Billy Elliott played outside-right, David Walsh was centre-forward, Jack Vernon centre-half. This goes way, way back.

"One of the first games, it was at Molineux, on Boxing Day. I remember looking up and watching the rain falling off my father's trilby. Wolves versus Sunderland. The centre-forward was Trevor Ford, and the centre-half for Wolves was Stan Cullis.

"In the early days, we travelled by bus. I can remember going down to Coseley to play, one day. We should have gone to a pub called The White Horse. Three of 'em biked it down and went to a pub called The White House by mistake. We'd got a cracking guy called Lochey Turner, a legend. He was a tremendous centre-forward – he's still alive. We'd got a chap called Duggie Newey, who used to put butter on his head instead of Brylcreem. He played outside-left, and we beat 'em!'

"We'd got Ducky, Ducky Howard, Lochey Taylor, Slasher Baker," he laughed again. "Smiler, Smiler Parsons. It played a tremendous part in our lives. Me and a couple of others, sometimes just myself, it was a ritual to mark the pitch out every Saturday morning with sawdust. I'd go down the sawmills down the Bumble Hole, and Darby Hand. Lochey Taylor, he used to keep the news shop, grocery stores there. You used to eat and drink the game, just waiting for one week to the next.

"We've got two teams now. We had three at one stage in the Brierley Hill League but, in these days I'm talking about, we'd operate with probably the whole season with about 15, 16 players. If you got hurt, you wouldn't show it, 'cos you'd lose your place. No way you'd admit you were hurt. Funnily enough, we didn't seem to get so hurt those days." He laughed again. "I can remember saying to Margaret, my wife, when she was about 16, 'Just forget the Saturdays, it's football now'. It was a huge part of the community. If we lost, we'd wander round the canal and discuss the match. Later on, we had a couple of trips to Majorca. For the weekend. The first year it cost us £19/2s. It was expensive the second year. It had gone up to £26!"

Yew Tree would have to keep going until 2048 to match Parkdale, I said.

"That's right," he nodded. "A lot of clubs we played have gone on 50 years. There's Quarry Bank Celtic, for instance." And virtually every team still owed some kind of allegiance to a workplace or a pub? "Or a church."

Before 1955, the Football Association wouldn't let clubs or players under its jurisdiction play on a Sunday. Five years on, Sunday leagues were allowed to affiliate to County Associations and, four years after that, the FA started the Sunday Cup for amateurs playing in the top division of their league. In 1966, Unique United defeated Aldridge Fabrications 1-0 in the first final, at Dudley. Fitting, I thought.

The switch didn't affect Parkdale, because they played on a Saturday. On a Sunday, they'd watch an 'illegal' game. The White Swan, down Baptist End Road, was one.

"They'd got a centre-forward called Johnny Plant. Bustling. He came from a big family down Spring Road. They used to go hop-picking. Year after year after year, apparently, everybody used to lose their garden lines the day before they went hop-picking, because his brother Georgie was cutting them down to tie his hop-picking bag! Over the park, some trenches had been dug. I remember George jumped the trench and broke his leg. Took him up to hospital. In plaster, six weeks. Came back, out of plaster, jumped the trench, broke his other leg!

"Around that time, I met Margaret, Tony met Iris, Ron met Mary, and we grew up like that. Unfortunately, we were never able to get a permanent ground in Netherton. Then it did start to split up and that's why, quite honestly, the comradeship isn't as good as it was in those early days," he added.

It was no surprise our conversation always came round to people. Like Ken Norton.

"You get your rogues, like any club does. We've had our characters over the years. The paper highlighted Andy Williams," he lifted the *Dudley News* cutting that had taken me there. "He was great, but by no means was he the best player we've ever had. Potentially the best was a guy called Ken Norton. I think he was 15. He was the perfect player, an inside-forward. Arrogant little so-and-so," the smile widened.

"It was at the time Netherton Town formed, and they played on Hingley's ground. They were run by a bloke called Ron Corbett, who had a garage in Netherton. They were in a higher league, and Ken said he was going to sign as a part-time pro. He went and, shortly after, Robson came in for Ipswich. From there, he seemed to drift. I've got a feeling he went to Manchester City for a time. He finished up, I think, at Southport. But probably Ken's biggest claim to fame… there's a bridge on Primrose Hill with 'Astle is King' on. Well, Ken Norton wrote that."

I leaned forward and flicked the *News* cutting over. He smiled again. "They located him," he said. "He went to Cornwall to be a disc-jockey. Apparently, he's still working in a hotel, but he wouldn't give them a story. Knowing Ken, he's probably scared of being done for the graffiti!

"I remember going to sign him. He came from a poor family in Cradley Road. He said 'Do I have to pay subscriptions, John?' I said 'A shilling a week'. He said 'Well, I can't manage that, but is this scrap metal any good to you?'" he laughed out loud.

"The other guy was Joey Truss, super name," he turned the cutting over again and thumbed across the picture of Parkdale's 1952 line-up. "Huge guy. Came from The Priory in Dudley, the same area as Duncan Edwards."

Duncan Edwards. A tingle started between my shoulder blades. It's there still, as I write. "Joe was always in trouble and he came to us. I said 'Joe, you'll enjoy playing for Parkdale, but any trouble and you're out'. He was a colossus. Why on earth that guy didn't get into league football, I shall never know. Centre-forward. Crikey! A hard man. One season, he'd had a cut eye and he'd had stitches. And the referee said 'Son, you can't play with those in'. He went in the dressing room and cut the stitches out," he winced. "He had a cartilage op that, those days, was six or eight weeks out. I think he played after three weeks. He was a bouncer at a nightclub in Brierley Hill. He was a real hard man.

"I remember playing a cup match down at South Road, Stourbridge. The week before we played this team, there was a league match and there was bad feeling. I remember going into the dressing room before this cup match, saying 'Forget last week. It's gone. Let's start again'. On his way out, he walked in to their dressing room and said 'I hope you've all got your shinpads on today!'

"He came off one pitch with a centre-half from the opposition. He'd been niggling him all match. There was suddenly a smack and the guy was out. No one knew what had hit him!

Having said that, he was a tremendous goal-scorer. You see people playing today in the Premiership, they wouldn't hold a candle to him."

John played his last game when he was "50-something". He was still training, the photos in a discreet corner clues to running the London Marathon three years before.

"I played a long time. But, it's incredible, in the club we've got..." he went back to the list "... Neil's done 25 years. He's late 40s. Paul Coley, our secretary, he's been with us over 40 years. There's Ron Barnett, the other founder member. Over 50 years, there's only been four secretaries. Treasurers the same, about four or five. First team managers? About three. Now, okay, in the early years we didn't have managers, you ran it yourself, but Ron Barnett probably did it for 20 years. David Pell, who's the son of one of our original players, was manager for a couple of years.

"I can never remember tactics being discussed in them days. You played centre-forward, two inside-forwards, wing-halves dropping back. Your two backs, their job was to watch the wingers. Your centre-half marked their centre-forward. It was played like that, really. I suppose the real effort came from your inside-forwards and your half-backs. Your centre-forward was usually a big guy who went down the middle."

I took a short breath.

"You'd have been how much older than Duncan Edwards?" I asked.

"I was exactly the same age," he said, and the tingle hit 4 on the Richter Scale.

"Did you... was there... he's still a hero in these parts," I finally spat the question out. John sat forward and pointed to the picture again.

"I was doing National Service, and I remember the guys come into the barrack room...," he started to move the story ahead to February, 1958, then reined back. "This guy here, Ronnie Barnett. I remember Wolverhampton Street coming to play the church school. Duncan was playing for them. There was a wall at the school, a punishment place. You'd get dumped over the wall. I remember Duncan Edwards holding Ronnie Barnett over the dong, threatening to bop him.

"How old would he have been?"

"Eleven. He was a big lad, and he played with the big boys down The Priory. He was a wonderful talent, but that's how he physically developed, you know. He was the sort of player," he nodded to himself, "... you can't say this of many players. Duncan could play in defence and then, if a goal was required, he could switch and score a goal. At whatever level. The nearest player I can liken him to was John Charles. A gentle giant. The same kind of player."

I took another breath, hoping for one answer, tingle nearing Richter Scale 6.

"Did you ever play against him?"

"I think I played against him in one school game," he laughed, but his smile hinted at regret. "I remember him coming to the ground. But I can't remember whether I played that match."

"Did you ever see him play professionally?"

"He was big." His expression this time suggested he was finding it hard to match the picture in his head. He finally settled on "He was just talented in every department. He could score goals, he could shoot, he could pass. Tremendous stamina."

"When he made it with United, d'you remember what people here thought?"

"Hero worship," he smiled again. "His mum was always being photographed. She still appears in the local press. He was a hero. I think Matt Busby used to come and see his mum. I think his caps and other memorabilia is still up in Dudley sports hall."

My tea was cold, but I sipped a few final mouthfuls to wet my whistle and moved on to John's memories of his own career, rather than a man he might once have faced.

There was one game that stood out in his long career, against Parks Hall Social, who came from up in Dudley. Their goalkeeper was notorious, a middleweight National Service boxing champion.

"They hadn't been beaten for a long time. On Netherton Park, down in the bottom goals, someone played a good ball forward and I chased. He came out, kicked the ball, and it hit me in the face and ricocheted past him and into the net. Shortly after, the same thing happened. The ball went down the middle, he picked the ball up and kept on running. He went straight through me and I cracked two ribs." He laughed.

"I was always pretty fit. I scored a lot of goals with my head over the years, but I never looked at going into it. I suppose I was too busy running the team and doing the secretary's job. When we started the club, I'd followed most of my family as an apprentice platemaker. Then I moved on and I did an apprenticeship in the builder's merchants trade, at a firm in Dudley. Became a salesman there and, ever since then, I've always been in sales. For the past 16 years, I've been self-employed, selling into the nursery trade. I'm still working, still slogging on. Earning a crust."

He watched them every Saturday, as chairman. I tried to imagine lads now setting out on a 50-year adventure, with the same bond, the same contentment.

"Things have changed," he said, without hesitation. "I don't know whether the villages, or little towns as was then, still exist. Sadly, you read so much about violence on the streets these days. That was never around. People wouldn't lock their doors in Netherton. You'd wander round the streets in a gang, for want of a better word. We'd take each other home. A guy called Smiler Parsons was always the last home. You could con him to walk the wrong way. He never figured it out."

Dandelion days. "Yes. Whether you've got that camaraderie now.... My brother still lives in the house I was born in. My cousin, Malcolm, still has the hair-dressing salon in Netherton. In the old days, next door was Jack Smith, a cobbler. Working for Jack was a guy called Brian, our first right-half. Most of the team came from that area. Johnny Bowers lived in the Square. He died a couple of years ago. Sadly. Fortunately, there are only a few who've passed on. The vast majority of those are still with us."

I had a theory to test. Your early life was governed by the war, I said, but your parents did your worrying for you. Your teens were a period of hope, after what had gone before. Life was stable. You did National Service, your adulthood started in the 60s. Work's available, people are more affluent, more mobile. You're established when the three-day week starts. Your generation had the benefit of the good things.

"Having said that, some of it did affect me," he answered. "My early job as an apprentice at Thompson's was tough. Early mornings. Not very nice working conditions. And several of the lads who formed the first team, I'm thinking of one in particular, he worked all through his life in really, really tough conditions. Foundries. Clay works. Having said that, that guy is probably the most family-orientated man of any of us. He is contented. So you're probably right, yeah. I know what you're saying. It was a little more stable. We had to make our enjoyment, and did.

"My first football boots were made by a bloke in Meeting Street. I remember looking under the table one day and seeing these yellow-coloured boots with bars. Those were my first boots. In the early days, one of my jobs was looking after the ball. They were leather then, with a lace. You'd seal the bladder with an elastic band and tuck it under. You had to keep the lace away when you headed it.

"I think I wore the first jockstrap that ever appeared in Parkdale! The captain that day, Les Hubble, big hairy guy, said 'What the bloody hell's that, John?' That wasn't the first unofficial jockstrap in the club, 'cos there was a guy called Stan Beard, and he used to wear a sprout sack round his privates. That's true!" he laughed louder than before. Margaret had long since retired to the kitchen, but something told me she was used to the sounds that accompanied her husband's reminiscences.

Then he began his own stroll down Memory Lane. It was less angry than John Acock's, more precise than Ken and Greta Wall's.

"In the very old days, at the bottom of Netherton High Street was Doo's, the chemist. Absolute chaos inside. Coming up from there was Grainger's, a meat shop. Opposite was The Maypole, a grocery store. One of my uncles worked there. They used to have this method of sending cheques with an overhead wire. And they used to have butter-patters. Up from there was Abner Walker's, the hair-dresser's. In those days there used to be an old World War One shell holding the door open. It's still there, 'cos my cousin has the shop. I do hope it's not live!

"In those days, they used to come in for their haircut and a singe. They'd pass a lighted spill round the back of the hair. I think it was supposed to seal the ends, or something. Prevent colds, I seem to remember!" We both sniffed. Laughter.

"Then, moving up towards the centre of the town, was a newspaper shop, Greaves' on the right-hand side, which was right opposite the Church School. Where all this started. The Midland Red bus shelter on the left, going up. There was a chemist's shop on the corner of the Marketplace and then Nancy Baker's which was, without doubt, the focal point of Netherton. I think they closed it down last year. Rhodes' fish-and-chip shop was next to Nancy Baker's. And Netherton was just all chapels and pubs. It was said that if you walked from Dudley to Old Hill, and stopped for a half at each pub on the way along the main road, you'd be absolutely paralytic before you got to the other end. You would have been too."

It seemed natural to poke around my bag and pull out a book of old pictures of the area.

John began leafing through it, his eyes widening more at some shots than others.

"I went there," he thumbed a picture of Northfield Road Infants School, taken at the start of the First World War. "Not in 1914! My first morning, I went into the school, turned and ran. The headmistress, Miss Clapham, she caught me about a hundred yards away, took me under her arm and took me back."

I switched the tape off. You have to at some point. But one name didn't take long to emerge one last time. I asked John if people in the area were already aware of the young genius Edwards already when Parkdale was formed. They were. Did they know how good he was? Yes.

Then John pointed to one face in the *News* clipping of the 1952 side.

"Wilf Foley," he said. "He was the only player spoken about in the same breath as Duncan."

The shudder between my shoulder blades nudged Richter Scale 8

"What happened to him?"

"Two years after that picture was taken, he packed it up."

A schoolboy as good as Duncan Edwards, who packed up at 17. They say Bobby Moore might never have risen as he did, if Edwards hadn't died in 1958. The irresistible what-ifs. Wilf Foley? My heart sank at the thought of a hero never discovered.

On the road home, my eyes were following the bonnet towards Stourbridge, but my mind was in the housing estates either side of Halesowen Road, and Cinder Bank, up to Dudley. Wilf Foley. Where was he now? And what might have happened, had fate played a different hand?

Then I heard John utter Edwards' name again, an echo bouncing round and round and round. If they'd been asked, how many men would have said 'yes', they'd played against Duncan Edwards, knowing they might not have, but safe in the certainty that no proof would be required or available? How many have said it? It would be easy. But John hadn't.

By the time I arrived home, February 6, turning to February 7, I needed to share the night with someone. But the lights were off. Too awake to think of bed, I picked up the paper. It opened at *Today in History*. My eyes dropped on "1958: Seven Manchester United footballers – Busby's Babes – were killed when their plane crashed in thick snow at Munich Airport".

My spine hit 10. I did the maths. Forty-three years ago this night, Duncan Edwards had been mortally injured in the Munich Air Crash. I ran upstairs, but Maggie was asleep. So was the cat, curled at her feet. I thought about waking her to talk. I thought about waking the cat. But, if I did, I knew neither would understand why. And that would have been worse than keeping it to myself.

14 THE BEAUTIFUL MATCH

THERE'S A PLACE CALLED BELL END, TEE HEE, close to Rowley College. The Hawthorns is the highest football stadium in the country and the college is perched just about as high, meaning that the long, wide road with the *Carry On* name is close to the end of a long, slow climb from south Warwickshire.

It consists of a series of steps, starting at base camp in Alcester, then rising through Redditch and Bromsgrove to the Lickeys, at around 170m above sea level, which is almost 600ft in old money. Once you're off the M5, you rise again towards Blackheath, then scale the south face of Mincing Lane (funah-funah). After Bell End, you pass the Providence Chapel and take a right for the final climb up Rowley Village to the college, with the Turners Hill TV mast – trig point 271m, 970ft – behind it. The higher you go, the greyer the light becomes and the more you shiver at the certainty that, with every foot climbed, the temperature's dropping by a degree.

The name on the caretaker's house was Hi-View. Sixties pseudo, but accurate. The game was on, so I twisted between the dull brick buildings and emerged on a rutted expanse of gravel that started red but blended to brown and green, making it impossible to tell where an abandoned all-weather pitch ended and the grass began. And there, far below to the right, was half the Black Country, spread out like a model.

One Saturday in October, 1933, on his *English Journey*, JB Priestley walked up Oldbury High Street. Dad was nine. He was running the other way, on an errand, unwittingly part of a shocking snapshot of 20th Century life. Maybe.

The same day, Priestley stood on the ridge overlooking Dudley, a few miles north-west.

"The view from there is colossal," he wrote afterwards. "You looked down and across roofs and deeply mounting streets and pointing factory chimneys. It looked as if a great slab of Birmingham had been torn away and then tilted up there at an angle of about 45 degrees. The view from the other side, roughly, I suppose, to the North East, was even more impressive. There was the Black Country unrolled before you like a smouldering carpet. You looked into an immense hollow of smoke and blurred buildings and factory chimneys. There seemed to be no end to it…

"I descended into the vast smoky hollow and watched it turned itself into so many workshops, grimy rows of houses, pubs and picture theatres, yards filled with rusted metal, and great patches of waste ground. There was a cynical abundance of these patches of waste ground, which were as shocking as raw sores and open wounds…

"Sometimes the raw fog dripped; sometimes the cold rain steamed; but throughout it was thick and wet and chill. I lunched in one of the smaller towns with a man in the metal trade. There were several Black Country businessmen there. Large hearty fellows, sturdy eaters and drinkers. There had been a sudden flurry of business in the metal trade, and my friend was going back to his office and warehouse in West Bromwich after lunch…

"My friend's warehouse was in Rusty Lane… He keeps sheets of steel there, and no doubt any place is good enough to keep sheets of steel in; but I do not think I could let even a sheet of steel stay long in Rusty Lane. I have never seen such a picture of grim desolation as that street offered me…. The whole neighbourhood is mean and squalid, but this particular street seemed the worst of all. It would not matter very much – though it would matter – if only metal were kept there; but it happens that people live there, children are born there and grow up there…." Children like Dad.

I turned the engine off and the only sound was the wind. I opened the door and it hit me, a blast born far, far beyond the distant blue remembered hills that had raced across the Bumble Hole of John Hingley's youth, then up this steep hill.

The college was a drab four-tier wedding cake, four bands of dirty brown separated by four more of dull blue rendering, the top one decorated with the white letters R-O-W-L-E-Y R-E-G-I-S C, then nothing, as if the lone C stood for centigrade or cold, or 'Can't be arsed to do any more.' Then I saw the Yew Tree lads as never before.

They were huddled, walking towards the far pitch, the one closest to the precipice, no stragglers, bodies tilted into the wind, 11 of them providing heat and shelter for each other. Rob's hands were deep inside his shorts, hunting warmth. Stan's arms were folded, like an old Black Country mother on the step, instinctively unimpressed. You could have put this line of men in any setting of the past hundred years, maybe more. Children braving the elements on the way to a street-corner game with a ball of rags. Pupils off to school. Youths stepping towards their first day of work at the chainshop, or down the mine. Dads walking home from a hard day's graft.

Mark Horton's girlfriend, Sam, complained.

"Dad warned her to wrap up," Lin said.

"Have you never been 'ere before?" Jezz laughed, and Sam shook her head. "It can be an 'undred in Netherton in the summer, and it's still three degrees below up 'ere."

Three officials marched in to sight. Three. It meant one of two things – a welcome break from the vagaries of club linos, or the grim prospect of three times as much inconsistency.

"So many games off," Rob remarked. "They want their money".

Princess Margaret's death, the day before, hadn't caused many tears among the Trees. I wasn't surprised. No one had mentioned The King, after all.

A phone went in Jezz's pocket during the minute's silence, and a Lowes sub teetered along the goal line on someone's shoulders, lashing net to metal, an odd high-wire act set against the bleak horizon. The whistle ended the silence, such as it was, and Lowes manager Craig Barnsley tapped Jezz on the arm and asked to borrow a pump.

"I want a spare ball in the net," he said. "It tends to go down the bank with our lot."

In the first 10 seconds, Ginger wellied the ball high. A gull wheeled 100 feet above the precipice, sensing every subtle change of current, every ebb and flow. But Yoss found it harder. He stepped back trying to track the ball's flight, then forward, then back again.

Then he gave a foul away. Nine minutes later, Ginger was handbagged after a clumsy tackle on half-way. The ref called them over.

"Let's have some proper football, lads," he told them. Proper football? If he wanted proper football, surely, we wouldn't have been here, head on to a gale. It didn't hold much promise for what would follow. Oh, we of little faith.

Pele didn't have a windswept Black Country hillside in mind when he called it The Beautiful Game. But, then, did Priestley dare imagine this "squalid" land might one day warm his heart, not fire his anger? Lowry, surely, would have recognised the light piercing the gloom, something special given by a higher hand to something ordinary.

I know what you're thinking. Football's simple but, to be the best, you need speed, skill, strength, touch, vision and belief. For all the gifts they lack, though, there's a perfection that plasterers and trench-diggers can dream about, too, maybe even reach half-a-dozen times in their lives. Days when an invisible string runs from toe to toe. When there's telepathy. When you believe pass-and-move is nurtured in the womb. If you think I'm off my rocker, you weren't at Rowley College on a vicious day in February, 2002. Because, though passions often overflowed, there *was* poetry. It was beautiful.

Tree were three up by half-time, and four ahead minutes later. The first came on 31, when Stan battled across the 18-yard box, right to left, but drifted the ball out to Tigs. On the wind, the pint-sized driver's mate dipped this way, then that, and threatened to take his man on around the outside, feet from the drop down Hawes Hill. Instead, he cut inside, looked up and chipped the keeper from 12 yards.

A minute later, the little winger skinned his full-back wide on the left, then rolled the ball in to Stan's sweet run. Twelve yards. Goal. His dad, Brian, turned to Bass.

"I taught him that in Netherton Park when he was 10."

I wondered whether Brian *had* ever told him, or whether this was another Black Country trait. I hoped it was. If Dad ever watched me play football, he was the first person I looked for on the line, when a break in play followed a sweetly-hit pass or a decisive tackle. I remember the occasional smile of satisfaction but, if ever we swapped words after a match, it was about what I could have done better, rather than what had made his heart skip.

It was the end of a good week for Stan. Minutes before, I'd stood with Lin.

"I know what I wanted to tell you," she'd said. "Craig had a call from his old boss on Thursday. Wants him to go back and be night shift supervisor."

Yoss, Naylor and her other son Robert were back, too. Yoss had said he'd learn to drive to spread the load. But no job for Carl. He'd kicked the door in when they sacked him.

"He's had a rise too," Lin added. "What he was earning on the forklifts is less than when he left school." She was pleased, but not as pleased as Stan, at that moment.

On 42, Craig Skidmore drifted out left to find the ball, let the wind blow him back inside and shot on the run. The keeper saved to his right, but Rob was the first to the loose ball. He was there again after 49 when Tigs went wide, glanced up and slide-ruled a pass between two defenders in to Rob's stride.

I was on my tenth tour of the pitch, seeking warmth in friction, when I peered in the ditch by the cliff-top goal. Amid the cans, unmistakably, was a blue johnny wrapper. A johnny. Up here. I stared across the valley, felt the wind rip more skin from my ears, then looked down again. Ah, Black Country women. They still made 'em tough.

Through it all, Tree prevailed. There were a couple of bad moments. The first came when Bran and Ginger watched Lowes' Number 9 force his way sideways before firing under Tuck. The second bad moment was my fault, when I asked Jezz why the ref hadn't lifted an arm for an indirect free-kick. One moment we were talking, the next he was ranting.

"Don't criticise me, Jezz," the ref warned.

"Yer give 'em a uniform," Jezz strutted away. Five minutes later, the ref dropped another clanger and Jezz was off again. The ref threatened to book him, this a man who'd ignored a Lowes player using the c-word so loudly in the first-half that the congregation at St Giles turned and looked at the door.

By the 72nd minute, my fingers were white. "Lowes no fight," I scrawled, and "Craig hit bar, Rob kicked off line", then put my notebook away. All feeling had gone.

That was it, anyway. A morning of surreal beauty. I walked off with Bran. The only blot had been the short period when they'd believed their own half-time talk.

"That's us though, innit?" he said, and put an arm round my shoulder. It was.

An odd thing happened in the car. One moment, I was taking a last look at Priestley's hell-hole as I fumbled with my anorak, the next I was inside the railway hut that passed as Lodge Park Juniors' changing room, 30 years before, losing the battle to undo laces with dislocated thumbs. This day, as then, I was home before they found their normal colour. I'd done some sums, ready to ask Jezz if he thought promotion was on, by the time I could bend them again.

He e-mailed me the day after, chuffed at the performance but reporting that Walsall Bengals had resigned. The table had Tree third still, on 24 points after eight wins and four defeats. Harborne were top, on 27, with Khalsa second on 25.

I'd had a chat to league secretary Peter Lowe, when Barrel dropped out of Division 1. The club had paid a £30 fine, and lost their £60 guarantee fee. If they hadn't coughed up, the debt would have been split among their players. And, if they hadn't paid that in 14 days, he'd have asked Birmingham County FA to suspend them.

The past couple of years had been horrendous, he'd said. The Premier Division had started 2000-2001 with 12 teams, and ended with eight. It had already lost five this year. Two had gone from Premier 1 and now two from Division 1. Clubs were finding it hard. My season mustn't end without talking to the people who made it happen.

Just now, though, there were more vital things, if Tree were to launch an unlikely promotion push. I tapped a reply to Jezz.

"When do you turn your minds to the possibility," I asked.

It's a quiz question, really, but it was a geography teacher who once asked me what geology had to do with a meeting in Fleet Street's Anderton's Hotel on March 22, 1888, the day Accrington, Aston Villa, Blackburn Rovers, Bolton Wanderers, Burnley, Derby County, Everton, Notts County, Preston North End, Stoke, West Bromwich Albion and Wolverhampton Wanderers formed the Football League.

Walls. Brick walls, in particular. The kind you kicked a football against in England's industrial back-streets. Had the Fleet Street meeting happened eight years before, the eleventh club in that list would have been the Strollers. They'd been formed in 1878 by a group of workers from the George Salter Spring Works. On September 20, 1879, they strolled to nearby Wednesbury to buy a ball, and renamed themselves. Their first match was a 1-0 win over Black Lake Victoria at Dartmouth Park, West Brom, on December 13, 1879. The suffix 'Albion' didn't enter the name for another year.

I'd wondered at the Tap House match how different things might have been if the Strollers had left a pub in the late 19th Century, not a factory. It occurred to me again at Lion Farm before the Hangman's Tree match. Would a kit-maker's name be spelt in white amid a sea of blue seats somewhere by a pub in Oldbury? Would children in some Third World hovel be earning peanuts stitching £50 replica Hangman's shirts?

Academic, really. Like Paul Gennard's over-ambitious '10 points from 12' plan. To be honest, it had died so long before that I barely remembered when it had been put to his players. I suspect they'd forgotten sooner than I had.

Lowes was always going to be hard to follow because, in his heart, a man who earns his crust with rough hands knows it's greedy to expect the same dream twice in two weeks. Instead, we were left with something more familiar, an unchanged, disjointed side that was 3-0 up by half-time through Rob, Craig and Tigs. Fluid football was hard to come by, though, on a pitch with tyre tracks running across its boggy turf. In short, it was disjointed because Tree let themselves hit Hangman's basement level.

Rob and Craig had made it 5-0 by the 64th minute, goals I watched with Ted Terry as he told me Little Greeny had been back in hospital. They'd had him on a drip to build his strength for the next round of chemotherapy. Ted was going to call soon.

I'd been doing my homework to check a hunch that the season would over before the lad appeared at the pub again. His parents wouldn't want a stranger knocking on their door, out of the blue, to ask about the Yew Tree. So I abandoned plans to try.

After the fifth goal, I bumped into Rob's Uncle Roger. We rambled through the names on the Parkdale photo. He'd been 14 at the time, a couple of years younger than John Hingley – and Duncan Edwards – but he still had a copy of the picture.

At the far end, apart from a first-half moment when Hangman's right-back had hacked Rob from behind, the home side had shown little passion in the mud. But they summoned enough from their caked legs with 16 minutes left to salvage some pride, though not before Tuck had produced 10 seconds of brilliance he'll replay till he's a grandad. Point-blank, shoulder pinned or not, he kept the first shot out high to his left, then flung himself low to his left to stop the second. The third – low to his right – was the best. His defenders were static as the ball bagatelled back into the six-yard box, but a Hangman reached it first and he couldn't produce a fourth.

A minute later, it was 2-5. This time, Tuck was a mile off his line when a free-kick sailed over his head. The abuse from the sideline would have been funny, if I hadn't already watched this scene unfold on countless days since September.

"Another goal will make 'em fucking panic," another Hangman shouted. He was right, but Roger Willetts laughed.

"The effing and blinding that goes on!" he shook his head.

That wasn't it, though. Ginger was lured into something ugly, eight minutes from time. The ref crooked a finger at Hangman's Number 6 first. In seconds, he was running towards

Sunday, muddy Sunday: Yode prepares a foray down the right flank, a move the opposition Number 2 clearly isn't expecting. Picture by Aaron Manning

the touchline, dismissed. Most men would have slowed to a canter, at least, nearing the spectators. Not him. He accelerated, ran beyond the front rank of onlookers – which was also the rear rank, if we're being picky – and put the bucket into orbit.

The keeper standing in front of us had been right-back until the booking for hacking Rob. Then he'd been stuck between the posts in the interests of Hangman finishing the game with a full set. He threw his hands in the air.

"Five-one down, and he gets himself bastard sent off!" I'm not sure if it was his team's first or second goal he'd missed.

Ginger had niggled the Hangman into nutting him. I learned that as Meesey, on as sub, rolled a pass to Craig in the area. He dipped a shoulder, then walked it into the net. He didn't sing "Georgie, Georgie!" I imagine he was too young to know.

"They don't listen," Jezz said as I yanked my clod-hoppers off, a few minutes later.

"It's the big 'un next week," Paul added.

Harborne. Our minds went back to September's aerial assault. We paused.

"I suppose the only thing you can do is not give throw-ins away," I said.

At home, I looked at the league table. If Harborne hadn't won today, we'd be level on points. On the Tuesday, I called Rob.

"If you win, you go above them," I said.

"Yeah, it would be nice," he answered, so I asked him how he saw things from here, a season which, he'd thought, might end proving that Tree had gone up too soon.

"Meself, personally, I think Harborne and New Fullbrook are two very good sides. If we can finish third behind them, I think we've had a great season. Sunday's the biggest game, to be honest, because the first time they destroyed us, like."

"But not very fast at the back," I thought I ought to offer a few positive thoughts.

"On a smaller pitch, now we've got a bit of belief in ourselves…," he said. "I'm going to get on to 'em to stop in Saturday, anyhow, I know that."

"What about training on Thursday? Much discussion?"

"I'd imagine there will be because Paul will be up for that."

I rang Paul afterwards and picked up where Rob had left off.

"Six-pointer, yeah," he said, and we took it from there.

"Did you ever think you'd get into that position?"

"Well, I've gradually brought them round to my way of thinking, some of 'em, like. I've told 'em about Saturday night. You cor expect to go and have 10 pints of lager and perform on a Sunday morning. I think a lot of 'em have took note. The training as well, the performances are getting better. I don't know what yo think, Mark?"

"Definitely," I said. I wasn't lying. Well, not too much.

"I'm trying to put into 'em, Mark, that two-touch, and playing a triangle, it improves the game. Which I think it has."

Then I asked the big one. "What's your game plan on Sunday?" He paused.

"We've got to adapt the same attitude as against Fullbrook. Close 'em down quick. I'll be playing five across the middle again. See how the game progresses, like… it's down to them. On Thursday, I shall emphasise this could make our season.

"But fair play to the lads," he finally paused for breath, "they have listened. As you know, Mark, you can only emphasise so much. They'm grown men, like, and if they don't want to listen, yo cor do nothing about it."

He finished off with Rob's display against Hangman's, the size of Yoss' waist, and Mark Horton's form. Close your eyes and, but for the names and the stretched Black Country syllables, it could have been Fergie. That's not meant to be a joke. It was football at its simplest, a manager assessing his players ahead of a must-win match, neatly wrapped in two minutes. Attitude, commitment, ability.

If only the Trees could put that lot together, not your flash-in-the-pan 30 minutes on a windswept hill, but game after game. They never would, of course, a reality I'd long since accepted as I e-mailed Jezz a questionnaire. You know the kind: Favourite drink, best goal, superstitions. Handy, I thought, if Ted Terry's cup final dream came true. As I hit the button, though, I was already worrying about the answers.

From: "Jeremy Dingley"
To: "Mark Higgitt"
Subject: Re: I've just realised…
Date: February 19, 2002 19:33
Hi Mark – Sundays match is a big 6 pointer. The lads know how important, this game is, but, they'll still get rat arsed Saturday night… See you on Sunday Mate. JEZZ

"The lads know how important this game is."
I don't know where to start, other than to say that, whatever intentions Tree had of topping of the table – even for a week – were conspicuously absent.

The team joked, walking down as one, unusually, to put the nets up. It was snowing. I tugged my collar high and my cap tight. The Turner's Hill TV masts were visible beyond the buildings running up Simms Lane. I thought I could see someone's outline, high on the side of Rowley Ridge. It must have been Titus Oates.

Paul asked if I'd seen training on Thursday, but I hadn't. Neither had he. His 16-year-old daughter had been in hospital with a skin infection, so he'd had other things on his mind. I wondered, aloud, if his players had been distracted too, last night.

"I don't know," he said. "Yo cor stop 'em drinking. They'm grown men."

Tree answered the bugle call well when two long throws bombed Tuck's goal in as many minutes after the kick-off. But things went pear-shaped the moment Mark rose for a ball in the sixth minute and collapsed in the mud, clutching his face. His eye was closing as he left the pitch and shut by the time Meesey replaced him, two minutes on.

After 23 minutes, the ball was turned in from the left and allowed to bounce. Harborne's Number 11 reacted first. A left foot swung from 18 yards. A lucky deflection past Tuck's outstretched right arm. Nil-one. End of story.

There's no point in going much further, because Harborne had all the time and space they needed on the ball. They could have been on the beach. I even counted the Trees – Tuck, Yode, Ginger, Meesey, Bran, Gav, Craig, Yoss, Rob, Stan, Tigs – to make sure they had a full quota on the pitch. They did.

Stan was the first to give in. The man who'd once chased lost causes like a Staffie loping after a meat wagon had long gone by the time I bumped into the old fella behind the top goal, and picked up where we'd left off weeks before.

He'd watched Old Hill play a couple of years earlier, and liked it so much he'd even been out on Boxing Day, "and no one entices me from my Boxing Day dinner easily".

The first game of the next season, he watched again, and hardly recognised a face. Most of them had signed for other clubs. They paid more.

"That's the trouble today," he said. "No loyalty." He looked at the top goal, nodding at the deepening quagmire. "Like Flanders," he said. Right on both counts.

"Yo ay done fuck-all," was the first thing I heard Paul snap as I drifted towards the half-time huddle, feeling like an intruder at my 21st game. "You'm thinking 'I done enough'. You'm a different side from last week. You don't fucking want it enough."

Then Jezz interrupted, quietly to start with, though the F-count was about to go up, which meant we were also perilously close to the point where an expletive split the first syllable of a word from the second.

"You'm thinking you'm gonna win the league. You'm gonna win nothing, I'm telling you. I bay being nasty. You'm winning fuck-all. Because there's too many… well, I'm going to be outspoken here. There's too many not thinking about Sundays. There's too many on the piss…" I looked around, Opple was saying "He's right lads!", Bran was nodding, Stan was very quiet. Jezz cranked the volume up.

"You'm still pissed up, half the time. It ay good e-fucking-nough. You got a chance today to go top of the league…" another notch on the dial "… fucking top! Not half-way. You've done the donkey dick work, and you'm gonna throw it away."

There was more pride in the second-half, and they could have scored seven in the last 10 minutes. But, as Paula Tucker put it when the last chance went begging, none of them could have hit a cow's arse with a banjo. And it would have been a travesty.

In the pub, later, I slid a stool up alongside Rob beneath the TV. Bran moved in too. The rest dribbled in after. Maybe they deserved a draw, they felt. Sod off.

To my surprise, Dave Green had been in, and I'd missed him. Rob told me they'd found a match with his sister, and he was pinning his hopes on a bone marrow op.

"That one I hit over," Rob shook his head after that, "if only I'd let the ball run on another inch, I could have put me weight over it."

"You can what-if everything, though," Opple answered.

"What if I hadn't started on these," Rob tapped his fags, then his pint and pointed to the TV, Sunderland players warming up at the Stadium of Light. "I coulda bin there!"

He turned away from the screen and, with a resigned note in his voice, named the three or four of them who'd been on the pop the night before.

"Stan day get in till squealing time," he said. "He was still drunk at half-past two. It don't matter how young you am, yo cor do that and expect to play in a few hours."

Paul joined us, and the conversation took a predictable path.

I drove down Cradley Road home. Ken Norton's 'Astle is King' graffiti had been vandalised, and so had the 'RIP' added after his death. A streak of yellow, aptly, had been painted through the white lettering, with the word 'Dudley' daubed in its place.

That was as depressing as the match. The *News* campaign to rename the landmark Astle Bridge, though, seemed a little more hopeful.

'Frank's behind us!' the paper had trumpeted a couple of weeks before. Actually, it wasn't Frank Skinner, as a closer inspection would reveal, but 'Frank's agent says Frank's behind us!' wouldn't have had the same crisp, optimistic ring.

Albion striker Jason Roberts, who'd paid a T-shirt tribute to the legend after scoring Albion's winner against Walsall, added his voice to the *News* campaign.

"The fans already recognise it as Jeff's bridge so why not make it official?"

Since that goal-celebration, a six-match winning run had put Albion third in Division 1, a point behind Wolves, and landed a place in the FA Cup Sixth Round.

Wolves hadn't done too badly either. Three wins and a defeat had taken them up a place to second the same weekend, with a game in hand.

Since then, Gary Megson's men had consolidated third, despite unexpected reverses at the hands Preston and Millwall. Wolves, though, had banged in three more wins, including 3-0 against Walsall that catapulted them beyond Man City to the top.

I'd expected to hear more banter between the Wolves and Baggies nuts. But it was hard to give it one day if, within a couple, you'd be taking twice as much back. I'd have been happy to see both teams go up. Football tribalism, though, is about who you hate as much as who you love. So, it was a view I'd never bothered to air. Risked, actually.

Hearts were worn on the sleeve elsewhere, though. On Albion's unofficial *Boing, Boing, Baggies, Baggies* website, Finbarr sounded as frustrated as a one-armed trapeze artist with an itchy arse. His trip to Preston had involved a dodgy RAC traffic report, a speed limit on the viaduct, a minor accident, five or six sets of roadworks and a two-lane wide lorry carrying the biggest Portakabin he'd ever seen.

"We were crap," he wept. "They were crap; Jason Roberts had his foot stamped on and hobbled off; We won a penalty and missed; They won a penalty and missed; We gave them a free header from a corner and they scored; They didn't return the favour."

Anyone put off by the dull exterior of the less-than imaginatively named *Wolves Stats* website would have missed the kind of view the likes of Stan, Mark, Rob, Bran and Co were probably only risking in quiet corners, among 'friends'.

"Can things get any better?" Bizket Wolf asked after Wolves had beaten Walsall to go top. "Eight points clear of Man City, 10 points clear of the stripey ones."

But even Bizket couldn't keep the carefree optimism going for long.

"Davey J will be undoubtedly crowned manager of the month for Feb – but how often does that signal a reverse in fortunes?" he said. They might have been within a sniff of the Promised Lane, but the years of expectation and disappointment had told.

So, reticent or not, the Black Country wasn't doing too badly. Back in September, thousands would have settled for the way the tables looked now, Wolves top, Albion third, and Yew Tree third or fourth, thanks to three wins before the Harborne horror.

From: Jeremy Dingley
To: Mark Higgitt
Subject: Sundays fixture
Date: February 27, 2002 18:28

Hi Mark (ar bin ya) – Just got over Sundays result, still never mind there's always next season as they say. Sunday away to Rhodia at Albright & Wilson in Oldbury. A/Z Page 57 Ref 5E. Got one new signing my cousins son Gavin. The signing date closes tomorrow. See you Sunday. JEZZ

I supposed he would.

15 UNCLE RAY

I INHERITED HALF DAD'S TALENT WITH A BALL, and most of his ability to be in the right place at the wrong time. Stop sobbing, it's true.

While I was an average Midland Comb player, he was only kept out of a Shropshire Light Infantry team by one Cpl Billy Wright – then being tipped for England's wartime international squad. Albion centre forward WG Richardson, and Johnny Hancox, the Walsall, Wolves and England outside left, also graced that side. I recalled from childhood chat that he could have gone to Spurs after the war, but had eyes only for the Baggies.

Football was in his blood. He was the fifth of eight lads and one girl. There was Len – born in 1914 – Joe, Fred and Lilian before him, with George, Sam, Jack and Eric, born in 1934, bringing up the rear.

I'd already nudged him into adding to his jottings when I packed him and Mum in to the car and headed back to his roots on the first day of March, in wistful mood. As this is what he told me, on a quiet afternoon a couple of weeks later, I assume that, on the way to the Coseley archive, thoughts like these he'd already committed to writing were flitting round his mind:

With Dad's interest and Len playing, Joe's interest and Fred's rolled rag ball, it's likely I kicked something from an early age. I know I kicked stones whenever I could. Footer, as it was called, wasn't played in the street, nor The Foredraught, where there was room, but on the playing field pitches, with real posts for "shots in". Sometimes we did pick sides, but it depended if anyone owned a casey or something bigger than a tennis ball. Practically no one owned a pair of football boots. I had one pair of boots for school, home, gardening, everything. With money so tight, it must have been a despairing sight for Mom and Dad to see sons kicking balls and, worse, stones.

Dad was short, stocky, and his flat cap – which he invariably wore – made his round face seem more round. His interest in and love for his family was evident in his treatment of all his children. He had an undying love for the Albion. He also believed passionately in a kind of Fabian Socialism that would lead to a more balanced society. His great hatreds were not against individuals, but institutions. Aston Villa and the Tory Party were invariably the focus of his scorn or his anger for most of his life.

According to your Uncle Sam, Dad played at inside-left for Worksop Town at around 19. He took a very lively interest in Len's burgeoning career. Len played for Oldbury United, Whiteheath Vine FC, in the Worcestershire Combination, and also Smethwick Highfield. He was about 17 or 18. Dad's wishes came true when Len was signed on amateur forms by the Albion. But, in his last match prior to joining Albion, he was badly injured playing for Redditch Town against Albion's A side. The player who tackled him was HE 'Tom'

Dollery, who played captained Warwickshire County Cricket Club after the war. I think that he may well have played for England, too.

Len was brilliant and should have made the move to higher Football League status. I have a memory that he had offers to sign for Sunderland and Leeds. But he chose to stay at home, because Dad was on the dole, and he was the only wage-earner.

He didn't play again until 1940, when he started to play for HDA, at the same time I began my adult career. I can't remember if Dad lived to see Eric play for Albion's youth team alongside Don Howe and Jimmy Whitehouse. I know Mother went to see them play Villa in a Youth Cup Final, so it's probable Dad didn't live to see that.

When Albion won the FA Cup and promotion to the First Division, in 1931, Len made up lines to the tune of *Covered Wagon*: "Pile 'em on little Baggies, pile 'em on; Pass it to the centre-forward Richardson; Their defence is in a hole; So here's another goal; Pile 'em on little Baggies, pile 'em on". I wasn't seven, and I still remember that. I still have a hankie with the players on it, a bit faded but recognisable, 71 years after. Another memory was when the team paraded the cup on an open top chara, past our house on the way to Blackheath from West Bromwich. The support for the back gate frame was a big stump. George used to climb to the top of it, like a monkey on a stick, watching the world go by. He was on his vantage point that day. He was five.

Johnny Lowe was living with his widowed mother by the playing fields when we moved to 567. He'd be in his late 20s and was unemployed. When we had a ball, we'd play shots in, using the top goals. Johnny would join in. He'd try hitch-kicks and scissor-kicks, and a lot of fancy Stanley Matthews dribbling. But he was never rough. I suppose, these days, he'd be regarded with suspicion for playing with small lads.

I'd started my football life playing for Good Shepherd School, in goal, at seven or eight, then for Langley St. Michael's School at 11. When I was made captain of Good Shepherd, I prevailed on Mr Cook to let me play in the forwards. Through my adult career, though, I always had a yearning to play in goal again, but wasn't tall enough.

Les 'Legger' Alsop was captain of the school footer and cricket sides when I started to play for both elevens. There was also Fatty Skett, the school goalkeeper. We used to pull his leg that it was because he filled the goal that the other couldn't score. Actually, despite his size – and he really was wide – he was a very good goalkeeper.

The *Birmingham Evening Despatch*, in the early 30s, started a series of league competitions for boys from about nine to 14. Boys around 11 became interested in playing in our age group in the Nig-Nog league. Yes, Nig-Nog! That was what the *Despatch* called their set-up. I've no idea why. Nobody would have associated the title with racism. To us, "he's a nig-nog" meant someone didn't use their intelligence.

So we formed ourselves into Whiteheath Albion. Whiteheath was in Staffordshire and we were in Worcestershire. What else could we call our team, when the boys from Blackheath assumed the name Blackheath Villa?

Freddie 'Tichy' Richards, whose parents died in an influenza outbreak, lived with his uncle and aunt, Mr and Mrs Harvey, who kept the fish and chip shop. Mr Harvey was co-trainer, with your Grandad, of Oldbury United. He was smaller than the rest of us – hence Tichy – and wasn't much good, but always wanted to join in. If it was footer, he was invariably the last to make the sides up because he wore glasses.

When we thought of joining the Nig-Nog league, he volunteered to do all the paperwork because we hadn't asked any adult. We walked to our away matches, and at times stripped under a hedge. We bought our casey by saving the football wrappers from nougat bars. You needed 50 for a ball. It was a sacrifice because, though you had the nougat to show for your pocket money, it meant we couldn't spend it on anything else. We found a wrapper for every team but Bradford Park Avenue. It took us ages before we got that ball. I regret to say that we folded after that first season.

Joe unfortunately had a suspect kidney and didn't play much adult football, though he claimed to have scored the fastest goal on record when he went to watch Len play for Oldbury Schoolboys, and was drafted into the side, as they were one short. Fred played in the Nig-Nog league for Langley Victoria. I remember playing for them, once, when they were short. I was about four years younger than most of the teams.

At outside-left for the Vics was George Sabin, who went on to play for Cardiff City in war-time football. Two former well-known Football League players who emerged from the pre-war Nig-Nog league to play in the post-war era were Len Millard, captain of Albion, and Jack Burkett, who captained Nottingham Forest at Wembley.

I've always associated Millard with Toll End Wesley, a Tipton team. Jack played for Hawthorn, even though he was a Villa fan in those days. He told me that when your Mum and I played him and his wife at bowls in Skegness, in the late 80s.

George played for Good Shepherd and St Michael's, and at outside right with me for HDA at 16. He was called up to the Worcesters in 1944 and demobbed, like me, in 1948. He never played again. What a waste. Sam, by his own admission, wasn't very good. But he'd join in if asked. Eric played for Ipsley Youth FC, one of the best youth teams in the Midlands. Of the Ipsley players, Tank Wormington, made the Blues first team. Jack and Eric both had trials for the Albion but Jack, according to Sam, was rejected, much to his dejection, on account of his very slight build. Eric played regularly in the Albion youth side, Erdington Albion. Don Howe played for the same side. When Eric was demobbed after National Service, he decided to teach.

I made my swansong for Alvechurch against Moor Green in a preliminary round of the FA Cup in 1958. We were badly defeated and I had a stinker, mainly because of unfitness. I didn't wait to be dropped. Could I put my loss of form down to having disturbed nights by newly-arrived twins, and having to rise sometimes six mornings a week before six, in time to catch the 6.30 bus to work for a 7am to 5pm stint of forging aircraft components? I was back there from 7am to mid-day on Saturdays and, while the Korean War was being fought, worked 7am to 4pm on Sundays, too.

Genetics? Mention Ray Westwood and Jack 'Eddie' Webster, the international runner. Granny Pendress was a Westwood, and it's likely Eddie's mother was a Westwood, maybe a sister of Granny. I recall Mother talking about her as Aunt So-and-so. At the time Ray

Westwood played for England, I can recall Dad saying he was related to mother's side. It needs to be substantiated. I know Sam, Jack and Eric all seem to remember this alleged family tie to Ray.

I'd like to think I did football-lovers the world over a service in the Coseley archive. I'd leafed through a book overflowing with cuttings about the events of February, 1958 – the Munich Air Crash. But it had been opened so often by people anxious to read the newspaper story of Duncan Edwards' fight for life – and his death at 2.15am on Thursday, February 21, aged 21 – that its spine was broken.

"Only after a fearful wait of three-and-a-half hours was it learned that Dudley-born Duncan Edwards… was among the survivors," the *Dudley Herald* reported on February 8. "Improved considerably," was its optimistic quote a week on, after a crisis with his kidneys, "but whether he will play football again is a different matter".

Then, seven days later, the terrible news. "Two weeks after sustaining serious injuries in the Munich air disaster, 21-year-old Duncan Edwards, Dudley's brilliant young footballer with Manchester United, died in hospital."

From then until his funeral the media replayed his career, from his Dudley school side to his last match. The *Herald* of Friday, March 1, described the tens of thousands of ordinary folk who lined the streets before his funeral. Arthur Hopcraft's *The Football Man* tells of Manchester's shock being followed by "lingering communal desolation". The Black Country felt the same thing, a feeling it hasn't forgotten.

"The body of Duncan Edwards was brought straight to his parents' home," *The Herald* said, "and taken from there to the church along a route which passed through the estate where he had spent his boyhood, and which was lined with people who had known him as 'that nice lad up the street'."

I could see everything I wanted, but the book wouldn't stand another copier flexing. It was probably the face I pulled, and the 30 miles I added in the telling of my trip, that persuaded them to take a master copy, and post me a handful of sheets.

Thirty minutes later, I celebrated with a bowl of faggits and pays at the Black Country Museum. Dad had the same, for old time's sake. Mum knew what old time's sake might do to the ozone layer, later, and left us to it. A wise move, for excitement and mushy peas have never mixed well in me.

The Black Country hasn't succumbed to making its hell-fire heritage a growth industry, but the museum at least keeps it alive for those who want a glimpse of how things were. Electric tramcars and trolleybuses transport you to a village of 30 buildings by a canal basin, with a mine and colliery buildings on its outskirts. As the faggits settled, we wandered past a chainshop built with two hearths from one of the last Black Country firms to strike handmade chain, Bloomers of Quarry Bank.

Bloomer. The name had a resonance in these parts. Still has. Football's first superstar, Steve Bloomer – the Derby County, Middlesbrough and England inside-right, whose career lasted from 1892 to the Great War – was born in Cradley, five miles south, in 1874. The town still honours his memory. Almost 65 years after his death, Derby's anthem remains *Steve Bloomer's Watching*. Heritage, in itself.

By the chainshop was a brass foundry, behind which was a row of back-to-backs. When I found him, Dad was in a bricked yard, looking at the 'brewhouse', but seeing his mum. It was five minutes before he said: "We had one like this."

The three-up, two-down I bought in 1983 kept a family of three in snug comfort. I only ever squeezed 10 or more in at a party and, even then, someone had to step into what passed for a garden if two people wanted to breathe at the same time. The tiny two-up, two-down Dad was back in, after 70-odd years, was home to 11. Eleven?

The Methodist Providence Chapel Greta Wall had told me of was up the hill. The wooden central pews had enough space for five either side of a wooden divide. The side pews sat two more each, beneath the wooden balcony. The wooden floor echoed to our footsteps, as it had echoed to a million others in the tiny, canal-side mining and nail-making settlement of Darby Hand – the Bumble Hole – from 1837 to 1974.

In the 19th Century, the chapel was affiliated to the Methodist New Connexion, which broke from the Methodist body in 1797, and was very strong in the area. Now, the Friends of the Museum arranged services there. A notice on the door announced the next would be on Sunday, March 31, the Easter Service (Limited seat availability).

Down the street, I walked through Emile Doo's front door and stepped back in time again. It was a replica of the chemist's the Walls and John Hingley had laughed about. The Doo family had donated the fixtures and fittings of the shop when it closed in 1974, 45 years after he bought it from a tailor. There was a man behind the counter, though whether he was a reconstruction of Mr Doo as well, I couldn't say. He was telling two small girls how Mr Doo made pills. He was more interested than them, it's safe to say. What's more, I waited 10 minutes, but he didn't whistle through his teeth once. In the interests of authenticity, I nearly told him Ken and John's childhood story. But, if he couldn't be arsed to do his research properly, I couldn't be arsed to do it for him.

We'd spent, what, three hours there by the time we wandered into the Hall of Fame, drawn as if to a back page by the ceiling-high picture display of Black Country sporting heroes. I asked Dad to go through the Westwood story one more time.

"There was Ray Westwood and Eddie Webster," he said again. "Granny Pendress was a Westwood. At the time Ray Westwood played for England, I recall Dad saying he was related to mother's side." It was good enough for me.

I sauntered off to the bookshop, smiling to myself that, if your boyhood dreams of playing for England somehow came to nought, it was reassuring to think you shared a DNA-profile with a former international star, even if the genealogical link was thin.

I was halted by a white book cover with a red-shirted figure on it. I recognised the image before I was close enough to read the title, *Duncan Edwards – The Full Report*. It was the story of the great man's short football career. I began reading, as you do.

"It wasn't that the scratched, ink-stained and rusted desk was too small for the fidgeting, tousle-haired primary schoolboy," it began. "It was, after all, the one he had sat behind for some time."

The original Brylcreem Boy: Ray Westwood, a family connection, according to unverified family legend. Possibly.

It went on to chronicle his childhood days, from his birth on October 1, 1936, at 23 Malvern Crescent, Holly Hall, Dudley – a 9lbs 8oz arrival – to the family's move, soon after, to 31 Elm Road, on the Priory Estate, and beyond.

Six pars in, this is what I read: "His parents could not be too critical of his interest in the game, as both sides of the family had footballing connections… His uncle, Ray Westwood, played as a professional with Bolton Wanderers in the 1930s, and also represented England."

I shook my head and read it again, "blah-blah-blah… His uncle, Ray Westwood, played as a professional… blah-blah-blah…." His uncle? I read it again.

Dad was half-way between the Hall of Fame and the bookshop when I found him.

"Read this!" I said. He did. Not a flicker.

"Read it again," I demanded, then took the book from him before he could.

"… His uncle, Ray Westwood, played as a professional…." I read, then looked up.

"Explain the Ray Westwood story again," I said. He did.

"Bloody hell," I gasped. "You know what this means?"

16 UP FOR THE CUP

STAN.

Ah. Stan. Where do I start?

Rhodia's ground was wedged between what was once known as Albright & Wilson's chemical factory and an exhaust and tyre depot. While I waited for the rest, I walked up Tat Bank Road, past Coronation Buildings, a row of terraced houses, and came across The Cottage Inn.

Its sign depicted a leafy rural scene. It would have looked only slightly more out of place in Baghdad. A mock-chalkboard beneath said: 'What's On Every Friday Karaoke with Woody 3pm Till 7pm; Sunday Turn Your Cards Right; Wednesdays Quiz Night 9.15 start win a gallon of beer.'

I had a question for the next quiz: "Will Stan turn up as pissed today as last week?"

It wasn't long before I had an answer.

Horns blew as I passed Club 99 on the way back, and I crossed Western Road to a sea of waves from the arriving Trees. Some used every finger of the hand, others just a couple. One or two tongues poked out, too, and I couldn't halt a shudder at the thought of where those tongues had been, and what they'd been doing, in recent hours. Stan, though, wasn't among them. That's because he wasn't there at all.

Rhodia's players were changing, even though no one had the keys to their dressing room. Rob and Tuck were outside, too, at the far end of what I took to be a social club. Tree's room was open, so I poked my head in. It was dingy. In the circumstances, the last thing they needed was for someone to drop their guts.

The door flew open a minute later and three or four men burst out like pop from a bottle, the sound of disgust following closely behind. Someone was laughing inside. I didn't need forensic evidence to tell me it was Bran.

That's when I bumped into Brian, Stan's dad. He shook his head, drew on a roll-up and admitted how far out of his skull Stan had been when he'd turned up the week before. This week, he hadn't even made it past Mitch's front door. While Brian went to collect him, Lin told me he'd been to an all-day birthday party.

"It wor a party," Sam corrected her. "Just a piss-up."

Mark wasn't happy, but at least he was there. With Paul away, Jezz was giving a game to the players who'd frozen their parts off on the line against Harborne. Most saw the point. While Wolves and Albion still had title ambitions, defeat had meant Tree couldn't win the league, unless results went for them. There were three Division 1 games left, and two cup ties. But Mark – his eye still black – was sub. He was also incensed. He moaned in the dressing room, and he moaned as we passed a roped-off cricket square. He moaned as we arrived at a massive pitch at the far end of a sports ground that had clearly seen better days. And he moaned as I gazed across its once-manicured acres. Anyone who remembered its legendary heyday would have wept at the sight.

"Jezz Dingley couldn't run a bath, let alone a team," he went on. "The bloke in my shirt must be some player to fill my boots." Then he told Sam it was going to be a bad day. He wasn't lying. Ten minutes on, he was still at it. Eventually, I couldn't take any more. Rob was running the line, so I sought sanctuary and the voice of reason.

"Go back and tell him he's got another 15 years of football in front of him," he tucked the linesman's flag under his arm and lit a cigarette. "He should worry when he can count the number of games he has left in his legs."

It was one of those games that make you wonder out loud why you like football. If I hadn't been taking notes, I'd have forgotten it within days, maybe hours. So, for the record, Tree completed a 6-2, 0-2 double over Rhodia. Other than that, I recall the home side's spindly keeper, a lad who looked likely to snap like a pencil if someone built like a brick-outhouse collided with him. Gavin Skidmore, for instance.

That hunch became reality early in the second-half when, for no reason I can still fathom, he wandered off his line at a corner and went down like a small factory chimney. For a few worrying moments, he lay very still. But he eventually found his feet and he seemed to twig when someone pointed out which way Rhodia were kicking. Give him his due, he staggered around his 18-yard box for the duration. No moaning, none that I could hear, anyway. I'm ashamed to say, though, that it brightened my morning.

"Are you starting to think about next season?" I said to Jezz at some point. Stan was what made me think to ask. I'd have washed my hands of him and done so with a sinking mix of disappointment and frustration in my heart. How I craved it to be different.

"Yes," he said.

"Some hard decisions to be made?"

"Ah."

I asked Rob the same thing, later.

"We need three quality players. But, I hope our showing this year might have encouraged some players to think about joining."

I'm not sure what time Stan turned up, or when Jezz told him "You talk to me about commitment and how important the team is, and you've let me down", but he said very little, apart from admitting he'd have been neither use nor ornament. He perked up slightly when Jezz explained how important the following Sunday's cup game was. Slightly, but not much.

I asked him about his new job, five or 10 minutes later. It was going well, he said.

"We played cricket most of the night, Thursday," he said, straight-faced. "We done a shift's worth in a couple of hours." I waited for the punch-line, but it never came.

When Mark went on in place of Yoss, after 70 minutes, the rotund midfielder sat down in what passed for a dugout and Stan asked him what time he'd arrived home.

"Five o'clock," he answered. Five o'clock, and he'd played 70 minutes.

And that was it, the first game of the season that felt like there was nothing to play for. I drifted back to that awful period in September, when the results had been bad and the football worse. I'd reacquainted myself with Sunday football. I'd remembered the rituals and rivalries. I'd forged new friendships, found common bonds. I'd followed some roots back into the iron and clay. And there was Duncan Edwards. But I'd wanted the season to stay alive to the last game. So, all we had left were the cups.

By contrast, all Wolves had was the league. But, then, it's all they'd had since January when Gillingham had dumped them from the FA Cup. Now they were starting to wobble there as well. A two-all draw at Forest had ended a seven-match unbeaten run and, though a 1-1 at St Andrew's saw them stay top of Division 1, the mood on the unofficial Wolves website was hardly optimistic.

"This takes us a small step closer to the Premiership," someone called Fat Stan said. "It also demonstrates one reason we've stayed in the division of death for so long."

The only bright spot was that Albion were still struggling, too, and looking like a play-off spot was the best they could do. A one-all draw with Watford prompted much shaking of *Boing! Boing!* heads, including this from one Dave Langston: "They scored, we equalised, it was like going to a wake."

It was more than Cliff Crancher could take. I don't know where he lived, but I had a picture of a fed-up West Bromwich housewife slamming his faggits and pays down on the table and saying: "Either shut up or give him a piece of your mind." He did.

"Typical," he typed in reply to Langston. "Last night, we gained a point while Preston, Blues and Burnley, all with hopes of the play-offs, lost. So with only eight matches left, we improved our situation. Two years ago we'd have dreamt of being in a situation like this." A voice of reason, but then he turned into Esther Rantzen.

"Why, why, why, why, why can't some of you just be happy with where we are?"

I was hoping Dave and Cliff might find themselves nose to tail in the Hawthorns pie queue at the FA Cup quarter-final against Fulham, the next Sunday. At least they'd have had Astle Bridge to talk about. Under a headline that, curiously, contained none of the words 'King', 'Astle' or 'Bridge', the *Dudley News* had reported that more than 250 Albion shareholders were putting their weight behind the paper's self-declared campaign to rename Primrose Hill after the recently deceased goal-scoring ace.

Dave Watkin, secretary of Shareholders 4 Albion, was taking their thoughts, and those of the West Bromwich Albion Supporters Club and the fanzine *Grorty Dick*, to a meeting of Central Dudley Area Committee councillors.

"We can put pressure on the right people who can make this tribute happen," Watkin, a Baggie for 45 years, said. But not enough. For the diehards who couldn't wait a week to find out, the *News* website brought disappointment the next day.

The elected members – representing not just Baggies fans, Astle admirers and proponents of *nouveau heritage*, but also Wolves supporters and little old ladies who, not to put too fine a point on it, couldn't give a monkey's about football – had other ideas. They opted for that knee-jerk reaction of councillors anxious to fill the allotted hours before a planning meeting

– a site visit, to "consider the full implications of a name-change", after receiving just three letters opposing the idea. Democracy in action.

"There are concerns that the name Primrose Hill Bridge, along with Primrose Hill Chapel, is all that remains of this small community," Councillor Phil Higgins said. It was a point. Then there was the Percy Sugden brigade.

"Some people feel it sets a bad example to allow this graffiti to stay," he went on, adding the traditional clincher, "and it could distract motorists and cause an accident."

Watkins was conciliatory at first – "I take the point about preserving the Primrose Hill community, but we could compromise and name the bridge Astle's Bridge at Primrose Hill" – and then defiant. "Even if the words are removed, they'll be sprayed on again because they've become a legend as much as the man himself."

I wasn't sure whether Stan would make an appearance at Woodgate Valley Country Park for the Warley & District Sunday League Cup second round tie against Selly Oak Eagles and, frankly, I didn't care.

As it happened, he turned up, but he was only sub. Unused. From the moment he took his place on the line, the atmosphere was as inviting as the sky. If I told you that the wind was whipping the rain in to spirals and flurries as I passed Lye Meadow, home of Alvechurch FC, you'd have an idea.

I mention this partly for meteorological reasons, partly as a yardstick for Stan's demeanour, but mainly because I was at the Meadow in the autumn of 1971-72, when 'Church began the longest FA Cup tie in history. The Fourth Qualifying Round battle with Oxford City lasted 11 hours before the men in amber-and-black won the fifth replay and reached the First Round proper, and, thus, the *Guinness Book of Records*.

I was born in the village. What's more, Dad had captained the club for years, so it was where I saw my first match. But a regret remains amid the pride in that feat.

After the first replay, an evening tie I couldn't make, most of the other replays were afternoon kick-offs. I thought about asking for a yellow slip out of school at lunch, and forgetting to go back. Lots of my mates thought about it too. Some did it. I didn't. Church went down 4-2 to Aldershot in the First Round. They'd played 12 games in three weeks. They must have been knackered.

I was reflecting on those heady days – and thinking of spraying 'Graham Allner is King' on the bus-shelter at the bottom of Tanyard Lane, the street on which I was born – as Ginger emerged from the dressing room, walked up and presented me with a fist, chest-height. I looked at him, wondering what the heck he was up to. Eventually, fed up waiting for me to meet him half-way, he knocked his knuckles against mine.

The opening exchanges set a game-long pattern. What light there was creeping through to the windswept hilltop turned Tree's orange shirts and the bright yellow of Eagles into fireflies against a grey Second City backdrop. If it hadn't been for the swirling gale, I'd have imagined that Tree didn't share my desperation to put a cup run together.

You could often see Fred Astaire in the 20-yard cameo Yosser normally put together three or four times a game but, this day, it was more Stan Laurel. Any pass knocked above head-height reared high, then hung or bounced off an imaginary mattress before returning to Earth. It was like playing on a beach with a lightweight Woollies ball, the impulse buy you regret making with the first kick.

It's not PC to say this, these days, but I once played in a Redditch County High School match in Stourbridge when our games master, Eric Jones, ventured out of a pavilion 50 yards from the pitch to tell us at half-time that we were like "a bunch of spastics". Jonah had played for Alvechurch with Dad, in the 50s, so, not only was I upset by his crude comment, I felt he'd let Dad down too. Thirty years on, I'm not sure whether I was more offended by an adult using the insult than his remote vantage point. Watching Tree and Selly Oak trying to decide where the ball would land, and when, then moving and having to think again, suggested what we Abbey High boys must have looked like all those years before. And we didn't have a gale to blame.

To be honest, there's something hilarious about an unco-ordinated man waiting for the ball to come to a cushioned first touch, then sidefooting fresh air when it balloons beyond. Or leaping for a header and landing again before the ball's within 10 feet.

The thinking footballer would have kept the ball on the deck and built play from a series of short passes. The playmaker who saw how slow the opposition back line was to turn would release someone behind the full-back. Shows how much I know.

On his left foot, Bran was cultured, one step away from his hero, Paul McGrath. Okay, maybe two. On his right foot, he was Sylvester Stallone in *Escape to Victory*, unsettlingly bad. The first goal came after nine minutes, when a wobbling ball hopped over his hesitant leg and ran into the path of Selly Oak's lanky Number 8. Tuck blocked the first shot, but the ball ballooned up and hit the bar. Ginger scrambled back to clear, but only managed to knock the ball into his own net.

I was standing by Jezz. Before he said anything, though, Stan had started laughing.

"Ginger scored an own goal! Ginger scored an own goal!" he yelled across the pitch.

"Thanks for caring," Jezz shouted across to him. If Stan heard, he didn't react.

There'd been times in the season when I'd laughed at moments like it. There'd been times when I'd thought to myself that Jezz should loosen up a little. But first I felt uncomfortable, because Stan had let the club – and his team-mates – down a couple of times in the past month, and being sub again today hardly made it sound like the joke of a man at the heart of the club, or with the club in his heart. Then I felt annoyed.

It looked ominous but, once they'd found their feet, in the space of 13 minutes Tree turned it around through Tigs and a hopeful long shot from Mark that went up, flattened out, then dipped, then dipped again, two or three crucial inches above the back-pedalling keeper's desperate flap.

Stan? He came to life a minute into the second-half when Gavin tanked across for a covering tackle and clattered Selly Oak's left-winger into touch. The ref gave the foul, but the brick-built defender insisted the ball had gone out first, as if that forgave it.

"Book him, ref!" Stan shouted, and laughed.

A few minutes later, he regaled everyone – Chubbs, Nigel Davenport, Craig, Opple, Bowe – with what sounded like the tale of a relative who'd been tried to hold up a bank with a water pistol. I wasn't sure what prompted the story, far less whether it was true. But his mum didn't look impressed.

Tree had a wake-up call, as the game died, when the dependable Yode lost his man and the ball flashed across the goal. I was talking to Paul Gennard as it happened. Mitch's cartilage had been shaved. Now he was concentrating on next season.

"What about you?" I asked.

"I'm frustrated by the attitude of some players," he sighed. You can complete the sentence by now.

They put effort in to training, and went through the routines, said the right thing.

But it was one good game, four bad.

They didn't listen, blah-blah-blah.

He said it five times in two minutes, each echo prompted by the action.

The struggle grew when Tigs limped away, badly bruised, after being hacked off the pitch. At times, they weren't even second-best and, suddenly, I could see it all going pear-shaped, my season over long before April began, a book without an ending.

"Tree, let's get our heads on!" Bran urged, out of the blue. To be honest, if he hadn't yelled it, I would. I looked around to see why the rest weren't as concerned and realised that – whether out of blind faith or resignation at Tree's fate – the touchline chat had already moved from Round 2 of the Warley & District Sunday League Cup, Woodgate Valley Country Park, to Round 6 of the FA Cup, The Hawthorns, and "Where are you watching the Albion game?"

Ten minutes from time, the ball found a Selly Oak forward, unmarked in the six-yard box. He fluffed his first shot, a panicky swing of the foot, but sent the rebound goalwards before Ginger stretched his little legs as far as they would go and cleared off the line. The home side has missed the equaliser they deserved, but my hopes were alive (it's worth reporting that Stan didn't cheer his team-mate).

In the car, former Wimbledon boss Joe Kinnear told *Sport on 5's* Mark Pougatch that Tree had done what was necessary.

"If you go out at this stage, it's the end of your season."

He wasn't talking about Yew Tree, exactly, but he might as well have been. He was previewing West Brom's FA Cup quarter-final tie against Fulham, "the multi-millionaires from fashionable West London against the working class lads from the Black Country". Tree hadn't deserved to win but, with three league games and the West Bromwich Albion Cup also still to be played, they'd extended their season by at least one game. Albion didn't. They played also badly but lost, 0-1.

On the Tuesday night, I called Rob and spoke to James first. He'd visited Little Greeny the week before and they'd played computer games. He was expecting to have his bone marrow transplant in a couple of weeks. He was in good spirits.

Jezz Dingley wasn't, however. He'd e-mailed me on the Monday, to say Hangman's Tree had been kicked out of the league.

"That's another six points lost," he wrote. "We planned a meeting for next Sunday, but that's gone out of the window. I told them in the changing rooms to find another f***ing idiot to be secretary. After talking to Bran, they think I'm joking. I'll see the season out. The way I feel while I'm writing this to you is that I just don't care any more. I've got loads of problems at home, so I could do without this shit as well."

I told Rob. He was surprised. Jezz had been unhappy having to run the line in the second-half, as well as run on with a bottle of magic water and a can of freeze spray. He'd told them he wasn't going to put up with it any more. In the pub, afterwards, Rob had asked him if he was feeling any happier. He wasn't.

"The trouble is, it's the same six or seven who put their hearts in to it, and the same six or seven who don't take it seriously," Rob said. "Look at the Harborne game. Some of 'em was getting in at five in the morning. You just can't play a game of football after that."

Stan? "He's been a disappointment. Full of the club when he's on a high, but doesn't like it when things don't go his way."

And Jezz? "He just needs a bit of loving-up from time to time. But we've got a lot to be pleased about."

17 THE WRONG TEAM?

I'M GRATEFUL fate didn't point me in the direction of a different Yew Tree when I set out to find a team to follow. A couple of months before I hitched my trailer to Jezz Dingley's towing bar, the unsavoury side of football reared its ugly head on a pitch in Kingswinford, and then in the *Dudley News*:

Referee determined not to be beaten by attack

A Clent football referee punched in the face by a player has returned to refereeing three weeks after the incident.

Match official Martin Grange of Mount Lane, a referee for more than 25 years, was left covered in blood after the attack during the Kidderminster and District League match between Yew Tree and Kingswinford-based AFC Borgfeld.

League secretary Ernie Pyke said: "Martin has put himself on the referees list for next season. He's put the incident behind him now and said he didn't want to finish his refereeing career on such a sour note."

Stourbridge footballer Keith Rhodes, aged 40, was fined £200 and handed a sine-die suspension – life ban, which he can apply to have lifted after five years – for the offence that left Grange unable to continue officiating the game.

Borgfeld have resigned from the league and the club has folded because most of their players have quit. Police are still investigating the incident.

A fine of £200 and a life ban for a 40-year-old. Like telling Stevie Wonder he'd lost his driving licence. It reminded me of a Sunday match I once played in, although 'played' isn't strictly accurate. I'd pulled the sub's tracksuit off when an opponent was dismissed for taking our left-back's legs away, then kicking him in the kidneys.

The same player had stamped on my right shin, laughed and told me "that's going to hurt" on Sunday, November 18, the same season (I remember the date well – it was a week before my wedding). On this occasion, I'd only given my first name to the ref before another player lost it. That set off the rest.

A mate of mine walked in to the ground as 10 men were sent off and the ref abandoned the game. Only the keeper was left, sitting on his penalty spot, bemused. If Uncle Len once scored the fastest goal on record, I must be close to the *Guinness Book of Records* for the shortest appearance as sub.

The bloke who'd reffed the Rhodia game, Eric Young, had a theory for it. Anyone emotionally attached to Elland Road or Highbury might want to look away now.

"The players see it on TV. I'm not just blaming them, but you see one or two of the

Arsenal players doing it, pointing, shouting at the linesmen, referees' faces… I tell you, if you see one or two bad instances on a Saturday night, on a Sunday you can bet your bottom dollar there's a spin-off up and down the country somewhere. I reckon it's drifted in since the Leeds era. That's one of the worst things that's happened. You'd got Don Revie who was part and parcel of it."

It was like listening to Dad.

Eric hadn't been that bad at Rhodia, even though one player had conned him into booking Yosser. I'd seen a handful of refs, some good, some bad, some excellent, some rank awful in the previous seven months. I'd seen some on the spot for every decision. I'd even seen one who was about five feet six and 18 stones, a man whose uncanny ability to be on the scene two passes after the ball had gone seemed to be matched only by his instinct for arriving at the pie shop at opening time.

I'd seen some players tuck the ref in their pocket, simply because of the way they treated him, a bloke with a job to do. And vice-versa. I'd seen the likes of Ginger practically beg for a booking – Arsenal fan, what do you expect? – time and again.

"You've got a general attitude of people today, as well, they will not respect authority," Eric told me when I tracked him down one night, a man in black turned social philosopher – and why not, after 40 years with the whistle. "Irrespective of whether you like police or not, or what you think of someone in charge, you're more likely to have people disputing what authority says."

His most memorable match was at the end of his six years in the Football League, when he joined 1982 FA Cup Final ref Clive White on an expenses-paid tournament trip to Madrid which ended with him running the line when Real met AZ Alkmar. Laurie Cunningham was in the home side. Three years before, Eric could have strolled down to The Hawthorns with the rest of us and watched him, though he'd have had to pay for the pie.

There were 100,000 in the stadium that balmy Bernebau night, watching the £995,000 Black Pearl and his international team-mates. The week before, he'd reffed Crewe Alexandra, in front of 3,500. Madrid, Crewe or Yew Tree. In essence, he said, the basic rules of the game were the same, you just applied them. There were things the likes of Beckham and Bergkamp did, week in, week out, that you wouldn't get away with on a park pitch.

"The chance of Rhodia or Yew Tree trying to take a quick free-kick, for instance… the players are slow-thinking. It's a different atmosphere and mode of thought." It was stating the obvious, but still worth saying.

He was 62 when we spoke, past the age where he'd rise at 4.30 in the morning and go on a training run, avoiding the traffic and the dog muck, then showering and going to work as an estimator. These days, he reffed youth games too, to "put what I've had out of the sport back into it". There were still "the odd one or two that still want to go out and kick something up the pitch, because they've had a bad curry, or got pissed, or hadn't got their leg over". He accepted that, just as he knew there were also lads who "like me, like to think they've had a hard week".

Over the years, though, his family had done without him, so he was doing less and less. What had started out at 7s/6d a game was about to come to an end paying him the princely sum of £16 a morning. Then it would be someone else's turn to be conned by cheats, someone else's turn to take lip off weekend prima-donnas, to watch grown men trying to play out their dreams once a week, to keep Warley & District Sunday Football League in motion. To ensure another part of the nation's heritage didn't end up at the museum. Sixteen pounds? I wouldn't have done the job for twice that, even with both knees in good working order.

Strange how fate knows when to play the hack a good hand, isn't it? Albion's key promotion trip to Bramhall Lane, the day before Tree visited Merrivale, had ended in an ugly fashion.

The match started badly for United. After eight minutes, goalkeeper Simon Tracey handled just outside his area, denying the Baggies a clear chance. Ref Eddie Wolstenholme waved the red card, leaving the 10-man Blades manning barricades that only Scott Dobie had breached by half-time.

The fireworks began at the start of the second-half. United manager Neil Warnock, no shrinking violet, he, made a double substitution, bringing strikers Georges Santos and Patrick Suffo on. Within minutes, Santos tried to remove Andy Johnson's legs at the knee without the benefit of anaesthetic. Wolstenholme waved red again. To be fair, a replay later showed Santos nicked the ball before rearranging the full-back's shins.

In the subsequent melée, Suffo headbutted an opponent and followed his pal to the bath. Thus the Blades found themselves with eight men, 2-0 down and with 26 minutes to save themselves from further humiliation. Scott Dobie added a third to Derek McInnes' 62nd minute goal and Albion's goal difference – worth a point in the battle to deny Wolves an automatic promotion place – looked like blooming.

By the 82nd minute, United had lost two more men, "injured". Some applauded Neil Warnock decision to pull them off as the act of a compassionate manager. Others marvelled at the benefits of an O-level maths education. Eight minus two equals six. The rules state there must be at least seven players for a game to continue. Game over.

Suffo's offence wasn't as heinous as the one that finished Keith Rhodes' career at Kingswinford, but the so-called Battle of Bramall Lane went down in history as the first time a game at that level had been stopped because of lack of players.

Wolves supporters were left cursing. Dave Jones' team had dropped another three points, in a 0-1 home defeat to Grimsby, a result JD Wolf – trying to make sense of it all on the fans' website – had once considered unlikely, on the basis that the Shrimpers had only won once at Molineux since the war. The one involving King Harold.

Before the game, he'd spoken confidently of "a safe bet and realistically only probably needing three more wins to secure the fortunes of the Promised Land next season".

After it, he'd tried to salvage a few rays of hope: "We're still eight points clear with only six games left. The title may be realistically out of our reach, but we can still show Keegan who's the better side," he said, referring to the table-top clash with Man City, two games hence. Some people never learn.

I'm left with JD's thoughts because, though I drove to Londonderry Lane expecting the dressing room to be alive with chat of Saturday afternoon, it was anything but.

Three league games left, two in the cups. There was still something to play for. Judging by the look on Jezz Dingley's face as he pulled the kit from his car boot, I was the only one who believed it. It was a look I'd grown to dread, to be frank.

"How are you?" I asked.

"All right, until I arrived," he said. They only had 12 men. Opple hadn't turned up. Jezz thought it was because he hadn't been picked for a few weeks. But, then, he added, he hadn't been playing well enough to be picked.

Then there was Stan. He was there. Trouble was, his kit wasn't. But he'd fetch it, if he was playing. You can guess the answer Jezz gave him.

Bran was injured. So was Nigel Davenport, Tree's new keeper. Jezz's relative, the other Gavin, was missing too. Jezz had forgotten to tell him there was a game. At least Blues had won on Friday, I smiled.

"That's the only bright spot on the weekend," he nodded, then shook his head. "It all looked so rosy a few weeks ago."

Craig Skidmore walked up and the pair moved away slightly.

"I shouldn't have said what I said," he told Jezz.

"I was out of order," Jezz said. "I was under orders to get back to see Mom on Mothering Sunday. That was what was on my mind."

In the circumstances, with hindsight, strolling up to Stan wasn't my smartest move.

"What's gone wrong?" I asked.

"I'm not playing for Jeremy Dingley again. I won't be playing for Yew Tree again."

"Why not?"

"I love the bloke but, when it comes to football, he does my head in. One time in four years I haven't turned up because of drink."

It wasn't a good time to mention that Paul Gennard wasn't there because it had been Scott's 21st the night before. So I changed the subject. Which is how I'm able to report that Stan's job was "going great. The best thing that ever happened to me was telling the boss where to shove it".

Five weeks on, he was back with a rise. Ah, a happy man. At last.

Then his dad, Brian, piped up. His boss had told him he couldn't go to his best mate's funeral, on the Tuesday, because it would leave him without a driver.

"Don't ask him any questions," Stan looked at me. "It'll only start him off."

It began raining heavily just before kick-off. The clouds were as black as a coal-miner's nose, so black that we could hear the sound of planes coming in low on the approach to Birmingham Airport, but we couldn't see them.

Merrivale started brightly, not like a team with three points to its name, following the departure of Barrel, Hangman's Tree and Walsall Bengals. They'd have been ahead on five minutes if their Number 9 hadn't swivelled, unmarked, in the area, and pulled his shot across the face of Tuck's goal. Tree looked disorganised, distracted by the ill-feeling. Only Yode was visibly trying to raise his game in Bran's absence.

"Fucking hell, Ginger, sort it out!" he yelled at the rugrat a few minutes later. Gavin told him to calm down, and Yode laughed at his own anger.

"He's doing my head in," he admitted. Tuck started to laugh too.

I ambled and found myself with Bran and Stan, a pitch width away from the usual gathering of Tree followers. Bran had picked up a knee injury at work, plastering. It was the first game he'd watched since September.

"Are we normally this shite?" he asked.

"There've been moments," I answered.

He paused, then talked about the over-reliance on Rob, the constant expectation that his pace would bring goals. He couldn't understand why, with so many ball-players in midfield. I looked at Bass, the enigma. He had it all, speed, control, a great shot, but never put it together with vision.

"Would it help if you trained on a full-size pitch?" I mused.

"Ah, maybe," he said. "Mind you, if Paul did do something, they probably wouldn't bother trying it in the game. They wouldn't take it seriously."

"Why?"

"That's just us."

"We just turn up and play," Stan joined in.

"Why?"

"Probably because that's what we've always done," he admitted.

"We're not bad, but we could be much better if we put our minds to it," Bran added.

The conversation was interrupted by a familiar voice. Ginger. Excited.

"Ant," he shouted at Bran. "Have a guess who's captain!" Bran shrugged. Ginger hoisted an arm in the air and pointed at himself. Bran's face was a blend of disbelief and betrayal, the look of a man who's been mugged by an old lady.

"How did that happen?" he wondered out loud.

"There was only five players on the pitch when the ref called the captains together," Stan said, "so Ginger took it on himself to say it was him."

Half-time, 0-0. As the oranges were savaged, the cigarettes were lit and the privates rearranged, Jezz wrapped his talk around Merrivale being a Route One team and told Meesey to pick his chin off the floor. Before they headed back, the ref asked them to mind their language. It was becoming too industrial for his liking in a public park.

It was an odd 45 minutes. Tree set off down the slope, a team that suddenly looked as if it was searching for something, anything. Merrivale played as if they'd reached the height of their ambition and expectations by keeping it 0-0. At least the sun had come out. It was a small mercy. The last time we'd been to Londonderry Lane, that grim battle with Barrel, it had been autumnal, a feeling that made you crave the sun again. Now it was warm, for a few minutes, at least.

Danny Baker has a theory. If you lean against a goalpost and randomly start talking to a parks keeper, without knowing, you'll always pick the one who's 9-0 down. I asked Merrivale's how come they were rooted to the bottom of the table. He turned and walked towards me, his back to the play, and held his hands out.

"Teams seem to get lucky against us," he said.

Georgie, Georgie! Rob Wall piles the agony on the home keeper. Picture by Aaron Manning

Lucky? A minute or two later, Yoss played a ball to the corner of the penalty area, calculated with slide rule, set square and theodolite to meet the angle of Craig Skidmore's run from the left wing. The keeper rushed out to intercept, but only succeeded in sending Craig sprawling. The ref had had a stinker so far and, predictably, Gavin and Ginger told him to send the goalie off. He didn't, to my relief. To my pleasure, someone in orange told the pair to shut up. Craig picked himself up and hit the bottom right corner from the penalty spot.

Lucky? Three minutes later, the keeper redeemed himself when Bass chased a ball beyond the byline and cut it back. The ref didn't see it. Bass cut inside and fired a fierce shot that was goalbound until the keeper arched his back and tipped it over.

Lucky? Two minutes on, Bass was brought down chasing a pass from Yoss. This time, Craig's penalty was palmed away from the inside the post. Not a miss. A save. The luck didn't hold out, though, which was a shame, for this keeper didn't deserve to be picking the ball out of his net again.

This time, Rob was brought down near the left-wing quadrant. A quick free-kick found Gavin Skidmore on the prowl from defence, and his shot was heading wide until it was deflected to the bottom left-hand corner. Three minutes from time, Bass flicked a Meesey pass into Rob's path. He beat the offside trap and poked the third home.

I sauntered back to the Tree mob near half-way, attracted by a sound I hadn't heard much in recent weeks. Laughter. Jezz had a smile on his face, Captain Ginger – substituted – was playing up as linesman and Stan and Bran were aiming insults at anyone and anything that moved. Ginger, mainly.

I stood with Jezz for the last seconds of the game and asked him if he felt better.

"It's took us 25 minutes to start the game," he sighed.

"They're an enjoyable lot to be with, a good team when they want to be," I said.

Saturday night and Sunday morning: Jezz Dingley (third from the right) and Stan Horton, hands in pockets, concentrate on the on-field action. Paula Tucker (second right) and Ginger, the reluctant lino, watch on too. Picture by Aaron Manning

"But so frustrating," he ended my sentence for me.

I switched the radio off on my way home. Frustrating was the word.

Stan. It would have been reassuring to see him don his kit, come on as substitute and prove a point to Jezz on the pitch. But his attitude was a disappointment. If I'm right, I reckon he'd disappointed himself. How can you expect to have a skinful, crawl in at five and play a game of football at 10.30? Wasn't it time he chose which one meant the most to him, before someone else did?

And what about the team? What had I been watching so far this season? A bunch of blokes who tended to draw their inspiration and example from someone who was looking down, not up.

It had been another low point, yet they'd won 3-0. Merrivale were the ones who could have grumbled. Yet they'd battled and battled and kept battling, not moaning, even though they'd been heading for their twelfth defeat of the season.

"Those sturdy knights of coal and hammer, who scoff at peace and joy at clamour."

It was beginning to wear off. Maybe I'd been following the wrong team.

18 DERELICTION AND DUTY

IT WAS A PIG OF A NIGHT. Lights flickered through the rain either side of the elevated M5 but, beneath, the streets of Langley were dark.

Mona's Transport Café faced me as I paused at the end of Popes Lane before turning up Tat Bank Road. But Mona clearly didn't work Thursday nights any more than she'd worked Sundays when I'd passed her corner before the Rhodia match.

The sign opposite the café read Engine Street, a no-through road. If the name described its heritage, the dead-end symbolised its fate. More dereliction. I pondered what it was like in 1933, when JB Priestley had been horrified by Rusty Lane.

On my wander up Tat Bank, 11 days before, I'd peeped through a gap between tall, decaying, padlocked gates that guarded another pock-marked parcel of dead industrial land. A rusting spiral staircase going nowhere stood amid dozens of old tyres, plastic bags flapping in the breeze around them. In another place – a traffic island or a shopping centre – it might have been an urban sculpture costing thousands, a powerful reminder of what corners like this had once meant to the nation's wealth, if not health. Instead, it was an indictment of what had been allowed to happen here.

The stale smell of cigarettes filled the Club 99 function room, a cavernous place with dartboards on one wall and bench-seats along the others, except where the stage and a sticky dance floor encroached. A hundred men and women – some in flat-cap weekday best, others in working clobber – had just finished their monthly league meeting. I was an item on the management agenda, after it, so I waited to 'come up'.

Paul Gennard emerged and wandered over, peeling each shoe off the vast, blue patterned carpet that didn't match the beige patterned walls, or the purple upholstery adorning the seats and the complementary mock-Georgian wall panels.

"Good party?" I asked him about Scott's 21st.

"Great," he smiled wearily and left it there. Then he leaned forward and, in a secretive manner, told me something about the Merrivale game. I can't say any more.

A minute or two later, he'd gone, and so had most of the others, so I sat on an armless dining chair at a red Formica table, facing double doors that led to a corridor. I glanced round. A woman was cleaning tables. She spoke momentarily in a soft Irish lilt that became East European, a speciality not unlike my own, when I start a joke in Cardiff and end it in Karachi. I hadn't a clue what she was saying, but nodded a lot.

Two blokes were at a table, one small and Asian in an obsolete Man U shirt, supping lager, the other thinning, in blue working togs, stroking a pint of Banks's. They were passing a phone between each other, trying to persuade someone called Dazzer to come out of retirement for a cup final. Dazzer had, evidently, chucked two stone on since hanging up his boots. And he was off on holiday. So that ruled him out.

"Maybe next year," Mr Banks said, and closed the call. He turned to his mate.

"When you said 'call Dazzer', I thought you was talking about a different Dazzer."

They were interrupted by the rattle of doors and my escort appeared. I followed to a room marked 'The Lounge' and blinked. It was dim. Ten or 12 people were sitting round the shadowy edge of the room. I saw a seat in the middle, facing a table that wasn't close enough to lean on. It had a Fat Man behind it. His name was Kasper Guntman.

"I distrust a close-mouthed man," he sneered. "He generally picks the wrong time to talk and says the wrong things. Talking's something you can't do judiciously, unless you keep in practice. Now, sir, we'll talk if you like. I'll tell you right out, I'm a man who likes talking to a man who likes to talk."

I was taken aback, I concede. I expected him to say "Well, well, Mr Cairo" too, but he didn't. He just looked at the chair, ripe for a confession.

Actually, that's not completely true. It wasn't Kasper Guntman, it was John Rochell, Chairman of the Warley & District Sunday League. And he didn't speak until I'd asked "Where d'you want me to sit?" and he'd pointed in front of him.

"The first thing I'd like to say is 'Not guilty'," I added, sitting down. Someone had the good grace to laugh. Not very loudly, but I did hear a titter. I was keen to see if it would grow into something bigger, but the Chairman had an agenda to stick to.

"For the benefit of those who don't know," he smiled behind his familiar grey beard and moustache, "tell us why you're here tonight."

On reflection, I put it down to the rain, the grim side streets, the cleaner, Dazzer, the long wait to be shown into the inner sanctum, the faces peering through the gloom. These were normal people, like you and me, doing a voluntary job that meant hundreds of other people didn't have a hole in their lives. I'd been in a few awkward spots on duty with HM Press, armed only with a pencil. But, here, I felt uncomfortable. This was their world. A secret place. I was an outsider. I breathed in.

"I'm Mark Higgitt and I'm following Yew Tree for a year…" I looked around, "…finding out what makes a Sunday football team tick, how it fits in to their lives and the community. I want to find out how the league runs."

There was silence.

"That's why I'm here."

More silence.

"My Dad was born in Oldbury."

The Chairman smiled again but, before I could ask a question, he leant forward and began. As he spoke, I tried to make eye contact with as many of the committee as I could. They were all sitting back, half-hidden in the gloom, studying me, with expressions that said they didn't expect to say much, they'd mainly listen.

I've thought hard since but, in the course of the next hour, I'm not sure the Chairman introduced anyone to me, unless the agenda pointed him in their direction. Not that it would have made any difference. I can name the Liverpool side that won the FA Cup in 1965 – Lawrence, Lawler, Byrne, Strong, Yeats, Stevenson, Callaghan, Hunt, St John, Smith,

Thompson – but I can't remember a two-item shopping list much beyond 50 yards from home.

"Marmite? You never said Marmite!"

See? So new names wouldn't have stuck anyway.

The Warley & District Sunday League had begun in 1972. Thus, it stood to reason, some of these people had been doing this for nigh on 30 years.

Not always here, though. I learned that within a couple of sentences. The league formed after the Warley Combination, a Saturday set-up, died on its feet because of a loss of venues and "other Saturday distractions". The chairman wasn't specific, but mentioned wives later. The chance of forming a Sunday league arose, and some members of the Combination council took it, with just eight clubs. At one stage, the roster hit 98, many run out of works, pubs or social clubs in the original Oldbury catchment area, others from Smethwick and West Brom.

The 2001-2002 season had begun with 90 teams spread evenly between the Premier League, Premier One, and Divisions One to Five. It had since dropped to 84, "though, frankly, we could have 190", he went on. "But it's governed by two imponderables. Pitches. Referees. There aren't enough private venues because any land that becomes available is snapped up by developers. If you pressed us, Mark, we could probably name 20 or 30 Class A pitches we've lost over the past 30 years. We have a clutch of private pitches, which we're very, very protective of, because they're dying out fast."

Tree had played on six private pitches. Hillcrest was one. Its state was disgusting, given what Jezz doled out to Dudley Metropolitan Borough Council every other week. I'd have had the chief executive on a fraud charge. Albright & Wilson, Birchley Park, Brum Uni, Woodgate Valley and the cliff-top Rowley College were the others. Few were better than Hillcrest. Neither were the parks pitches maintained by Sandwell Borough, though I didn't have to risk being rude in saying so before he hinted at it himself.

"We're close partners with the local authority, who have to let us use their pitches. We're the biggest user of Sandwell pitches," he added. "We're forever having battles about the quality of venues. Every year we try to get something. So the showers are a bit better than last year...," he trailed. "It's a difficult task."

He pointed a finger in Peter Lowe's direction as he said "showers". A few minutes later, he had me turning again when he outlined the members' designated jobs.

"Bob, our financial wizard, has ensured that, for 30 years, we have never, ever shown a loss on our balance sheet. We've always been healthily viable," he sat back and smiled at me. Then he rattled through a series of thoughts I'd taken for granted, both as a Yew Tree-watcher and as a Sunday footballer, 20-something years before. So, I guess, would anyone who farted and pulled on an orange shirt every week.

"It's a very, very large machine. The mechanics of Peter having to make fixtures monthly... bear in mind that many of our venues are also used by other leagues. We have to ensure they're away when we're at home. Some teams share a pitch. It's not easy. Peter produces the fixtures monthly, shows them to Herville," he pointed left to a large man in the shade of a 30-watt bulb, "who puts the referees on."

Refs. I'd wanted to talk about refs and did, eventually. But it's worth mentioning them now. I hadn't remembered there being so much on-pitch confrontation with the man in black in my day, though maybe that was just my eyes opening wider. The language probably wasn't any worse than the 70s and 80s, either, but there seemed to be an edge to it now.

"Lack of respect for authority," the Chairman said.

"Is that what's causing the problem recruiting referees?" I turned to Herville.

"It is to a certain degree," he looked at the Chairman, not me. "Two of our experienced referees have asked me not to put 'em on certain clubs. It's never happened before. It shouldn't happen, really. They should be able to referee any team. I've had teams tonight ask me not to have certain refs. And, sometimes, I'd rather say to them 'No, you're having that ref'." He paused, then stretched out a massive paw that said 'on the other hand', and added "We've just got our first young lady. Sixteen-year-old girl…."

"Sixteen-year-old girl, taken up the whistle," the Chairman intervened. "So, again, that brings us problems when you think of changing facilities. Peter brought it up in the week at the local authority."

Changing rooms were important, naturally. But I was more concerned about welfare. I had a 16-year-old daughter of my own, and couldn't help bringing her to mind, whistle in hand. Was this girl from the same mould? I'd seen the aggression and heard the foul language. How would the players put up with it? Only joking.

I guessed she'd have her hands full. I knew the league's Premier Division attracted blokes who played semi-pro on a Saturday. But the stars didn't all end up in the top flight. The Chairman had already admitted that, occasionally, new teams would advise Lowe they weren't any good, then take their place in a lower division and hammer everyone in sight. The Handbook allowed for clubs to be put in a higher cup competition, to give them a tougher time, maybe even wipe the smug grin off their faces. Indeed, The Handbook covered just about everything. The Chairman passed me a copy across the table. I opened it from the back – old habit – and saw 50 on the last page. It was big.

"Strict," he called it. "Those that don't like it soon fall by the wayside," and smiled a Guntman smile.

He didn't mention them by name but, in Division 1 alone, Barrel, Khalsa and Hangman's had already found themselves unequal to The Handbook's demands.

"Clubs of poor discipline and administration," he smiled again, without even a hint of regret that something tangible – someone's Sunday morning passion – had passed.

"They can't improve," he added, and I suspected he wasn't the dewy-eyed kind.

"Bad apples," he finished, sounding like Guntman again. Not dewy-eyed at all, then.

"We've got quantity," he moved on. "We want quality now. We don't need to take on any more clubs because they want to come in. Not for revenue. We're in the black. I don't think any of our rivals can say that. So, if we're looking to bring in quality, we'd be happy with 80, 90. Always there's this looming spectre of pitch availability."

"There's been a phenomenal rate of change socially over the past 30 years, hasn't there?" I said. I hadn't asked a question for 15 minutes. What I really wanted to know was where they thought Sunday football would be in another 30 seasons.

"When we first started," he looked around for nods, "football was all you'd got on a Saturday. Sunday football didn't exist. Then Sunday did. Now there are computers, TV, DVDs. The average age of your league is higher, certainly the average age of refs is frighteningly higher. If you follow that to its logical conclusion, you'll run out of referees before you run out of players. We hope that situation never comes.

"This committee's been in-situ for a good number of years. Life members? We've got two, one of whom is deceased. The other, Frank Giles, was a founder member. I was a founder member, Ken and Pete, Bob came in soon afterwards, and Jean."

I swivelled to see if Ken, Bob and Jean were taking a bow, but they were merely smiling.

"Without sounding pompous, we do it because football has been good to us. When the day comes, as it must, when you have to hang your boots up, it's nice to think you've put something back. When you walk away, you haven't just taken.

"We patently don't take, because we don't get paid," he emphasised. "It costs us to run the league. Another corny statement," he looked beyond me, "how many players, Andy, did we say we'd got?"

"It's 2,336," Andy had the answer at his fingertips.

The Chairman smiled. "We're providing football to 2,336 young men."

Not many of them were as sociable now as in earlier years, though, if Bob was right, picking up my question about social change.

"Fifteen, 16 years ago," his voiced lowered, "our presentation at the Night Out, 15-hundred people. Sell every ticket at £30 a head, and we could've sold them again. Top name cabaret. A very good night. The apathy is such today that we'd have very great difficulty selling 250 tickets with a discount."

"Less social off the pitch," I said, hoping he'd keep the exchange rolling.

"Cost," Bob shrugged his shoulders. "Quite a few people are out of work."

The Chairman interjected. "It became like pulling teeth. We even changed the rules to say that each club must take five tickets. It was a pain in the arse so, in the end, we didn't bother. Think back to how we started. Ken'll back me up."

I looked around again, but I'd forgotten which one Ken was.

"I'll bet every player knew every player. Now, I don't think they want to know their opponents. It's tribal. Society's like that. Win at all costs, and we don't want to fraternise with them. So it's less of a family league than it was."

So what of the future?

"We've just had a meeting now with some people who've been trying to sell us a package," the Chairman leant forward again, "which is rather expensive."

It was Bob's turn to intervene, bluntly.

"It sounds catchy," he said, "but it's not our money. It's the clubs' money." He didn't expand.

"Sixteen-year-olds coming in now, they'll be hanging their boots up in 20 years. What kind of a league will they be playing in?" I asked, when I realised he'd said enough.

The Chairman drew breath.

"We'll probably level off at 50-60 teams," he answered, "because this is now not the be-all and end-all for young men. The way it used to be."

I heard someone behind me start his own conversation.

"To set up a team now, you're going to struggle unless you've got £1,000," he said to someone else, not me.

"The honest answer, Mark, is we don't know," the Chairman added. "We'll provide football for these young men as long as they want. And as long as we're elected to."

It sounded like a conclusion, but Bob hadn't finished.

"The plans we spoke about are very exciting," he said, sounding positive this time, threatening to reveal a secret.

"It's our own venue, which we can own, practically," the Chairman interrupted. "It would be pitches, facilities, training facilities. It would be our own home. If that were to come off, that's a big plus. But it's a long way away yet."

Bob was undeterred. "In terms of attracting younger players, and refs, it's harder…."

"The thing is, I suppose, Mark," the Chairman picked up the point again, "to put the tin hat on, all of us are above 40. Many of us above 50. How long can you go on? It's not because there aren't many young people to come on the committee. Though, frankly, I can't think of anybody. Again, if you follow that to its ultimate conclusion, when we say 'It's too much now, I'm going to retire', who is going to take over?"

Minutes later, someone walked in, and a soothing, fresh breeze lifted the light. The Chairman folded his agenda and put the top on his pen. I recognised the signal.

The man in the shadows who fronted this remarkable, dedicated, ordinary bunch leaned in to 30-watt territory.

"Anything else you want to know?"

"As a matter of fact, there is," I shifted to the edge of my seat. "In the back of the Maltese Falcon…."

From: jeremy dingley
To: Mark Higgitt
Sent: Monday, March 18, 2002 5:00 PM
Subject: Yew Tree

Hi Mark (ar bin ya) – After the match Sunday, myself Robin and Paul had a little chat about a few things. We all came to the same conclusion that we wanted to go as far as we can. I surgested that we can just have a normal pub side and go into division 5. Both Robin and Paul said, "they would pack it in if we did that". Then we called Stan in to see what the problem, with him was. He told us that he was unhappy with what I had said last Sunday, about if you don't turn up, you don't get a shirt. Some times I say things without thinking first. Fullbrook next Sunday. We can still finish second (I think). See you next

Sunday. JEZZ.

PS Can't give league table A drive playing up. (soz)

Oh, well. It's out now. Paul's whisper in my ear. Stan.

"I don't know what he's got against Jezz," Paul had said. "You can't have a bloke telling you he'll only pull his kit on if he's guaranteed a place. That's not the way to run a team."

Then the chat had hit familiar territory, commitment, drinking, potential, young men, "in our day". You know.

That night, I hadn't been certain whether Paul would be there next year. Or that Jezz would retract his threat to call it a day. I e-mailed Jezz about Stan. The Rhodia no-show, Eagles after that, then Merrivale. The man I'd once thought most epitomised Rob Wall's 'all-for-one one-for-all' spirit had been a let-down, I said.

So, what did he have in store as they drifted to the pitch for the game against New Fullbrook at Hillcrest? God alone probably knew, and I even had my doubts about that.

It was the last-but-one league game, with second place still possible. If someone had told them that in September, they'd have laughed. But there were reasons, if they'd cared to examine themselves honestly. Tuck had played his socks off since returning between the sticks in the wake of Chubbs' broken ankle. Gavin had been a rock in defence, Tigs full of poise and precision, Bowe was Mr Patient – if not Billy Whizz – now Yode was back. Mark still thought he was Stevie Gerrard, and Rob was still striking blows for the Old Uns, and digging for England. Life as a sub since injury was testing Opple's humour, Meesey was still an enigma, and Bass was still less than the sum of the parts, if inspiringly loyal. Stan was at the tail end of that line, in sub's kit, as they sauntered down to the pitch. I watched him go, then sought Jezz out.

"If Stan and Mark decide to leave, then that's what happens," he told me. "I won't risk the club breaking up for the sake of two players."

With Bran back for the injured Gavin, Tree kicked off uphill 20 minutes late, on account of ref Bob Griffin forgetting his whistle and flags.

"I've never done it in me life, but I'll give it a go," Stan said, and held his hand out for the lino's flag. Only Osama bin Laden turning out for Fullbrook at left-back would have surprised me more. That or Yode scoring.

As the game started, Tuck's dad John turned up.

"He had a good send-off"," I heard him tell Brian Horton about the funeral Brian had wanted to attend. More than 200 people had. I hoped he'd been one, though – in this day and age – it had long since stopped shocking me that a boss would even think of preventing someone seeing his mate off. It wouldn't have happened in Dad's day.

On the pitch, there was a slickness about Tree I hadn't seen since Lowes. Even Meesey and Yoss looked like they'd slept. In contrast, the Fullbrook *Prize Guys* were niggly, unable to cope with being denied the time to roll the ball beneath their shiny Adidas boots and knock it around, yellow shirts and embrocated thighs glistening in the low sun.

Both sides could have scored in the opening four minutes, but both missed easy chances. I joined Paul on the line, desperate for this to be his good day, for once, but apprehensive that Lady Luck would act the prat.

"Most on 'em stayed off the pop last night," he said, by which he probably meant they'd had five instead of six. Still, they were playing the brighter, more passionate football.

A mate insists he once saw a steeplejack drop his radio from a girder high in a Sheffield steelworks. As it smashed into a million splinters, he yelled "Fucking hell, the fucking fucker's fucking fucked!" I'm prepared to believe my mate as he now works for the BBC.

In one early Hillcrest match, I'd heard this exchange. Half of Netherton had:

Manager: "Fucking hell, how many fucking chances you fucking going to fucking miss?"

Number 9: "That wasn't a fucking chance!"

Manager: "They were fucking queuing up for the fucking ball. People are working their fucking bollocks off here. And that's what you fucking do!"

Number 9: "And I'm fucking not?"

Dad had been feeling well enough after his cancer op to hint at venturing out to his old stamping ground, one Sunday morning. I'd been hesitant, and had felt bad about it, even though, in my heart, I believed I was doing us both a favour. He might have spent a working lifetime in a drop forge, but I knew he'd be left shaking his head in disgust at the language coming from that football pitch. Part of me still wishes I'd risked it, even if the next few minutes say the opposite.

Bob Griffin's pre-match prediction of a trouble-free match took a nose-dive as Mark Horton's opposite number collected a faceful of mud on 19 minutes. Mark was booked. Craig Skidmore followed him two minutes later for a tackle that made my legs hurt, 80 yards away. Until then, he'd been so anonymous, drifting up and down the left, that two passing bobbies had already done him for loitering with lack of intent.

"Ref, you should book 'im for divin'," his sister Paula yelled, and, when the ref didn't, "Ref, you'm a fuckin' disgrace!" The head-down midfielder responded by collecting Yoss's inch-perfect pass and scurrying off on a jinking run that ended with the bar being grazed. Fullbrook responded by scoring, however.

I wondered out loud what Tree's reaction would be, and it came in the shape of Yoss being booked for a very late tackle. Ginger had been giving the ref the benefit of his opinion at every turn, and he did again. So Griffin booked him too, with the message that, if he had to caution one more man, the game would degenerate.

"Yo bin warned three times already!" Jezz yelled at Ginger. I was by Paul at the time.

"He can't even put a challenge in now, or he risks being sent off," he groaned.

I think I mentioned that, if it had been me, I'd have subbed him. A moment later, Paul told Tigs to warm up. Meesey heard the call, and that was him off on one.

"You're fucking replacing him because he's been booked?" he screamed at Jezz.

Jezz: "One more tackle and he's off anyway."

Meesey: "He should never have been fucking booked!"

Jezz: "He's been warned three times. Yo cor talk to a ref like that."

Meesey: "He can say what he likes. He's his own fucking man." And on like that.

"They'm only one down. Why are they losing it?" Lin Horton shook her head as a predictable half-time loomed. Predictable as in reflect, repent, repeat, oranges, fags, forget.

Paul: "We seem to be winning the midfield but drifting up and we ay getting back. They'm comin' at us. Keep closing 'em down."

Bran: "We did it over their place, boys, we can do it again, cor we? It's gonna be hard. We got the slope. Calm down, play a little ball. We'm still panicking."

Jezz to Ginger: "Why d'you 'ave to go on at the ref?"

Ginger tried to defend himself, but Jezz had none of it.

"No, no, no! Meesey's right to 'ave a go at me. But I'll back meself. I haven't got a problem with blokes backing folks up with tackles. But when you'm talking 40 yards away and he's already told you twice, yo ain't got a defence. Keep it shut!"

By now, you can probably see where this was heading. If I'd been a betting man, I'd have nipped up to Wilf Gilbert's and put a few quid on the outcome. In six minutes, it went 0-2, 1-2, 1-3. I was instinctively glad not to be standing by Jezz.

Between the goals, I ventured into the depths of the trees beside the pitch to retrieve a ball and found the remains of a bloke who'd done the same several years before, and never come back out. Stan had replaced Bass by the time I emerged. The little winger had chased hard, but his touch had been predictably unpredictable and much of Rob's running had been wasted. Concede one, score one, concede one, score one?

A minute after Fullbrook's third, Tree went through the agony of seeing a shot cleared off the line, but they reduced the arrears again when Stan turned and shot from 18 yards. I looked at my watch. Thirteen minutes left.

Could they equalise? They tried. Sweet Turf, how they tried but, as Netherton bloody-mindedness overcame Walsall poise, the pitch was the decider. It was abysmal. Jezz had handed nigh-on £200 to Dudley Metropolitan Borough Council for this patch and they hadn't once bothered to cut or roll it.

Rob went one-on-one with the keeper, dipped the shoulder and watched his shot beaten out. Then, two minutes into added time, Bowe, the stalwart, uncomplaining clubman, slow, unfussy, straightforward and reliable, somehow stole up from right-back – a journey he'd set out on before Christmas – and unleashed a right-footer. We turned as one and followed its arc. It rose. It dipped. The keeper took the last steps of his hopeless retreat. It rapped the bar. And flew over. And Bob Griffin's whistle went.

I still don't know how to describe Paul's body language as I helped him collect the netbag and the balls – the few that remained – or the note in his voice when I asked him if that had changed his thoughts about next season.

"Stupid bookings, stupid goals… big fight… character… the best and the worst of Yew Tree… potential to win the league next year… bear in mind most of their lot play Saturdays… if we can just get ourselves fit during the summer…."

Maybe he'd be closer to an answer in seven days, Swan in the West Brom Cup. Struggling in the Premier Division they might have been, but they were still two steps up.

That would be the real measure of this frustrating, engaging gaggle of brothers, cousins and old schoolmates. And it would either stretch or shorten the season.

What I'd heard from outside the dressing room, so far, told me the manners hadn't changed in 20-odd years. I ventured into Tree's inner sanctum afterwards for the first time, in search of a loo, and realised how foul mud, sweat, wind and steaming socks smell when yours aren't among them.

I found relief in the main school building and, a couple of minutes later, returned.

"Will it be in the book?" Ginger reminded me of his Beckham free-kick goal as I picked my way past soiled shirts and humming underpants.

"Only if I can find out how to spell 'magnificent'," I replied. It had been.

Then Bran called to me, agitated. I'd given them all a questionnaire, remember. A bit of fun in the hope – rather than anticipation – of a final. You know the sort, name, nickname, superstitions, usual Yew Tree drink, other family members.

"Ay, Mark," Bran shouted above the din. "Don't believe Ginger. He ay my cousin!"

19 WHO'D RUN A * FOOTBALL TEAM?

FROM THE BOGGY END OF BIRCHLEY PARK, by a high, tree-covered bank, I could just make out the rooftops of the row where my grandparents had lived almost 80 years before. They died before I was close to a twinkle in the old man's eye. He was born just down the street, in 1924, in Thurston Buildings. Long gone, too.

Birchley Park was where he'd played football as a boy, so Tree's trip there to play Abbey, five months before, truly had been Father's footsteps. That match had been the second round of the West Brom Cup. West Brom. Dad's team, man and boy. So it was fitting that my second visit was also a West Brom tie, the third round, against Swan.

My problem in March had been bearings. I'd looked at the A-Z and a 30s OS map and couldn't marry the location of Birchley Park on the two. Weeks later, Dad had realised that, while his back was turned, the Town Hall planning department had built on his old stamping, tackling, shooting ground, then spotted Accles & Pollock's once-grand sports ground, over the road. And he'd renamed it Birchley Park instead. I felt diddled when he told me. But he'd played at A&P, as well. So that was all right, too.

Beyond the bank at the furthest point from a shabby social club was the site of Pratt's Brickyard – the bottom end of Lion Farm – where he'd worked as a 14-year-old. When he was 10, up to leaving school at 14, he delivered his brothers' breakfast there every day. It was a peep into childhood he'd given us when cancer came calling.

With bacon sizzling on the range, my grandmother would hold a loaf below her throat and cut an inch-thick crust-end slice. She'd scoop out the shape of a fried egg, cut a second slice, slightly thinner than the first, and dip both in the bacon fat before laying the egg on its bed. Rashers covered the egg and, with its bread blanket, it was wrapped in the *Evening Despatch* or a brown paper bag. The original takeaway breakfast. If they'd called it the Bacon McHiggitt, they'd have made a fortune.

The children witnessed by Priestley would have thought they were on another planet if they'd made Dad's journey to Pratts. It took him over playing fields, past ponds, a brook, a cow field and along tracks cut over decades by men trudging to work. His final steps, probably still at running speed, skirted three wharves off the main stream of the Titford Canal and up a mountain of broken tile and brick scree.

The half-past-eight 'bull' was the signal to eat, so Len, Joe and Fred expected him to be there. The tile-making shop was up a wide wooden plank, reinforced by long steel plating, then across floors thick with fine grey-brown dust and raised several feet above ground level. Beneath ran the hot water pipes that dried the wet tiles. If Uncle Len had decided to work before breakfast, Dad would go to him first, watch him work for a couple of minutes, then cut through the drying racks to Uncle Joe and Uncle Fred. Then he'd run back to start school. No health, no safety.

Sixty-five years later, give or take, 300 yards across the waterlogged grass was the same New Wolverhampton Road, now with the M5 high behind it, cutting a line across the horizon. There was no M5 in the 20s splitting Birchfield Lane in two, of course. Nor the One and Two Halves pub on the corner, close to where the Wolverhampton Road once crossed Birchfield Lane. The pub sat by Joseph Street and an npower building, all glass, brick and curved roof.

Birchley Park Social Club car park was as scruffy as ever as I waited for the Yew Tree wagon train to roll in, listening to Wolves boss Dave Jones on the radio, discussing the Easter Monday table-top clash with Manchester City at Molineux. He didn't sound like a man whose team had brought fanatics like Nero Wolf to the cusp of a stroke.

Still embarrassingly short of an inspiring moniker, the *Wolves Stats* website was the usual confusion of blind optimism and ill-disguised despair. Mr Wolf had listened to the last 10 minutes of Albion's game at Forest on the radio the night before Wanderers' meeting with Norwich, and so had heard Bob Taylor's late winner.

"You could also hear the 'boing! boing!' of the single brain cell they share as they realised that they could yet catch us," he whinged. "Only a win could settle the nerves as the scum embark on an easy run-in and we face Burnley, Man City and Millwall."

Then Norwich had left Molineux with a point, and it seemed touch-and-go whether he'd filed his *Wolves Stats* report before or after calling the Samaritans.

"Two weeks ago, thinking the unthinkable meant preparing for the Premiership. Now I wish someone would wake me from this nightmare. To be robbed by moaning Megson's B*ggies would be hell on earth. It can't happen. Can it?"

The horizon looked a shade brighter after the 2-3 win at Burnley, only their second win in six games, even if it came at a price. In denting Burnley's play-off hopes, they had guaranteed the Baggies at least a tilt at the end-of-season Cardiff shoot-out.

Albion added victory over Barnsley to the Forest and Crewe wins. Nine from nine. On March 6, they'd been 11 points behind table-top Wolves, with a game in hand. After their 4-1 stroll over Crewe at the Hawthorns, the spare game had gone, but the gap had been narrowed to three points – and Man City were top by five.

"I don't pretend to know what's going on," Dave Jones confessed to his *Sportsweek* inquisitor. "A lot of people don't."

Any Wolves fan tuning in at that precise moment and recognising the Scouse accent might have panicked, and unnecessarily so. Jones had played the City match down, but couldn't make sense of the continuing ITV Digital cash crisis. "I don't pretend to know what's going on." It summed up how most paying football fans saw it too.

I confess, I'd paid only fleeting attention to the run-in since Tree's season had begun to depend on the cups. As Jones spoke, a red Toyota hurtled into view, and two young women let two young men out of the back seats. The driver took a fresh packet of cigarettes from her pocket, ripped off the wrapper and chucked it on to the ground. It was blowing down the potholed drive as the Trees convoy arrived, looking unlike a team that had spent the night on the pop, or one that was worried about facing a team two divisions higher.

Five minutes later, Meesey blasted into sight, in his tatty blue Fiesta. He grabbed a tatty rucksack and walked after them. Five minutes later still, Jezz arrived and humped the kitbags out of the boot.

I leaned on the railings outside the Social Club door and watched a secretary and manager in a mild state of panic, two players short of the starting 11.

"Navi," the manager answered the ref's enquiring expression.

Navi? The name had appeared on a list of suspensions I'd liberated from the league meeting, "Larry Reid, Navi Rovers, 112 days from 14 January, 2002, plus 28 days from 25 February, 2002". One hundred and forty days? Reid was one name that wouldn't be on the team-sheet.

Some players were already wandering out. If my deductions were right, Navi were the motley-looking bunch in white, some neat, others with last Sunday's mud on their boots, all with black tape wrapped around their left arms. I studied their shirts and tried to remain expressionless. I didn't know Reid from Adam, but I instantly had an image of some poor ref waving red at a seething, shaven-headed psychopath while the name of the club's *Forever Lace Bridalwear* sponsor stared back from his heaving chest.

Paul Gennard was the next to emerge.

"This is it," I said and nodded at the Swan players warming up, one player knocking corners for the keeper to take, others doing shuttle runs. "Tall lads."

"Ah," he said, then "they complain about not being given a chance, then they don't turn up." He meant Opple, Bass and – surprisingly – Bowe. "And Meesey got lost trying to find the ground," he went on. He didn't deserve this.

"Nigel Davenport's not here either," he added. "Tuck's going to have to play with a swollen elbow. No choice."

He wandered off, and Brian Horton appeared.

"What about the Queen Mum, eh?" he said. He was the only one who'd mentioned her death, the afternoon before.

The minute's silence was observed in the same manner as those that had marked September 11, Remembrance Sunday and Princess Margaret's death though, this time, the smell of freshly-cut grass filled the air as the pitch fell quiet. Some, like Bran and Rob, put their hands behind their backs and bowed their heads. Yoss stretched his hamstrings and fidgeted. Mark stretched his quads and whirled his arms to loosen his back. Stan yawned, though at least he was there. Ginger looked bemused. A coach drove past on the New Wolverhampton Road, and its passengers gazed across at the two teams lined up in the breeze.

Me? My eyes scanned the horizon for Grandad's old house and my mind wandered.

"Come on, get yer 'eads on," Bran broke the spell as the silence ended.

After four minutes, "Get yer 'eads up!" would have been better. Gavin Skidmore mistimed his leap to meet a long throw and Swan's tall, unmarked Number 10 had stretched an unnaturally long leg and knocked it past Tuck.

By the time Yew Tree carved out their first chance, Yode and Gavin had argued and been warned to moderate their language, and Swan might have been five up. Yode had limped off, too, holding his right hamstring after making a last-ditch, covering tackle on Swan's marauding Number 2. Yode's passion and commitment had been pivotal in Tree's change in fortunes but, ironically, the injury turned the match. Little did we suspect it at the time, but it was about to change the course of the season, too.

Tigs' arrival in left midfield pushed Craig Skidmore to right-back and also put paid to Swan's Route One plan. Instead, in a game that should already have been beyond the visitors' reach, Swan began to do the worrying and lost their shape. Tree began exploiting the space behind Swan's fullbacks, the kind of simple, schoolboy ploy you often see used against England. Suddenly, the ball wasn't in the centre of midfield when a move broke down. Suddenly, Swan weren't picking up those vital knock-downs. Ginger had clocked the fact that the right-back was terrified of Tigs' pace. So had Bran. Now Tree were making Swan turn and chase.

At some point, Yoss must have looked up and felt the penny drop. On 29 minutes, he collected a pass, bearing down on the penalty area. He cut one way, then the other, went past one man, feigned to pass another and shot past the keeper. The ball began to squirm wide off the bumpy surface, but Rob arrived on the back post. One-all. I couldn't hear what he said when he turned and shouted at his team-mates as the ball was rolled to the centre-spot, but Ginger yelled "Come on, he's right!"

Five minutes after the equaliser, Tuck raced out to smother the ball at the feet of Swan's Number 9 and clutched his elbow. Jezz sprinted round to the goal, but it was obvious he wouldn't be able to carry on.

I looked across the pitch. No Tuck, no Chubbs, no Nigel Davenport. Not even Opple, who'd spent 40-odd minutes between the sticks earlier in the season. I was still running the dwindling options through my head as Nigel ran on. He'd turned up soon after the game started, following this phone conversation with Jezz.

Jezz: "Nigel, what time is it?"

Nigel: "It's 9.30."

Jezz: "Look again."

Nigel: "Still 9.30."

Jezz: "Nigel, the hour's gone forward."

Nigel: "Oh, shit!"

Swan tested him twice, then retreated. Craig looked natural at right-back, Yoss looked shagged, Meesey had picked his game up and Tigs was running Swan's young right-back ragged. The poor lad looked like he'd turned up on the wrong pitch. When the ball went out, I threw it back to Ginger.

"The kid's terrified of Tigs' pace," I said to him, then felt a little ashamed, because he could hear me. Ginger was less concerned.

"Lads, they'm shite!" he yelled, almost in disbelief, a minute later.

Half-time was a strange affair. No one shouted. No one moaned. No one argued. This team could be beaten. All they had to do was carry on playing the same way.

"You're gonna have to dig in," Jezz sent them away for the second-half. "This is the kind of team you'll be playing week in, week out next season."

I went for a walk as the whistle blew, and paused for a brief conversation with the Swan keeper, then met Brian Horton walking the other way.

We stood in silence as Tree searched for their rhythm. Swan pressed briefly, but more in hope than expectation. We looked at each other as Ginger was booked.

"Keep it shut!" Bran bawled.

"I day say nothing!" Ginge remonstrated. Not unless you counted opening your gob and letting a sound out. We tutted.

"It was Mark's 21st birthday last night," Brian said, out of the blue. I stared across the pitch, to check the lanky, loping midfielder I'd seen rushing round like a hyperactive giraffe was, indeed, the person we were talking about.

"He doesn't appear to be a person with a hangover," I mused. He laughed.

"I spent mine helping to put a special edition of the paper together on the Queen Mum," I went on.

He paused, then said: "I had the great privilege of meeting her once. Lovely lady."

"Where was that?" I looked at him.

"Windsor."

"What were you doing?"

"Guard duty. Seventy-two or 73, Windsor Castle, Christmas Day."

"In the Army?"

He nodded. "Second Battalion, Grenadier Guards."

If this were a film script, he'd have gazed into the middle distance, the sound of Black Countrymen unconcerned at the Royal death fading into the background, and you'd have been left thinking that here was a man whose fondest thoughts had rolled back 30 years. That's exactly what happened. It was strange for a nicotine-lined voice like his, normally only ever a couple of words away from an obscenity, a joke or a mickey-take – often all three at once – to be talking with reverence.

"She walked up to me and said 'Happy Christmas, young man! How are you?' just like we're talking here, just like she was a commoner. Marvellous lady."

We talked about how old you had to be to know what her death meant. Meesey had just been booked for arguing about a throw-in. The ref waved him over, and Meesey argued again, claiming he'd been talking to Stan. Bad timing. Brian considered my question and said "They've got no respect these days, no time for authority".

"I don't think they understand the importance of knowing what's made the country what it is," I picked up his point.

In two sentences, we'd condemned an entire generation. Later it occurred to me that, without realising, I'd turned in to an old git. Still, for now, the evidence was strong.

Meesey then tried a dribble with Rob straining at the leash. Brian gestured with a half-smoked roll-up as the bulky Number 7 was dispossessed.

"He'll never make a footballer as long as he has a hole in his arse," he said.

I had no reason not to like the lad, but I'd never been able to strike up a conversation with him long enough to find out. Maybe his bull-headed, sometimes thoughtless manners on the pitch gave way to a shy man off. I didn't know then, and I don't know now. Still, I thought he'd had one of his better games, once he'd woken up. One-paced, granted, but that was nothing unusual for someone who looked like he'd already played 90 minutes when a game started, socks at half-mast.

We were still being old gits when Tigs floated a 76th-minute free-kick from the left and Rob, coming off his marker with precision timing, cut back towards the near post and nodded home. One-two. One-two? Swan were shell-shocked. For a split-second, we waited for the goal to be disallowed. But the ref pointed to the centre-circle.

In the last 14 minutes, Swan threw everything into attack, but big Nige was equal to it all. What didn't reach him was repelled by last-ditch tackles. What didn't require that was snuffed out in midfield. There was a price, though, just as there'd been in the final moments in the victory at Fullbrook. Stan was flagging, Meesey and Yoss were digging deep to track back. Meesey resorted to hoofing. Yoss relied on feet that would have still made Fred Astaire look like a shuffling amateur. He knew no other way.

As the clock ticked past 87 minutes, Rob found himself one-on-one.

"Hat-trick!" Mitch yelled from the line, but Rob slid the ball wide. He wheeled into Stan. They knew how vital it might have been, but the near-miss had brought a joy of its own, for it had been worked out of nothing. So, once they'd gasped, they hugged.

But that wasn't it. Yoss wasn't done. From somewhere in the depths of his steaming boots, he dredged the energy and control to plant a final pass into Rob's path. The 38-year-old made one last sprint, but the keeper saved on the edge of the area.

Mothers, daughters, wives, lovers, brothers, sons, distant cousins. We've all sat through final minutes that go on forever. We can all name a dozen games that were the most nerve-wracking. This was it. When the whistle went, I stepped on to the pitch and reached for Rob's hand. He hugged me. Then Stan. A Biblical comeback. Another hug. Then Ginger. The same. I don't need to tell you how I felt.

On the walk back to the dressing room, Rob reminded me there wouldn't be a game the next week. They were going the Grand National. Aintree on the Saturday morning, Blackpool Saturday night. They'd see their way through £400 each, he reckoned. He laughed. I was thinking £400 wouldn't be enough.

Before I left, Jezz mentioned the presentation evening, at the Woodside Liberal Club, near Dudley, on June 22. He showed me a sample of the whisky tumblers he was arranging as a surprise keepsake for the players. Brierley crystal. Black Country craftsmanship for Black Country blokes in a Black Country Liberal club.

"Bring the wife and family," he said.

By the time Jezz's e-mail arrived with me on the Tuesday, Wolves had lost to City. It was more than Bizket Wolf could take, far more.

"It all started going wrong from the very start. Our mate (Wolves chief executive) Moxey asked everyone to get to the ground early as the pints were going to be cheap. Wot happens?" he asked his *Wolves Stats* surfers. "You get inside and 'Due to unforeseen circumstances' the beer was at the usual extortionate price. Typical."

He'd been relatively harmless till now, then he lost it completely.

"There was supposed to be a minute's silence before the game in respect of the Queen Mum, but Moss Side scum decided to spoil it... I thought Brummie inbreds were bad, but these inbred mono gene pool tadpoles are the scum of all England."

And, as the rant climaxed: "To think Dave Jones was out-thought by Keegan is like a Mini being out-manoeuvred by a Chieftan tank. It was April Fool's day wasn't it?"

It's a guess, but I imagine he arrived home as Bob Taylor scored the only goal of Albion's game at Coventry. The 11-point cushion had gone. One other thing. Blues were up to sixth and into the play-off positions. Jezz would be happy.

From: jeremy dingley
To: Mark Higgitt
Subject: A BIG Thank You.
Date: April 02, 2002 00:55

Hi Mark, (ar bin Ya).... It's nice to see you yourself get emotionally involved with our club. Unfortunately the season is coming to a close and it's obvious that we won't see you. I just hope it's not good bye forever. It's not very often you meet good folk by chance. Ok that's the soppy bit out of the way. We have a game on the 11th April (Thursday night) away at Fullbrook, 1/4 Final of league cup. I won't be there. Sunday 14th at home last league game. (Merrivale). Look forward to seeing you soon. JEZZ

I sent him a reply on the lines of "You soppy saft get!" Then I sent another. I'd forgotten to ask what time the Fullbrook game kicked off. The old butterflies were beginning to flutter. A couple of days later, he replied. It almost made me cry.

From: jeremy dingley
To: Mark Higgitt
Subject: Re: I forgot to ask....
Date: April 06, 2002 00:17

Hi Mark – KO 6.15 or there abouts. Spoke to Paul earlier and he is not very happy. He's in Blackpool For the weekend and National. He told everyone about the 1/4 final, the response he got was a disaster. Meese said "I'm at work" with the attitude he didn't care. Tigs will try and get there. Tucker at work. Yoda injured. the best to come. Gavin & Craig Skidmore said, "the bowling season has started so they might not come. They will phone me in the next few days, so we might not have a team. (not bad for a 1/4 final). Paul's had enough, so we going to have a talk about the future, with in the next few weeks. An idea for the title for your book. 'Who would run a f*****g football team'. See you soon. JEZZ

20 THE TRUE THEATRE OF DREAMS

THE NIGHT YEW TREE PLAYED NEW FULLBROOK is a night I won't forget until I'm old and grey. Actually, until I'm old. I'm grey already.

It started with the realisation that nerves aren't like fear, cup nerves especially.

Nerves feed anticipation, the prospect of a surprise.

They promise a reward.

Fear, though, is the death of such optimism. Fear, that night, was too few players showing up.

Or that it didn't matter enough to miss bowls.

Or finish work in time.

I feared for many things, that night. But, most of all, I feared feeling let down.

The good news was that Craig and Gavin were already there as I emerged from the M6 rush-hour. But only Tuck, Ginger and Bass were with them. And Mitch. He was having a kick-in, limping slightly. The knee was coming on. It was hard not to watch and wonder how different the season might have been if he hadn't been injured.

Yoss arrived soon after, then Stan with Mark, and Bran with Rob. That made 10. Fullbrook were changed and warming up, the brightness of their yellow shirts, green shorts and yellow socks – and the plantation of embrocated thighs – already hinting that the light wouldn't hold. They went through their ritual sprints and stretches, lay-offs and touches. Their heads were up. Confidence wouldn't be a problem.

If Bowe was the last-but-one to appear, Nigel Davenport wasn't far behind, though it might have been Meesey. By the time Paul Gennard turned up, with the kit, the game should already have kicked off. I looked at the sky, then my watch, and mentally wound it on two hours. They'd be pushed to start the game in daylight, let alone finish. Extra-time, extreme optimism anyway for one fearing a tonking, would be out of the question. Penalties? Hah!

When Tree finally trickled out of the moss-stained dressing room block, the cigarettes of condemned men glowing like fireflies, Fullbrook had stretched so much their midfield quartet were playing Vivaldi on their hamstrings, and a greater fear had gripped my heart. The fear of capitulation, humiliation. I felt bad for it then, disloyal even. I feel bad for it now because, of course, I know how it ended, and you don't.

I've often imagined how a dozen *Match of the Day* cameras, twisting and turning above and around the pitch, would have witnessed and replayed this night. I've wondered what words JB Priestley would have chosen to describe these descendants of Rusty Lane. I opened my notebook, primed my pencil and looked for numbers, a formality, given that everyone who'd turned up was on the pitch – bar Bass, Tuck and the unfit Mitch. With each name I scribbled, the weeks and months rolled back, a couple for some, all the way to

July for others: 1 Nigel Davenport, big, brave, reflex keeper; 2 Paul Bowen, fast for a yard, then not, wouldn't stray; 3 Ginger, fiery, lippy; 4 Mark Horton, battler, sometimes sulky, talked the talk, needed to walk the walk; 5 Bran, one-footed, committed; 6 Gavin Skidmore, rough, tough driving force; 7 Meesey, head up, head down, match-winner, match-loser; 8 Yoss, 70-minute man who needed 10 seconds to win a game; 9 Rob, inspiring; 10 Stan, unpredictable; 11 Craig Skidmore, day-dreamer, hot or cold. You never knew which.

The 10 orange shirts took position, Nige touched his crossbar, maybe for good luck. This was it. Frustratingly awful on their worst day, frustratingly good on their best, as Fullbrook knew. Now they needed to be better than they'd ever been.

As the whistle blew, word came that each half would be 40 minutes, and Tree began as if they meant to have it done before their mums arrived to tell them it was too dark to be out playing. Either that or before they'd run out of steam.

The first 10 minutes lifted the heart. They picked up where they'd left it against Swan. Stan was the first to try his luck, an overhead kick the keeper claimed at the second attempt, under the bar. They closed opponents down and, as the first two games, Fullbrook didn't like it. They weren't able to stand and pick their passes.

But the home side, inevitably, didn't roll over. They probed, threatening little incursions, like the anxious moment that had Gavin charging across to intercept a knock-down as Fullbrook's Number 7 was set to pull the trigger.

"It's going wrong all over the park!" Bran yelled, but that wasn't how it looked to me, even though Tree needed to find some composure. "We've got to want to know."

A minute later, he was at it again, and it began to look as if Tree's opening hurry-harry-rush-cover-run spurt was over. Forget postulations. Whatever Paul had said, they'd resorted to habits picked up on street corners and school fields. And maybe that was only ever going to be equal to the task for 10 minutes. Maybe they were already spent.

It was Gavin, ironically, who nearly gifted Fullbrook an opener by letting his man hook a cross from the byline. The bloke who'd wrecked Chubbs' ankle watched his header blocked, then took the rebound 12 yards out. Nigel closed the angle, but the shot was already heading his way. It passed him. But it went wide.

It marked the start of a sticky patch. As the sky darkened, Yoss lost possession and fouled his man. Tree fell for the little training-ground feint inside, and Ginger was in No Man's Land as the ball went right, instead. The cross cleared Nigel's head and the home players turned to celebrate. But Gavin made them pay for such presumption. He reached the ball as it reached the line and hooked it to safety.

He was having another robust game but, suddenly, I wasn't sure if the rest knew how to win. Bran's pumping fist suggested he was wondering, too, and I could almost hear him saying he'd seen epidemics come and go quicker than Bowe. What the right-back lacked in speed, he was making up for by being in the right place at the right time. But how long before they sussed him? Ginger was sticking tight to his man, but how long till he found himself in a tight corner with a short fuse? Mark, though, was dominating midfield, not talking a good game this time, playing it.

But. The lack of pace in Meesey's legs, in front of Bowe, meant little was happening to Mark's right. And Craig was too deep on the left, despite sister Paula's demand that he "Push on! Push on!"

Stan, carrying his lager sluggishly, was having to back-track. Rob must have gazed from his isolated outpost and wondered when he'd receive supplies.

A minute after Gavin's goal-line clearance, Bran came second in a two-man race to the near-post and Nigel watched Fullbrook's Number 9 stab another chance wide. A minute after that, the half-time whistle went. Forty minutes. The ref was still clearly accounting for the possibility of extra time. How we laughed inside.

But, hang on. Fullbrook still hadn't scored. And hadn't Tree shown twice already this season – and in the opening 15 minutes – that they knew how to niggle them into looking ordinary? The home side, all *Prize Guy* flicks and feints, might have looked the part, and they weren't a bunch a moaning, bickering brothers, cousins and schoolmates. But there was something Tree had that Fullbrook lacked.

So, when Paul gathered his men, barely pausing for a breath in the two-minute break, and told them "Let's put our foot on the ball", they nodded. When he chased that with "We're not supporting the forwards", they sucked oranges and listened.

"We ay put a 10-yard pass together," he went on. "We'm trying to put the ball over the top, and it's coming back. Think about it. Think. Tremendous half, Gav," he turned to the stopper. "Get this ball under control. We've got to look up. Meesey! Come on, son. You've got to get more involved."

He wasn't wrong, though the bigger picture said something different. You needed not to study the detail to see it, but to stand back. It was something you had to feel, not analyse. The ref blew his summons, and Rob, Stan and Bran peeled away.

"Scurve," Rob drew a lungful of nicotine and called to Stan. "We got 'em rattled."

Stan nodded. "They'm just a big bunch of babbies."

The first-half breeze had subsided as Tree kicked off down the slope, away from the railway line. It might have been the coming of dusk, but the clouds seemed to grow darker within themselves, as if they'd dropped anchor 2,000ft up the day Priestley visited in October, 1933, and hadn't moved since.

It's tempting to link that dimming light and Stan's mood-change on 45 minutes but, in truth, it would be a metaphor too far. He couldn't see any better than me if Craig was offside when the Fullbrook lino waved his flag after a quick free-kick, and I was closer.

"You fucking chate!" Stan pointed a loaded finger. The lino, to his credit, retained his dignity as Stan was shown red and ripped off his shirt, telling the lino all the way what he thought of him – "Chate! Chate! Yo'm a fuckin' chate!"

The tone in Bran's voice was angry: "Why don't we learn our lesson?"

In the gloom, it was hard to see his team-mates' faces, but body language spoke volumes. Bowe turned his back and walked towards the far line. Mark had hands on hips and feet rooted in disbelief. The two most likely to inform the ref of his mistake did nothing. Meesey stared at his boots. Gavin sank to his haunches. Two yards to my right, Stan's mum looked on, expressionless. Paul was stunned, as if he'd come across a terrible accident. He watched Stan hurl his shirt against the filthy dressing room wall, then called Bran over.

The change was swift, but not the one I'd have made. He switched Bowe to right midfield, pushed Craig up with Rob, and left three defending Nige. Mark, Bowe, Meesey and Yoss would have to run till their feet bled or burned, whichever came first. If they didn't, Fullbrook would make the extra man pay.

Before we had a chance to find out, Rob had run through the home side's left-back. Through, not past. As the pole-axed man in yellow rolled around, a team-mate squared up to Rob. I didn't hear the words, but I recognised the bulging neck veins and the lip movement.

The turning point at the true Theatre of Dreams as Stan prepares to hurl his shirt away.
Picture by Aaron Manning

I don't know much about boxing, but this much seemed certain. Rob would surely dispense with the formalities of a range-finding left jab and simply launch a right as straight as a shovel handle, then take what followed. But he didn't. Instead, he looked the man straight in the eye.

"Fuck off!" he laughed and went. He meant it. It was the language of the street, the verdict and sentence of a working man, not the gratuitous response of a superstar reciting the soccer hard-man's manual. Few such people have seen the inside of a factory on a night shift, or the bottom of a gas-pipe trench, in the middle of winter, when it's chucking down.

"Fuck off!" Rob had said. The Fullbrook man didn't say 'Pardon?' He backed away.

Tree struggled to pick men up in the gathering dusk. Passes went astray, and they chased shapes and debated whether to play deep or push on and risk a ball over the top and lose a foot race to the trains.

Then something remarkable happened.

First, Fullbrook patently didn't discuss how to use the spare man. Second, Meesey and Yoss dug deep. Inch by inch, yard by yard, run by run, they picked up their work rate. And they started turning on the tricks. If Fullbrook found the space to open the scoring, fine. But they'd have to defend first, then go back to defending afterwards.

After 55 minutes, Tree gave them a taste of what was to come. They won possession on half-way, probed the right, but ran out of options. They tracked back, switched the ball inside and two-touched across midfield, until it arrived at Yoss's feet. His marker backed off, a small step but a big error. It was the space the burly 20-year-old needed. He toed the ball two inches off the deck and fizzed his volley inches over.

Fullbrook were stung and sent the ball straight back at the men in orange, via Route One. Gavin lost his man but the free header was hurried and sailed over Nigel's bar.

Two minutes later, the same forward rolled out to the back post to meet a lob. He lifted his shot towards the goal, but Nige made ground and tipped it over. Tree cleared the corner, breathed a sigh of relief and set off again down the slope.

Before long, the loose ball arrived in a gaggle of players and took a nasty skip off the bone-hard surface. Yoss was first there. He took it on his chest. As he did, alarm bells ought to have been ringing for the three Fullbrook players nearest.

A ball cushioned on the chest in such tight confines plays into the opponent's hands. The chester must let it fall and then move in to Phase 2, either controlling it ready for Phase 3, or knocking a pass and hoping. Or he can shield it, buy time.

But the opponent has more options. He can step up, make the chester commit, hurry him in to something negative. None of this is voluntary. It's all reflex and instinct.

Yoss's chest drew the first man. The yellow shirt had closed the gap by half a step as Yoss knocked it over his head, right-footed. That drew the second man, his options already diminished by the space Yoss had given himself. The *Prize Guy* stretched his neck, but found fresh air as Yoss chested it past him. That left one man. He had to do something, so he stepped forward, then back. But they were token movements.

Before his heels were pivoting on the dirt, the warehouseman had lobbed the ball beyond him with the outside of his right foot. Rob was waiting. The Old Mon let it fall over his shoulder, cut outside his man to put the ball on his left foot and fired. The ball glowed like a Size 5 meteor. But Fullbrook's Number 6 twisted a leg and diverted it. Applause echoed down the line, and not just from the Yew Tree following. It was a moment that unites football-lovers, regardless of colours, a flash of genius that would have had Sir Bobby Robson, a man whose silky skills had graced The Hawthorns 45 years before, dancing a jig of joy.

Along the line, two and three deep in places, spectators were stunned. They hadn't all been there for the start. Maybe they'd finished late shifts. Maybe word had spread around Walsall.

Fullbrook didn't have time to regain what was left of their composure, though. Within 60 seconds, Mark Horton won the ball on the ground in midfield. He turned and broke, shrugging off his marker. Another defender stepped up, but he bounced him, too, and strode forward until he could scent the keeper's sweat, 25 yards away. The ball crackled this time, but the keeper stretched till you could hear his joints click and tipped the ball round the post. It only served to drive Tree on.

In the next three minutes, it became more punishing and passionate. Craig picked up the gauntlet. He shrugged off his own defender and let fly from 20 yards. If the keeper saw it leave his boot, he could only guess where it was going. He scrambled behind the shot and watched it bounce away again, but no one – orange shirt or yellow – had the legs to close him. He picked up the scraps, then knelt and said a prayer.

On the line, three dozen people talked at once, animated chat where, seconds before, the tension had brought a throttled silence, a kind of church-like respect for the working men, jobbing players, over-achievers, under-achievers, dads, sons, lovers, scrotes, nice blokes, road diggers, plasterers, builders, telecoms engineers in front of them, playing their hearts out, or defending for their lives.

Could Tree keep it up for the last 15 minutes? They'd done it once, remember, come from behind, 1-2, the day Chubbs had his ankle broken. But with 10 men?

Eleven minutes from time, Nigel Davenport tipped a long shot over the bar. Fullbrook only had a three-man defence to overcome, but they hadn't twigged that they could run beyond it, deploy their extra man from deep. They were either trying to go round Bran, Ginger and Gavin, or shoot from distance. They were waiting for Tree to wilt, instead of making them turn, but they were beginning to win corners. And, with 30 seconds to go, they won another.

Tree pulled every man back, bar Rob. Fullbrook sent every man bar one up. The numbers didn't match. The corner was a good one. In the gloom, six or seven players ran to meet it, dipped at the knee to spring, then realised it would go beyond them. With 20 seconds left, it dropped at the back post, beyond Bran's despairing leap. Nige scrabbled past bodies on the line, then became a spectator again. Wumph! The ball smacked the Number 9's forehead. But he was falling back as it did, and the ball clipped the bar. Twenty seconds to go. It would have been heart-breaking.

Tree took the goal-kick short, knocked a couple of 15-yard passes and Ginger began a brief run down the left. Up ahead, Rob was on the move, and Ginger saw him. He rolled the ball a yard to one side, took a steadying step and knocked a 40-yard pass between two defenders. The Old Mon outstripped them, but didn't touch the ball until he shot, at as close to full speed as 38-year-old legs would carry him. He was in his follow-through as another leg stretched and deflected it inches past the post.

Craig hurried to take the corner and found his brother advancing on the penalty area. He set himself up for the volley, swung his leg, but snatched the shot and watched it skim the bar. And the ref blew his whistle.

The Fullbrook players walked straight to the dressing room, but Paul gathered his men in the middle. "Ten minutes each way," he said, then "golden goal or penalties."

"If it goes to pens," I said to Tuck, "we'll have to park our cars behind the bottom goal with their headlights on."

"Otherwise, the keepers are going to have to hope the ball hits them," he replied. "It'll be 47-46!"

Extra-time took a few minutes to catch fire, unsurprisingly. Tree were bushed, if you'll forgive the pun.

The opening exchanges were cagey, until Gav collided with Fullbrook's Number 10, running back into the area. The forward went over and pleading yellow arms rose across the pitch. Gav mimicked a dive. We held our breath for another of those seconds that pass like an hour, and the man in black pointed for a goal kick. Paul puffed his cheeks. I took a walk, unable to stand the tension any longer, and ended up behind the Fullbrook goal.

On the stroke of the change-round, Rob twisted past a defender, about 25 yards out, and found himself picking dry earth from his knees for his efforts. He did what any bright, fouled forward does and walked straight to the full-back who'd fouled him while Yoss placed the ball for the free-kick.

The area was packed. Yoss took three steps and hit a swerving drive. Out the dark it came. The keeper saw it late, and the ball cannoned off his chest. Rob was first to the rebound. He knocked it goalwards, but the keeper threw a hand up and changed its course. The ball rebounded from the bar and, for all I could see, bounced over the line before spinning out and finding a Fullbrook boot. We leapt, but the ref waved play on. No one argued. From where he saw it, there was no way he could give a goal.

Chances from then on were few, thank goodness, for the light was too dark to take notes. The play switched from end to end, that much I know, Tree still trying to two-touch it within striking distance of the top goal, Fullbrook content with hit-and-run. It's difficult to say who had it right. The game slowed, but if you blinked you still lost the player you were following, the yellow or the orange shirt a staccato image on a grey back-cloth, as if someone was using a ropey strobe.

Then the 96th minute came, and Fullbrook launched another raid. Ginger dealt with it, but at the expense of a corner. The players shuffled as the kick looped and dipped into the six-yard box. Nigel back-pedalled through the pack and palmed it over the bar, then staggered behind the goal, gripping his stomach. Tree could ill afford to defend without a keeper whose eyes were adjusted to the light. The ref halted the game and, by the time Paul reached him, Nigel was doubled up.

It took a couple of minutes but, eventually, the second corner was floated over.

Nigel stayed on his line this time. The ball was half-cleared, but fate intruded.

Instead of flying clear, in to the path of Ginger moving off the front post, it hit a Fullbrook player's shoulder and rebounded above the little full-back's despairing leap, on to the inside of the post – and in. Nigel flapped. In vain.

There was silence while the moment registered. Then the men in yellow threw their arms to the night sky and yelled cries of victory and relief. Yew Tree heads sank. Nige ran from the pitch holding his guts.

It had been an epic, but it was no way to lose a game. On the other hand, the longer it went, it was the only way the game was going to be won. I felt safe suggesting the same to Bowe as they traipsed off, one by one. He'd had a massive game. We walked in to the dressing room block and heard Mark Horton's incensed voice, predictably, complaining that "The ref sent Scurve off but done nothing about them lot".

It wasn't the time to tell him they'd played better without Stan than with him.

Some stripped off, pulling steaming boots from steaming socks and rubbed steaming, stinking, blistered feet. Others just sat, head in hands. Rob shrugged his shoulders.

"That's a bastard," he said to me.

"Better that than losing after a mistake," I offered, though I didn't mean it.

I'm not sure where Stan was, but Paul walked in soon after.

"Well lads," he shrugged too. "What can I say?"

I talked to Bowe for a few minutes as they hauled weary limbs to the showers.

"Nige has had the shits all day," he laughed. It was the only thing that brought a smile to anyone's face. The effort of reaching the last-but-one corner had been one jolt too many. He was still fully occupied in Trap 1 when I left, 15 minutes later.

How could you be unhappy, after such a night? Disappointed, yes. But unhappy?

It was only a Thursday night Cup match.

Millions weren't riding on it.

Wars would not be fought over the outcome.

Anniversaries would not be marked.

People would not be asked if they could remember where they were the night Yew Tree played New Fullbrook.

But, give the players five yards in their legs, and 10 in their heads, level the pitch, squeeze another 40,000 in between the railway line and Bescot Crescent, and it would be selling on video. Not really, but you know what I mean.

I'll tell you this, though. The stars planning a World Cup summer could have done worse than stand and watch, and ask themselves whether the game that gives them a working man's lifetime earnings in a few months finds its greatest expression at places like Broadway Playing Fields, on nights like that, and not – sorry to go on about it – in the Theatre of Dreams. They owe their pampered money-bags lifestyle to it, because these blokes pay to play and watch. Thank-you would be a start.

On the way home, filtering off the M6, some bastard in an artic forced me to put two wheels up the kerb, within six inches of the nearside barrier. I thought about indicating the scoreline, using one finger of my right hand, but scenes from *Duel* flashed through my mind. I dictated the registration number and the firm's phone number into my tape recorder but, by the time I reached home, all I was thinking about was the game. I have the number, though. I might still complain.

21 UP FOR THE CUP

JUST STOPPED CRYING. Fullbrook had been the game of the season, but the man who'd agonised for every minute of almost every other match had missed it. Jezz had spent the night making Vauxhall camshaft rockers, picking 'em up from a tin, dropping 'em down a chute. Seven thousand of them. You might once have had one in your car.

The night after the golden goal, I e-mailed him. "Oh, deep, deep despair…." I started. A day later, he replied. "Just stopped crying…." So had I.

Paul Gennard laughed as I locked the car at Hillcrest on the Sunday. By the look on his face, it was that or weep.

"Rob's injured," he said, then "Stan ay turned up…." Only one of those worried me.

I enjoyed the company of both men, but I connected more with Rob. He was old enough to be my younger brother. Stan, God forbid, was young enough to be my child. I watched how Rob applied his talent and I wished it were me. I saw Stan's footballing brain come second best to a pint, replayed the stories of scouts who'd queued to watch him, and sighed for him and every other 23-year-old who's realised it's too late.

Georgie! Georgie! The image I'd take away of Rob would be the joy of scoring. The picture I'd have of Stan would be less happy. That was a big, big shame. Still is.

The Fullbrook defeat meant Tree were on a rolling two-match countdown, one league game against Merrivale, and whatever the WBA Cup brought. On the one hand, the season seemed to have gone quickly. On the other, the start of this cup quest, the 2-0 defeat of Midfoam in September, felt an age away. Round 2 had been 2-0 over Abbey, at Birchley Park, in November. Then there was the win over Swan a fortnight before.

Rob's reward in that game for being hit by the keeper had been a rib injury. He'd played his heart out on the Thursday but, as we walked to the pitch, talking about the Grand National, he could hardly move.

The National. In the drama of Thursday night, I'd forgotten to ask about it. I'm not a betting man but, for the first time in my life the year before, I'd tasted success in the big race. I'm not sure where Smarty was when he arrived at the Canal Turn, but he was second when he landed, having picked his way through the flailing legs of 10 horses that had gone down. Second of two, but that was good enough for me. When I'd picked Smarty in the office sweep, Sports Editor Paul Ricketts made his annual call to the trainer and RSPCA to suggest he pull the 16/1 chance. With good reason.

I'd splashed the *Birmingham Daily News'* 1987 National spread with 'It's Dark Ivy's day!' By the Monday, the headline was stretched across a composing room pasteboard with 'last' inserted before 'day'. The nag had made it as far as Becher's.

In 1998, I had Celtic Abbey in the sweep and it fell at the fifth. In 1999, Suny Bay dobbined in 13th, but at least it was alive. In 2000, Royal Predica went so quickly at the first that its only *Grandstand* name-check began "oh, by the way".

The Trees had shared my 2002 luck. Wicked Crack never cleared a fence. They had each, as predicted, made £400 disappear, and nobody had won a brass razoo. But, Rob smiled, they'd already booked for 2003. Blackpool had 12 months to prepare.

At the pitch, we turned and walked back. He needed to change for a team picture.

I don't often watch a man undress and dress, for the sake of it, but there's something compelling and comical about one who pulls a shirt and shorts on, then plans to walk through a public place with ankle socks and shoes finishing the number.

"There's nothing more unsexy than that!" Jezz pointed at his legs and laughed. In fact, there was, though it still involved blokes with socks on.

Jezz had shuttled from one extreme to another most of the season, either laughing or shouting, smiling or cursing, planning to sort things out, or ready to jack it in. As we left the dressing room, we talked about the Fullbrook match and he declared there'd have to be changes before next season. You-know-who, particularly.

Rob and I left him to lock up, and picked up the chat. I couldn't think what Jezz would do without football. He might complain about this lot, but no other bunch would have given him much different, from what I'd seen.

Would he really leave? Could he? Rob would be content watching his boys and handing out the oranges. Maybe that was the difference between the shovel and the factory handle. They both had a rhythm, but only one encouraged you to be philosophical.

As the picture was taken – several, to account for the likelihood of todgers hanging out – there was a sweet scent in the air in front of the Cabbage Patch goal by the rusty Cinder Bank railings. The mid-morning sun, creeping higher with every passing Sunday, added to the air of expectation. There are only two smells of England that I'll carry through the years. One's the whiff of Castrol R that trails a vintage racing car at Shelsley Walsh. The other's newly-cut grass. For a £110 deposit and £16 a match, we'd reached the last-but-one home game before seeing some return for the cash Dudley Metropolitan Borough Council had mugged from – sorry, charged – the club.

I breathed deeply once the picture was done, partly relief Ginger hadn't mooned, partly summer's beckoning finger. I was beginning to rewind the year – the days I'd have gladly been somewhere else, those when I'd wished I could pull boots on – when Brian Horton broke the spell.

"What's wrong with you?" he shouted at Rob.

"Wounded," Rob rubbed his ribs.

Brian nodded behind. Stan was walking towards us, hands in pockets, dragging a little thunder cloud similar to the one his brother had towed at times this season.

"He got stopped by the federal agents last night, coming out the Lion at about 4.30," he said, but didn't elaborate. He meant am, not pm. It wasn't said as a boast, or in disgust. It was just information. Then he looked down the pitch at Nigel Davenport.

"All right, cacky legs!" he bellowed.

Opple headed wide before 60 seconds had gone and, for the next 88 minutes, you'd have thought Rowley were the team eyeing fourth in Division One. Chances came at regular intervals but, sweet turf, it was so frustrating that, at times, I was in danger of doing a Jezz. I wanted Yoss and Meesey to tell the strikers where the killer pass was going. I wanted Bass and Opple to start a run, point five yards behind the defender, and tell them where to put it.

My mind went back to Eric Jones, the games master who'd told us poor 13-year-olds we were a bunch of spastics. Honest. "Triangles," he'd tell us before a match, and "Triangles" at half-time. He was the only bloke I've ever seen link stick-men on a blackboard with three lines. If he'd seen Tree that morning, the game gagging for an opening goal, the quarter-final beckoning, he'd have nipped behind the hawthorn bushes to light a fag and rehearse his 1973 speech.

Oh, the chances that went begging. Meesey, Mark, Ginger, Ginger again, Bass, Bass again. They looked like a team who didn't believe they had a right to score against superior opposition. Bass was the biggest culprit. The little forward had the control, the speed, the shot. But he wasn't putting them together.

Stan had cut a lonely figure on the far touchline at the start of the second-half.

"I still think that lino was chatin'," he'd said, hands still jammed in his parka.

"It's one thing to think it, another to say it," I suggested. He paused.

"I'd do it again," he went on. "I've thought about appealing and telling 'em I was right," he added. "Mind yo, they'd probably come down on me even harder."

"What are you expecting?"

"Seven weeks."

While we talked, the Rowley lino flagged for offside.

"Yo chate!" Opple shouted at him. Stan's jaw dropped.

"Ay, ref!" he boomed, "I got sent off for that!"

And still the chances came. Bass pulled out of a one-on-one with the keeper.

"You sat it out!" Tuck and Stan yelled in unison. Bran ignored them.

"It'll come, Bass," he shouted. But the head was dropping.

"Time they brought Tigs on," Stan said. "He'd be my first pick."

"He'd be my second after Gavin," I replied.

"I day expect to play, not after Thursday. But if I had, I'd have been on by now."

Tigs or Stan? Academic, first on account of the fact that Stan still had his hands in his pockets, second that even Blind Lemon Jefferson would have put the little midfielder on ahead of the warehouseman, and then written a song about it.

With four minutes left, Tigs teased the right-back, feinted outside, then cut in and found Gavin Skidmore. The centre-back stepped inside too, let the ball roll and shot. The keeper blocked, but he couldn't hold it. He lay helpless as the other Skidmore, Craig, seized on the scrap like a starving man and, thwack, people were suddenly leaping skywards.

The joy was loud enough to make a Sweet Turf pastor rethink his morning sermon. The ref blew and turned, until one Rowley man pointed to the Rowley manager, on the line, flag held high. The ref walked over. They spoke for 15 seconds, then he turned back and pointed to the patch of grass where Tigs had won the ball. Offside. Never in the reign of Sam.

"I thought yo was 'aving a great game till now," Jezz yelled, hurling something imaginary at the pitch. How long would it take to reach coronary care? I looked at my watch. The poetic riposte to Thursday. Gone. Tree wouldn't have the legs for extra-time twice in four days, surely, to keep their dream alive and, let's face it, mine? They needed one last chance. One shot. One header. One deflection.

Eight-seven minutes. Tree prodded and probed.

Eighty-eight. Rowley pulled every man behind the ball.

Eighty-nine. The visitors were happy to hunt a golden goal.

Ninety minutes. Tigs took delivery on the left, a carbon copy of the move that led to the disallowed goal. He rolled it inside to Yoss, who slid it to Craig, who let the ball run half-a-yard to his right. He didn't look up. But, then, he hadn't most of the season. Some players operate on an unseen awareness of what's around. Craig wasn't one. He pressed on with a vague idea of direction, like Ted Terry's spaniel Robbie on the scent of a crushed bottle. Eighteen yards out, he whiffed the keeper's embrocation. As his right boot swung, the ball skipped an inch off the stud-pocked earth.

The boom echoed down Cinder Bank. It was a moment you want to recall in slow motion, the backing-track bass-line pumping adrenaline, watching the ball swing this way and that. A moment when the beat grows louder and the Mitre logo spins into view, then out, then in. When the ball takes a deflection, its track altered by a degree, and curls past the keeper. When the stretching defender grimaces in his final effort, and a cannon-fire rush of drums turns tension into an explosion of joy.

In truth, it whistled inside the post. Half-a-second. Done. Before the net bulged, the men in orange were going wild. The Rowley players looked at the ref, then the line. God knows why. Hope, maybe. Disbelief? No flag went up. We went nuts.

"Ay!" Ginger tracked the ref to the centre-circle and, for the first time all season, said something polite. "How long left?"

"Twenty seconds," the man in black replied. Excited? I thought Ginger was going to wet himself. Twenty seconds. Rowley threatened once, but lost possession and Gav's boot cleared. And that was it. The whistle went. Jezz screamed. We all did.

In the Bar, I opened a packet of peanuts, waiting for the crunch Wolves-Wimbledon game to start on TV. Young James Wall sat by me, a mini version of the Old Mon. I asked about Little Greeny. He'd had his transplant, he said, although his sister had had a hard time, because the harvesting had to be done twice. But the doctors were pleased. They were hoping he'd be out in two weeks. I still couldn't guess what the tension must have been like in their house. It made a last-minute winner trivial.

We moved to the Lounge a few minutes after, an armchair Liverpool fan amid a sea of Wolves or Baggies followers. It was fun. It was noisy. It was a match Wolves had to win. The Baggies had cemented second place behind Man City by remorselessly accumulating points while Wolves – who'd come out of the City defeat level on 82 points, but ahead on goal difference – threw them away, like a loss at Millwall.

Nero Wolf had anticipated the game in an acute state of excitement.

"They don't come any bigger than this," he said on *Wolves Stats*, and he was right. "Win and the pressure's on W*** Brom. Lose and W*** Brom look favourites to go to the Premiership automatically."

In his misery afterwards, he prematurely condemned his team to a play-off battle, "while the moaning, cheating negative playing Hand B*ggies get to the Promised Land. Football's never fair or predictable, but it can rarely have been so unexpectedly cruel and unusual".

If he'd blown his nose, wiped his eyes, taken a big breath and looked in the mirror to practice a smile, he'd have realised Albion still had nine points to win or lose. They'd finish anywhere between 91 and the 82 they then shared with Wolves. Nero Wolf had two more games to endure – against the Wombles at home, and Sheff Wednesday away, the last day of the season.

Rotherham helped soothe the pain a little by holding the Baggies to a 1-1 draw the day after Wolves' Millwall disappointment – though, on the *Boing! Boing!* site, one David Watkin was incandescent.

"The TV evidence showed incontrovertibly that we were denied a valid late goal. The officials should be ashamed…. This could easily cost the supporters and team the glory of promotion and the club literally millions of pounds."

The best Wolves could do now was 88 points, so Albion still needed to win against both Bradford and Palace to guarantee 89, and promotion. A cool, 90th-minute Igor Balis penalty took the points at Valley Parade. The Baggies in the 20,209 crowd boinged, chanted and sang for 20 minutes after the players left the pitch.

Mind you, very little of the anxiety had seeped away by the time Dave Watkin's trembling fingers began an exhausted journey across the keyboard and purged himself on the *Boing! Boing!* site.

"Was this game as memorable as Oldham 76?" he asked when he arrived home. "Well, almost, and – whisper it softly – but we're almost there… Just one more fully-committed performance in front of a full house next Sunday."

In the Yew Tree, Tuck was as nervous as Rob, Bran, Stan, Mark and Nige. He tried to play the nonchalant, heckling gate-crasher, but no one was fooled. If Wolves lost, his five team-mates would go home in despair. Any other result, and Albion would need just a draw with Palace to be certain of playing Premiership football.

He soon quietened down, and I was sure I knew what was going through his mind. Fate had often punished me for being cocky. Because of me, Nigel Mansell's rear tyre exploded in Adelaide, 19 laps from the end of the 1986 Australian Grand Prix, 19 laps from a world title. I'd poured a celebratory Guinness. The same when Liverpool lost the 1988 title showdown with Arsenal.

Jezz and Paul were talking, but not about Wolves. The topic was Tree's potential to be a good Premiership One side. The state some of them had turned up in this season, they wouldn't last long. As they spoke, laughter was following a piece of paper from table to table. It dropped in front of me. It was a copy of the referee's report on Ginger's booking in the Swan game. Ginger had been cautioned, the ref said, for "shouting unintelligibly whilst frantically waving his fist above his head".

"You should take out a direct debit to pay your fines," someone suggested.

I left, reluctantly, with Wolves leading 1-0 – a quietly-received goal – and the news that the quarter-final would be against Premiership One Lighthouse. Or Fullbrook.

The rest of the TV game generated more heat than light, a fact curiously absent in JD Wolf's webcast, a heart-on-the-sleeve outpouring that stumbled between those old familiar companions, blind optimism and painful reality. He allowed himself one extravagant moment, recalling Blake "twist his head in true Exorcist style, without jumping to head the ball home".

It wasn't the goal I'd seen. That was a simple near-post header. What was incontestable was that it had been Wolves' first home goal in nigh on six hours.

Otherwise, a couple of hundred words later, it boiled down to a bald fact that every Wolves fan understood, the Molineux men among the Trees wandering home for dinner, those traipsing from the ground, those switching off their sets at home.

"It all goes down to the last day," he finished, "a scenario I wasn't expecting or even wanted to envisage. After the way we dominated the league in February, it's understandable that Sir Jack and all fans are a little annoyed. We only have ourselves to blame, as our fate's in the lap of the gods."

From Halesowen on, you enter *Express & Star* territory. This Sunday, the newsagents' bills yelled things like 'Albion v Wolves: Final Countdown' and 'Battle of the Black Country: Latest'. The radio chat was wrapped around the same, the last game of the Nationwide Division One promotion race. Albion and Wolves.

While I wondered whether Ginger, Bran and Co had toned Saturday night down for the biggest game of the season, against Lighthouse at Cradley's Bearmore Playing Fields, on *Sportsweek*, Jim White asked Wolves boss Dave Jones if his team had prepared for Sheffield Wednesday like a Cup game.

"No, like a league game," he said. "a league game we must win. It's come down to one game, but it's been a long season and I think everybody's looking forward to this one. I know my players are. I think the fans are nervous, which is expected."

Then writer Patrick Barclay spoke about how great it was for the Black Country to be the centre of the nation's sporting gaze again. I'd have liked him beside me in the passenger seat, talking about Jezz, Paul and the Yew Tree season. He'd have made that sound important as well.

"Some people will go to work tomorrow feeling the worst's happened. Others will be glowing after the best day of their lives." How right he was.

Near Cradley Heath Army Stores, a line of men in best bib and tucker, with old gold cummerbunds and old gold bow ties, were watching three stretch limos glide up. Wives and mothers in shell suits and slippers were pointing camcorders and cameras at them, laughing. I thought of Dad and Uncle George watching Albion's FA Cup and promotion-winning side going past 567 Birchfield Lane in 1931, parading their trophies on an open top chara, on the way to Blackheath from West Brom.

That day had stayed alive in him for 70 years. What of this one for the Wolves faithful?

I'd first driven this journey eight months before, praying Tree's season would stay alive to the end. Otherwise, what would there be to write about? A relegation fight would have done, in a sad kind of way. But 33 teams had started the year in the Warley & District Sunday League's top three divisions, so to be in the last eight of their own FA Cup was a success by any measure. I'd have settled for it in September. My blind trust had been given some kind of reward, after all.

This part of Cradley Heath was a confusion of side streets, rows of terraced house with high doorsteps, interrupted by new, redbrick Wimpey interlopers. The A-Z had me looking at the pitch from the wrong side of green railings. A bloke with a sponge, a battered Sierra and a thick Cradley dialect put me straight. He gave three sets of instructions before settling on a final version. A couple of weeks to go and my ear was, finally, tuning to the 'ays', 'days', 'bays' and 'you'ms'.

Titanic's anchor and anchor chain leave Lloyds Proving House after testing. Copyright unknown

The pitch was firm, wedged between the back of houses and the brick walls of old, industrial Cradley. The only colour came from a play area. At the far end was an anonymous relic of Black Country heritage, Lloyd's Proving House. It was to here from

Hingley's Chain & Anchor Works that a cart pulled by 20 horses brought Titanic's 16-tonne main bow anchor for testing in 1911. The White Star liner's two eight-tonne stern anchors and its anchor chains – three-and-a-quarter inches thick, 1,980 feet long and weighing more than 100 tonnes – made the same trip. What a sight they must have been.

Team news. Tuck's voice was the loudest I could hear as I pulled up – "Come on, you Baggies!" – so he was all right and, for all I could tell from those four words, confident. As they headed for the dressing room, Ginger hung back to give a petite young lady a peck on the lips.

I rubbed my eyes and looked again. Ginger. A peck on the cheek. Had I misjudged him? I wondered whether she was from Willenhall, but realised it would rude to ask.

Rob? His ribs were hurting, but he was ready to be sub. I caught Paul by a graffiti-scrawled door opening on to an unlit corridor whose inspiration had clearly been drawn from a prison punishment wing. The American architect Louis Sullivan coined the phrase "form follows function". He had a lot to answer for.

"I'm giving the kids a chance up front," Paul said, deadpan.

That meant Bass and Opple. If they didn't click, he'd put Yode in defence, move Gav into midfield and push Craig up. Seemed reasonable.

Stan? My heart sinks as I write. He was asleep on the settee at pick-up time and arrived with Lin, Brian and Sam as his team-mates emerged. His ban was through, 35 days from August 26.

"I've give him three chances, he's chucked 'em back in me face," Paul had a note of resignation in his voice. "I've heard he's going to play for the Red Lion. Let him."

Tree were everything in the first-half they hadn't been against Swan, Fullbrook and Rowley. Average. The yellow-and-green stripes of Lighthouse seemed everywhere, not because they were running the game, but because the Netherton men were back to their old tricks, shapeless, rushing, playing deep, and moaning a lot.

It wasn't the way to win a quarter-final, not when the game was so clearly there for the taking. That was confirmed when Lighthouse's right-back hobbled off. Not because he hobbled off, but because he hobbled on again. They had no sub, apart from their lino. And he was a keeper doing a mate a favour. In fact, he admitted as the game went on, they didn't have a centre-half in the side, or a fullback.

Unfortunately, Tree were a goal down by then, a lame deflection after Ginger – wearing new Adidas boots and distracted, presumably, by the lingering scent of last night's perfume in his nostrils – had gifted Lighthouse possession.

Tree had spurned their own chances regularly enough to work out what was happening, and what was possible. In fact, if one thing had me as frustrated, game after game, it was that no one on the pitch ever looked up long enough to see how the game was developing, and respond. If Jezz grimaced, pointed, stamped and shouted "Am I talking to myself in the shagging dressing room?" once, he did it a dozen times.

Like this.

Ginger. Warned over his language after complaining about a two-footed tackle to a ref who'd already shown that he didn't mind anything physical, but wouldn't have people swearing at him.

"Am I talkin' to meself in the shagging dressing room?"

And this.

Twenty-three minutes. Craig shuffled past the right-back and hit the bar from 10 yards. The keeper, who didn't even look like a footballer, held at the second attempt. No one was following up. No one.

"Am I talking to meself in the shagging dressing room?"

Twenty-five minutes. Craig, unmarked, headed over the bar. Lighthouse defenders? Like lighthouses.

"Am I talking to myself?"

Bran sensed the tension: "Come on, Tree. We've had our 10 minutes now!"

Thirty-two minutes. Opple, all arms and legs, won the tussle for Mark's cross and fed Craig, who traversed the 18-yard line. He was tripped before an opening emerged or someone ran into the space in front of the man whose dressing room hook had somehow held the keeper's jersey. Bowe wasted the free-kick.

Shaggin' dressing room.

See what I mean? Now I've started!

On 44 minutes. Craig jinked past five men. He might have laid it off three times before his heels were clipped. Yoss's free-kick was headed clear. Not a Tree in sight.

"Am I talking to myself?" Jezz asked me. I pretended not to hear.

Late in the first-half, a move broke down and, suddenly, the despair was catching.

"It's schoolboy stuff!" Bowe shouted as he turned his back on play. "It's shit, ay it?"

I didn't listen to the half-time team talk, but you could probably write the script as well as me by now. However, this time, it stuck.

Before the lid went back on the orange-box, Craig had turned two defenders and stabbed the ball back to his brother. With an instinct absent in the first-half, the man in goal tipped Gav's shot over and it soon became apparent that, if Lighthouse had limped to the break, they'd turned into a side intent on hanging on. For the final 43 minutes.

On 51, the keeper – for we can call him a keeper now – pulled off another remarkable save from a point-blank Tigs header. But he didn't have a prayer two minutes later, when his tiring defence failed with the offside trap. Bass met Opple's through-ball and fired home. Jezz ran on and hugged the little striker, proving the emotional line between unconfined joy and abject misery was razor-thin. Tuck joined in and pulled Bass to the ground and they all piled on. Bass emerged, eventually, counted his limbs and headed for the centre-circle.

"I take it that's your first goal?" the ref asked him as they went.

The relief was palpable and, I confess that, momentarily, I too fell into the Tree trap of thinking the hard work had been done. Then chairman Ted Terry appeared on my shoulder and whispered "Barrel, Gornal Bush, Netherton Hillcrest". Score one, concede one. Tree started pushing the ball around arrogantly, carelessly. Ted and I looked at one another, and we knew what each was thinking. Two minutes later, it happened.

Gavin had never lost possession, out of position. Not until now. Lighthouse's big Number 8 strode away and, as Bran jockeyed, he unleashed a thunderous shot. Nige tipped it on to the bar, but it rebounded in to the empty six-yard box. Well, it would have been empty, if a forward hadn't been there to nod into the net.

There came a point in most games when I'd join Jezz on the far line and, in doing so, through some careless remark, set him off on one. The Trees probably don't know this, but most of the arguments resulting from Jezz's spontaneous observations were sparked by my attempt at conversation. Mind you, he was on such a hair-trigger that Ted's dog might just as easily have nudged him too far.

At 2-1, Paul had to do something. Bass and Opple went off, Gavin pushed into midfield, Craig moved up to partner Rob.

If Tree were going to extend their season, stand 90 minutes from a final, someone had to decide how much they wanted to win. Rob had done it a dozen times, but this seemed a gamble too far. The 38-year-old was running like what he was, someone trying to protect an injury. Then up stepped Yoss. While his mates were either too hasty offloading the ball, or held it too long, the 20-year-old was prepared to put his foot on it, and knock a telling pass.

Little by little, Tree twigged. On 75 minutes, Gav beat his man on the right, stepped inside and rolled a five-yard pass to his brother. Craig looked up – looked up! – and nudged it to Rob. The Old Mon dropped his right shoulder, winced, went left past his man and shot from 12 yards. Two-two.

A minute later, it should have been over. Craig, brought to life by Rob's arrival, sent Gavin away. The defender-turned-midfielder thundered forward and shot, but the ball skimmed the post. He slid to his knees and pounded the pitch in torment. Within 60 seconds, he'd shot wide of a gaping goal. Howls of derision came from the touchline.

Thoughts flashed to Fullbrook until Mark Horton turned on a sixpence and saw his shot tipped spectacularly over the bar.

Tigs' deep corner threatened to find a telling touch, but it was knocked away. A Yew Tree head sent it back into the danger zone, but again it was rebuffed. Back it went. And back out, beyond Bran's late run. The captain didn't hesitate, though. Stretching his left leg further than all season without farting, he hooked it over his shoulder and watched it sail over the keeper's head. I'd dismissed this man on the flimsy evidence of his appearance. But he didn't deserve this. Two-three. I felt sorry for him. Sorry, but only for a nanosecond.

There were nine minutes to go, this week, not 20 seconds. Would Lighthouse find a reply, like Fullbrook? Or were they done, like Rowley? We found out when Craig forced the keeper into another wondrous save four minutes from time, then watched a final shot tipped wide a minutes later. Between, Ginger had looked set to join the fun.

"Keep yer shape!" Jezz yelled.

"Calm down, you're not helping!" Bran bawled. As Jezz didn't mutter a sentence ending in "shagging dressing room", I assumed it was nerves, not anger. Whichever, within seconds, the whistle blew and every Yew Tree man leapt in the air.

Paul sauntered out of the dressing rooms, 10 minutes later. The Old Mon had come through. Yoss had sparkled. Craig too. He had one of those 'guess what' faces on.

"Stan come up at half-time and asked if he can be sub next match," his head shook.

I followed the Wolves and Albion games on the radio, relieved that my morale for the coming week wouldn't depend on the results. The intoxicating anticipation they'd bring for one set of fans would be mine, anyway, as the countdown to the semi-final began.

Wolves needed an early goal at Hillsborough to settle nerves, and it came after less than a minute when Noel Blake powered through the home defence like Rob Wall and squared for Colin Cameron to slot home.

"Could justice really be served today and the moaning Brummies get their just deserts?" Nero Wolf would ask later on the *Wolves Stats* website.

In short, no. Sixteen minutes after Cameron's strike, radios crackled in Sheffield and the news broke Wolves hearts. "The scum had scored," Nero added. "We fell apart."

Albion added another, and so did Dave Jones' men. Unfortunately for Nero, JD and Fat Stat – and Rob and Bran and Nige and Stan and Mark – Palace didn't reply at The Hawthorns, while Wednesday hit two to lead 2-1 before Joleon Lescott equalised.

"Never can a season which went so well leave such a bitter taste," Fat Stat started his web wail in poetic fashion. "At the start of the season, who wouldn't have accepted going into the final game with a chance of automatic promotion? Despite the air of gloom, I think we need to put a few things into perspective and dispel a few myths." It wasn't long before his despair dragged him beyond the edge.

"I don't think that we should be too harsh on Dave Jones as I think it's difficult to psych out a psychopath," he wrote. "The Ginger Whinger has the look of someone who was continually bullied at school. He certainly has enough hate to go round...."

Then this. "The talk coming out of Molineux is about Sir Jack withdrawing his money. This would be a mistake. As my Mum says, what can he do with his spare millions? Buy another 20 yachts? I'm grateful to Sir Jack, but let's face it, he's had plenty of free publicity out of his money...."

A little harsh and ungrateful, I thought. Then I stumbled on Nero Wolf's final word.

"Now we face Norwich in the lottery of the play-offs," he typed. "How can this really have happened? In France, the National Front got through to the second stage in the Presidential elections. Today the Devil looked after his own."

'Boeuf a la mode', Del Boy might have said. Or 'bollocks', as Paula Tucker would have put it.

"Let's just gloat over the final table," Dave Watkin suggested on *Boing! Boing!* It had City top by seven points from Albion and 10 from Wolves.

"None of this seems real," a near-blubbing Simon Harris admitted. "I'd like to thank the board, the playing staff, the ground staff and the tea lady for putting the pride back in this part of the Black Country... A quick note about Wolves. If they don't go up in the play-offs, it'll be a travesty." But even he couldn't resist a dig.

"To Lee Hughes, Kevin Cooper, Jason Koumas, Ray Harford, Rodney Marsh, Clinton Morrison, Jack Hayward, Dave Jones and Sir Steven Bull – hahahahahahha!"

I prefer this to end on Gordon Lynch's picture of noise, nerves and happiness.

"When *The Liquidator* came on you could see waves of people in the East Stand raising their arms in spontaneous delight... Then, 10 minutes from the end, something I'd never heard at The Hawthorns – a chant of 'Going up'."

Blues won 2-0 at home to Sheffield United, finishing fifth. A play-off place. Jezz would be pleased.

The Thursday after the Lighthouse quarter-final, I drove past more chip papers and derelict land and turned left up Church Road, by what used to be Netherton Junior School. A dad was playing football on the car park with his kids and a few mates, two jumpers on the kerb as goalposts. One lad weaved past the others, a shimmy here, a feint there and sidefooted a goal. Flowing, balanced, blissfully unaware he was little more than a free-kick from where Duncan Edwards had done the same thing to John Hingley's schoolmates, 50 years before. He looked like he could have done it all night.

Ten minutes later, I leant against the wire fence and watched Tree playing five-a-side. They looked like they wouldn't score if they'd stayed until morning. Craig and Gavin were at bowls. Bowe was looking after his daughter, Ginger was missing.

Stan was in goal. After five minutes, he let one in. That shouldn't be taken as a measure of his ability, just the fact that the ball never came in his direction.

"Stan, you only had one thing to do and you got it wrong!" I shouted.

"Ah," he laughed, "I'm crap!"

"Sunday's game's against Quinton Rangers," Paul stretched out a hand. Quinton. They'd won the Premiership by a Black Country mile.

"They put five or six past Swan," he added, and suddenly the semi had perspective. This would be Tree's final. This was Arsenal vs Huddersfield in the last four of the FA Cup, and Huddersfield had put out Villa and Blues already.

"Nothing to lose, then," I said, because, in my book, anyone who's pulled boots on for an April cup game knows such games are simply about playing as well as you can.

"I told 'em," he went on, a sentence that – after 29 games – he didn't really need to complete, "anyone who turns up after being out on the drink won't pull a shirt on."

"Have you decided what you'll do next year?" I asked.

He watched a couple of shots slam the sideboards, and another sail over the fence.

"I might give it a rest," he said. "What's worn me down is the attitude of some of the players. Some games, half of them have still been drunk on the pitch. If their fitness and commitment matched their potential, I'd be happy to continue."

He paused. Another shot flew high with Dudley written all over it.

"Fullbrook won that cup 4-0," he said afterwards, and I couldn't help thinking that Ted and Lin's dream of welcoming a cup-winning team might just have come true. Maybe if Stan hadn't been sent off. On the other hand, maybe if he'd called the lino a chate earlier....

As we talked, Yoss and Tigs were on form, doing step-overs and drag-backs where others would have kicked and run. Such feet, playing in a Sunday league. Not for the first time, I mused over what must be like having such talent. Not for the first time, that thought led to another, lager and cigarettes, and on to the change in players' attitude to their Sunday sport since my day. And, before I knew it, I was saying it. I must have sounded like Dad. Paul nodded.

"You can have all the skill, but it don't matter if you can't look after it. I used to play with Sam Allardyce when I was a kid," he said, and the conversation took a turn.

"The lads are talking about training through the summer," he added, out of the blue, then "Stan's signed on at a gym".

About 40 minutes after I'd arrived, the whistle went. Training over. The next time they'd kick a ball in anger, Quinton Rangers would be facing them. The players left the pitch, glowing in the late spring night air.

"See you Sunday," Stan said, then strode down to his car for the drive to Leicester and a night-shift in a medical supplies warehouse, playing cricket.

"D'you think you'll watch next season?" Paul asked as he went. I watched Stan go.

"Jezz asked me the same thing a few weeks ago," I said....

I took a different route out of town, past a row of old terraced houses towards Netherton Reservoir. As I did, two young lads emerged from the shadows with fishing rods over their shoulders. I mention this to let you know that not all the old, simple pleasures in life had been abandoned in the face of Mr PlayStation. These two were walking in the footsteps of how many thousands of young Netherton lads, over the decades? Mind you, they probably stopped off at the pub for a swift one on the way home.

22 PAIN

SO, THIS WAS IT. A cup semi-final. Huddersfield vs Arsenal. Yew Tree Rangers vs Quinton Rangers. An unlikely outcome for a season that had started with half a team and a weary fart. I'm talking about Tree, of course.

Where else across this football-mad island – Liverpool, London, Manchester, Glasgow – was this scene being played out? Around the time this cup run started, I'd found a disjointed collection of players in need of something inspiring to go with their willingness to share communion every week. Most of all, I'd hoped they'd prove they weren't completely out of their depth. How I'd hoped. Now this.

I was the first to arrive at the ground, way too early, but it gave me a chance to sit quietly and think.

Think of what Paul had said at training.

Think of the game he'd ask them to play.

Think of what they'd end up doing anyway.

I couldn't honestly say whether I'd ever played there, but the ground was familiar, a relic of the days when big companies – like Albright & Wilson, where Rhodia played – provided entertainment, as well as employment. It wasn't called Bass Sports Ground any more, though the Cape Hill brewery was still just down the road. The social club had seen a lick of paint, but the fading green cricket pavilion at the end of the pitch hadn't. There was an old armchair in the middle of the bottom goal, but no nets.

By 10, I realised it was too quiet. Even by Tree standards, the sides were cutting it fine. By two minutes past, I was back on the road – there were two grounds on P72 3C of my tatty A-Z. By the time I arrived at the right ground, 800 yards away, Quinton's subs were warming up in blue tracksuits. They looked the business.

I passed Stan and Tuck in the corridor by the Tree dressing room. They were going out for a kick-in. There was nothing in Stan's mood that would have even hinted to an unsuspecting observer what the previous months had been like.

I eased the door open. It squeaked. Rob looked up and smiled. Jezz and Paul were there, fiddling. I gazed around, moving clockwise, sniffing embrocation, ahh, and wished it were me. Sweeping my gaze clockwise, Mark was by Bran, with Yode next, Ginger, Rob, Bowe, then Tigs, Gavin and Craig. Nigel stood and left, clutching a toilet roll.

"Poo bear!" Rob laughed.

"Best go now, rather than leave it to the 28th minute of extra time," Bran shouted.

Then Ginger's mobile went and I learnt something new. In these parts, you don't just navigate by pubs.

"It's where we shoved Deep Heat in Scurve's pants," he said.

Apart from that, most people were quiet. Yoss walked in, sat down and said nothing.

Bran was doing most of what talking there was, and tapping his studs.

"That's beginning to get me nervous," Jezz said. Ah, bad move. Everyone followed suit. Tap-tap-tap-tap….

If nerves were jangling, it was also the wrong time for Jezz to say "This is the biggest game in this club's history". Rob added "… so far", and Bran joined in with "Let's hope this lot have been on the piss, thinking all they have to do is turn up".

"Mind you," he added, "them out on the piss is probably less than we'm drinking, and we'm cutting down."

It wasn't a signal to stand up and walk out, but it was somehow fitting that they did.

"Do your best," Paul told them as each passed. "You make the final if you want to."

Lin Horton and Sam were on the touchline, two ever-presents. Brian was there too. And Tracey with the lads, hoping Rob's sore ribs would hold out. Carl was standing with the subs, as he had all season, asthma or not. So was Mitch Gennard. Not much being said. Nervous. We all were..

Tree maintained the kick-in ritual of losing a ball over the fence before Jezz called them in to a huddle for a final team-talk. Rob's boys found a place in the circle.

"This is your chance to show how good you are," Jezz told them, and his voice wobbled. No tactics, no confirmation of who'd do what, just that.

The huddle broke up and I was half-way through scribbling a list of names and numbers in my battered little green notebook – 1 Nige 2 Bowe 3 Ginger 4 Mark 5 Bran 6 Gavin 7 Yode 8 Yoss 9 Rob 10 Craig 11 Tigs 12 Bass 17 Stan – when Jezz walked past me, wiped an eye and laughed at himself. Soppy sod.

The opening exchanges aren't always a reliable guide to what will follow but, on this day, they were. There were early warnings that Tree would have to be careful not to leave the back four exposed, because the home side counter-attacked like lightning, as you'd expect a team littered with Midland Alliance semi-pros. But Quinton could be put on the back foot too. In fact, at times, only the odd show of poise marked out the men in blue as something other than Division 1.

If Gary Lineker had asked Alan Hansen to pick out two moments from 45 end-to-end minutes to illustrate Paul Gennard's half-time talk, these would have been them.

The first came on 16 minutes. Two fast passes took Quinton from defence to attack. Ginger was drawn towards the corner flag as Yode and Bran back-tracked, one eye each on the impending cross, the other on the blue shirts arriving in the area. The cross came, as it was always going to, but Bran's weak clearance was deflected invitingly to one of three players steaming in unmarked at the far post. Number 9, the executioner. One touch to control. One to fire. Point-blank.

Big Nige had started to come, but took a step back as the bullet left the gun. Thirty inches from the line, no more, he fell back and threw out his left hand. The ball cannoned into his glove and speared off at 90 degrees. We watched from 50 yards, this time unarguably in slow motion. The ball crashed against the underside of the bar and bounced once in the vacant six-yard box, begging the coup-de-grace. Before Nigel's instinctive hand had intervened, though, the forwards had turned, breathing a sigh of relief at the first goal, sure the rest would follow. A rebound wasn't in the script. Two turned back to seize it, but it was Ginger, scrambling from the corner flag, who reached the ball first.

Jezz turned to me, his eyes as wide as mine. We'd stared into the same mirage, seen the ball go in. No question. Neither of us could believe what we'd actually seen.

"Fuckin' 'ell," he gawped. "That wuz better than Banks."

That was the first Lineker moment. The second came on 40 minutes. Looking up was a new habit for Craig, after a season scurrying, head down, up to and sometimes past defenders. This time, he spotted Rob hunting space beyond his marker. The crossfield pass dropped in to the Old Mon's stride. He took it past the defender on his left peg, but it ran a foot too far ahead and, as we held our breath, the keeper saved.

The body language on the half-time whistle was telling. Quinton walked to the dressing rooms like men who hadn't been given the respect they deserved. I lagged behind the Trees as they gathered mid-pitch and hesitantly passed the oranges and fags round, like they'd been distracted by an imaginary scoreboard reading 0-0, and disbelieved their eyes. I glanced around the orange shirts as they milled, waiting for Paul's half-time talk, a message they'd doubtless ignore.

Nigel. That save. Bowe. He was doing what he did best, nothing fancy. The firing-squad chance apart, Yode hadn't given the Number 9 any change, even if he'd thrown himself into the occasional tackle. Ginger? Still occasionally caught out, but he'd been feeding Tigs with what he needed to trouble the right-back. And he'd kept it shut. Hard to believe, I know.

Gavin had more room than he knew what to do with on the right of midfield, but he wasn't seeing enough ball. Mark Horton was having another massive game alongside Yoss, whose feet were doing most to reduce the home side to ordinariness. Rob and Craig? This is where it fell down. Here was a back four that hadn't shown an inclination to play an offside trap. A pass behind the line… Oh, for just one.

"Every time they get a free-kick, they'm moving it quick," Paul opened. "It's training ground stuff. Stand over the ball. Let the ref push you back. Make 'em tek their time." That was more or less it. Then they began talking themselves.

Opple: "No arguing with the ref, lads. Let's get back into position."

Tuck: "Yoder, yo've got 'im in yer pocket."

Bran: "Boys, at times we'm looking down-hearted. Get our heads back up, man."

Paul: "You've done the 'ard bit. You've played against the wind."

Ginger: "For fuck's sake, we can beat anybody!"

I wish I'd said something to Rob and Yoss as the gaggle broke up for the second-half, because then I'd have looked like a genius. Within 60 seconds of the restart, 10 or 12 yards inside the Quinton half, three men closed on Tigs as Yoss used the outside of his right foot to lob a pass to him out left. Tigs drew all three, then lobbed his own pass beyond them all to Rob. The blue-shirted centre-backs hoisted their arms in unison, but the flag stayed down. That left the Old Mon, 10 yards from the nearest defender. The keeper sprinted out but Rob, composed, slid the ball past. Time froze again, until Rob's turn to the left wing confirmed what we all hoped, and feared. Nil-one. Quinton were stunned. So was Jezz.

"This is gonna be the longest 'alf of me life," he turned to me.

I've told you about my uncanny ability to affect sporting history with one twist of a Guinness bottle top. Well, I've never been equipped to stand the tension of watching my team at 1-1 either, let alone hold on to a one-goal lead. Thus, I can tell you where I was about 9pm on Thursday, May 25, 1977. I was wandering the Lodge Park estate in Redditch, staring in to people's living rooms, hoping for a sign that Liverpool had turned 1-1 into 2-1 against Borussia-Moenchengladbach in the European Cup Final.

There were no front rooms to stare in here, though, nor – for all the fantasy of the Lineker half-time studio inquest – a TV to watch it on. So I had to stay.

The next 10 minutes brought more bite from Yew Tree, while the home side played like a team who still thought that, in the last 30 minutes, their time would come.

The tension standing next to Jezz was draining, so I drifted away and found myself with Paul just as the first worrying cracks began to show and he yelled "All right, Yoss?" The key midfielder was holding his knee.

"Twisted it," he winced, sweat pouring off him. It was hard to tell. He looked knackered anyway. So did Mark. Paul glanced at me. He looked worried too.

"I can't change things now," he said.

Within a minute, the scene in Tree's area resembled the scramble for Lin Sanders' post-match chips. A long Quinton throw-in caused panic. The ball wasn't cleared properly and ricocheted twice before, from the midst of the melée, a Quinton boot turned it goalwards. No slow-mo this time. Nigel stuck a right foot out and the ball cannoned back to Gavin, who took an agricultural swing. How we gasped.

Two minutes later came another long throw, this one from the left. A posse of players went up for it, including Nigel. Suddenly, he lurched backwards, off-balance. He clawed at the ball as Ginger moved off his post to intercept, but both were falling as it crossed the line. The ref looked to his linesman, momentarily hinting that he'd seen the shove we'd seen. Then he pointed to the centre-circle. One-one.

Jezz went ballistic. I can't tell you what he said because I didn't have Dad's *Black Country Old Testament* to hand as a phrasebook. It was more than Yode could take too. Within a minute of the restart, the stocky defender went right through Quinton's trappy Number 10 on the edge of the centre-circle. He'd been niggling since the start. He stood to confront Yode, yelling at the ref, but Bowe was in his face first. The rest leapt in, Yoss among them, with a push in the chest of another blue-shirted player that said "This has nothing to do with you".

The ref finally intervened, booking the 10. Ginger could contain himself no longer. He'd seen what the player had escaped with so far – the ankle-taps, the elbows, the constant mouthing – and gave the ref chapter and verse, red-faced.

Within seconds, Bowe tried to clear the free-kick and was hammered by the same player. Bowe fell, holding his ankle, but no red was waved. The ref, I assume, hadn't seen. It was turning nasty, but that was playing into Tree's hands because, while the tension had risen, Quinton's composure had gone. They should have been stamping their Premiership superiority on the tie, not legs. Instead, either they still believed in divine right, or – like Fullbrook, a few weeks before – hadn't worked out what to do with a tiring, retreating Tree midfield. Quinton had been harried, hassled, closed down and shown no respect. Nevertheless, the longer it went, with no sign of Tree finding their second wind, an inevitability grew. Quinton would score the winner. Strangely, at the time, it mattered and it didn't. If they won, they wouldn't have deserved it.

Thirteen minutes from time, Tree cleared a corner, but it fell to a Quinton midfield man, 25 yards out. He swung a hopeful boot, nothing better, when he had men wide and the defence running out. This time, Nige saw the shot coming from the moment it left the boot. He told me so afterwards. He took two steps to his right and dived, but then something horrible happened. Yode flinched as the ball speared at him and it glanced off his nut. In mid-air, Nigel watched as the ball and history changed course.

The relief on Quinton faces as they raced for the line was as obvious as Tree's despair. The cocky git in the Number 10 shirt shouted "Oh no, not another final!"

Two dubious goals in 15 minutes. It left 13 more for Tree to salvage a draw, or to win and wave two fingers at Number 10.

Seven minutes from time, Ginger hoofed a long pass down the left to Mark. The loping, lanky midfielder gained ground. Then, as the sapping heat turned his run into a moonwalk, he released Rob. The 38-year-old turned for goal, but he was clattered.

Quinton's wall formed. Mark stepped up, dragged his socks from his ankles, and hit the 30-yard free-kick. It flew, it dipped, and it grazed the bar. That, surely, was it.

It was for Rob. Six minutes from time, he made way for Bass. He jogged off, feeling his ribs, then grabbed a bottle of water and sank to the grass. Aaron walked up to him.

"All right, Dad?"

"Too old, son," Rob smiled and rubbed his boy's crew-cut. "Too old."

Gavin followed five minutes later, hobbling, and Stan stripped off. By my watch, Bowe's injury meant he had three minutes to redeem himself, to grab the equaliser. Villain-turned-hero. But don't raise your hopes. That would have been too much to hope for, greedy even.

Tree launched a final assault. The ball was cleared and flew over Tuck, on the line. I was near enough to see that it would fall for me, and began pacing backwards to catch it, as you do.

I'm not sure what numpty left a cast-iron table five yards from the pitch, behind me. My legs, they laughed later, hung momentarily in the air, twitching like a disco-dancer who's stomped on a live cable. I'd intended to return the ball for a quick throw, the start of a move that would drag the game in to extra-time. They took the throw, but the last hurrah didn't happen. They were pissing themselves too much.

The ref blew. Quinton were jubilant. I looked at Jezz. The gobby 10 swaggered off.

"Someone should have hit him near half-way early on," Bowe glared. Someone? Yes. Me. The Git's team-mates were honest enough to stay quiet. They should have won by six.

"No way they'm good enough to be top of the Premiership," Ginger moaned as he trudged off. Maybe.

I stayed long enough to watch Jezz shake every hand, only guessing what he felt because, though I'd lost in semis and finals, after 20 years the pain fades. I slid out and sat on a railing with Big Nige and Paul. Fitness had cost them.

"It's what we bin saying all season, ay it?" Paul said. We had. "That was the hardest game we've had all season,"

Quinton's manager walked past a moment later. Paul had barely digested the thought when another blue shirt passed.

"I was surprised the ref and linesman missed the shove for the first goal," the opponent said.

Big Nige looked at me and shrugged his shoulders. No good admitting it now.

While we were yacking, Jezz appeared and asked Nige if he was signing next season.

"Definitely," he said. So, they had a keeper three months earlier than last season. It was also my signal to go. One game left, Merrivale at home. No silver, but a voyage of rediscovery that had stretched further beyond the horizon than I'd dare hope.

As I limped to the Escort, a group of Trees trudged towards their cars, disconsolate. A couple of them asked me if I was all right, and I said "Yes", even though bones were graunching in my back and hip after the table's tackle from behind. Then Tuck appeared, pulling a top over his green-and-yellow Baggies away shirt. He laughed. Bastard.

From: jeremy dingley
To: Mark Higgitt
Sent: Monday, April 29, 2002 2:12 PM
Subject: P*** Up Sunday Night

Hi Mark (ar bin ya) – Getting over Sunday slowly, the Blues match didn't help, but, the Wolves match lightened the grief. Anyway that's the end of the sadness. Next Sunday night were are having a end of season P*** up. Hopefully we will be getting a Karaoke, so this is an invite to you and your family to join us. I and the lads woe tek no for an answer. Please tell the wife to expect anything. (I hope they don't get offended to easily). Hows yer back, hope you didn't hurt yourself to much. See what I mean about getting any sympathy from us, loosing in a semi final with a couple of minutes to go, all we did is laugh at your down fall, sorry mate. See you soon. JEZZ

Ah, the Wolves match. Blues had led until the last minute of the play-off first leg at St Andrew's, when on-loan Villan Dion Dublin scraped Millwall a draw. Still, there was everything to play for.

Not for Wolves, though. They'd already blown it.

"Is there anything that's more of a cruel and unusual punishment than being a Wolves fan?" Fat Stat wondered after his team lost their first-leg 3-1 at Norwich. Three days later, Wolves won the return 1-0, but it was too little. Suddenly there was only an empty numbness in Fat Stat's life. Not my words. His.

"Jones will have to find what went wrong, in what must be one of the most spectacular collapses in form in recent history," he declared. "I have a strong suspicion that the real problem was a poorly-fought PR/psychological war which gave impetus to our opponents and drained the self-belief from our team. But the real problem for me is that I'll never believe that we can ever be promoted again. This relationship only ends with pain...."

Pain? Unless he'd been mugged by a table, he didn't know the meaning of the word.

23 ROOTS

"YOU GONNA SING?" Tuck said as I slipped in to the Yew Tree at about 8.30, hoping I could slide up to the bar, buy a fruit-juice and watch from the shadows.

I rubbed my throat, a well-rehearsed move topped off with a shrug to say thanks for including me, and I'd love to, but this throat. You know....

"You gonna sing," he replied, and I realised he was telling me, not asking.

Paula caught my eye across the Lounge. She had a book with a million songs in it. I held my thumb and forefinger an inch apart and pulled a pleading face. Sign language hadn't made a stunning start to the evening, but she had to know I wanted something small. She ran a finger down the pages and came back with *Do You Wanna Dance?* My mind went blank. Hysterical dysphonia. Blighted with it all my life, a rare anxiety-based syndrome, the vocalist's equivalent of merciless stage fright. I couldn't remember the tune. I understand many other top musical performers suffer the same crisis.

I chatted with a few folk while the noise from the mic grew more pitiful. Music's usually as big a part of the culture as the food or the dialect in meanderings like this. In my year with the Trees, though, I hadn't as much as heard a car stereo on loud, except for one deaf twit on the car park at the first Fullbrook match, the day Chubbs had his ankle shattered.

"They've said they'm training this summer," Paul Gennard told me, without even a raised eyebrow at the din or the news. "Stan too. Said I'd take 'em up Clent Hill."

The manager's yearning to be optimistic had too often given second best to straightforward despair since September. Training? Summer? The look on his face said he'd believe it, not when he'd seen it, but some weeks after, once he'd had a chance to digest the evidence and ensure he hadn't been hallucinating.

My nerves settled when Stan went on before me, singing Shania Twain's *Mon, Ah Feyul Liyke a Wummun,* dressed in his Friday night best, swivelling his considerable hips, pointing at the audience, but this time refraining from telling someone they were an effing chate. He was dreadful, and we loved it.

The highlight of the night, apart from discovering that Bran could knock out a tune and Opple couldn't, was the latter's *Evergreen* duet with Bass. Worryingly, Bass knew all the words without bothering the screen. So, maybe the musical tradition had died around here.

Opple's first song had almost been faithful to the Grade II listed joke that he sang all the right notes, but in the wrong order. He sang all the wrong notes in the wrong order, and the duet proved it was no fluke. We all joined in, apart from Scott and Mitch, who were trying to persuade Yode to do something impolite as he danced with a tall blonde. Yode, the gentleman, blushed. They didn't risk suggesting the same to Ginger.

Gavin and Bran followed with Spandau Ballet's *Gode* and, as the evening stretched towards half-eleven, more people drifted in from the Bar on the basis that, if you can't block 'em out, join 'em. Then an old fella was persuaded to take the floor and belted out *Delilah*, accompanied by the entire ensemble, proof – should it be needed – that, if another war broke out and we found ourselves huddled in an air raid shelter, we'd skip popular modern standards like *Smack My Bitch Up* and Mr Eminem's *Slim Shady* and head straight back in time.

I'd intended to ask Rob what had disappointed him more, Wolves missing the play-off final or losing to Quinton. When Tuck led a loud "Boing! Boing! Baggies!" chant, I didn't have the heart. The night was about to become tribal and, though – if we'd cared to dig – any of our family trees might have crossed 70-odd years before, it was time for a third cousin twice removed to slide out. So, with Jezz close behind, I did.

All together now! Ginger and Mark serenade each other while the rest try to hit the same notes at roughly the same time. Picture by Aaron Manning

"Enjoy yerself?" he looked at the sky, stars lost a gazillion miles beyond the sea of Merry Hill neon. I had.

"The Merrivale game might not be played," he said, and I felt a pang. Every season has to end, but there's something about the last game already being history, and not having known it was the last game, that makes you feel your home's been burgled. The dismay lasted until the Wednesday, when his next e-mail arrived. "The game with Merrivale is on," it said.

My first Sunday had been the morning after Germany 1 England 5, our toe-hold on World Cup qualification. The last was as warm, the M5 stretching north was flanked by dappled fields and trees, and a tiny cloud did nothing to spoil the deep blue sky.

Tord Grip was on *Sportsweek*, describing Sven-Goran Eriksson's calm nature and admitting to being the one who did the shouting. For every Sven, of course, there are 100,000 Paul Gennards, for every Tord as many Jezz Dingleys, for every Stevie Gerrard, a million Mark Hortons, and every Michael Owen a handful of Rob Walls.

I'd suspected the Old Mon had been right in the Smoke Room months before. Now I knew he was. England, Juventus, Wolves, Yew Tree. Football's genetic. Same stuff, different bricks. Mind you, I'd be hard-pushed to name the last England left-back named on the subs bench who turned up without his boots, like Ginger.

Tree won 4-0, Rob and Bass scoring in the first-half, Mark and Bass in the second. It left them fourth, nine points behind champions Harborne, four behind Khalsa, in third.

Early in the season, Paul had talked about survival. They'd done that, and more.

Over the year, a heap of other things had found a home in my little green book but, if I wanted any page to speak for the whole story, the Merrivale game would be it.

Things like this. Walking to the pitch, Paul said Ginger wouldn't be signing again. He owed £40 in fines and subs, yet he always had enough cash in the pub.

"Priorities" and "responsibilities", Paul said. You know the rest by now.

The players were waiting for a ball.

"Seventeen they've lost this season. Seventeen!" Paul muttered. Jezz walked past, a ball in each hand, and Bran shouted for one.

"You ay gonna lose another," Jezz yelled. He wouldn't chuck one.

The man in black was the bloke from the Barrel match at Londonderry Lane in October, the darkest day of the season, a morning so chillingly disconcerting it was unbearable. He hadn't been the most mobile of officials that day. But now he had two knee bandages on.

"It's worrying when the ref's carrying more injuries than the players," Jezz said.

Rob. His opener came after a minute, a step this way, then that, after Mark and Gavin had worked the ball down the right. Georgie! Georgie!

The pitch. Early on, Yode sprinted across to cover right-back Pete Cutler, and drew the ref's attention to the fact that there was no touchline. I wandered round. He was right. The corner flag quadrant formed a loose right-angle, but the first hint of a line was 30 yards away, where it had been painted on last summer's bare earth. It had taken Dudley Metropolitan Borough Council nine months to cut the grass, now the players would have to rely on guesswork and honesty about when the ball had gone out. They'd be better at one than the other.

Yode. After five minutes, he picked the ball up in defence and strode on, making only the slightest deviation in a run plucked from a Roman road-builder's manual. He looked up as he neared the area, with players making rare runs this way and that. The closer he came, the closer he was to having to make a decision, and we knew it. It was only a short run in the context of the pitch but, within his season, it was an odyssey. He hesitated after cutting in, and let the ball roll into his stride.

"Yode hasn't scored for four years," I remarked to Paul, recalling something the bustling defender had told me. As I spoke, he tried to chip the keeper. Paul allowed the ball to bounce once beyond the far post before he picked up the point.

"He still hasn't," he said.

It was a shame. Of all the Trees, I reckoned, Yode most closely resembled one I remembered from my own playing days. Me.

Then there was Bass. A few minutes on, he hit a snap-shot with the outside of his right foot, a sharp chance on the edge of the area. No time to think. It nicked the bar. When he operated on instinct, instead of mithering over the choices, he had it all.

Tigs. A trademark through-ball, delayed, perfectly weighted. One last time, Rob strode on to it and, ignoring the calls for offside, fired a left-footer an inch past the post. The pleas for a flag were pointless. Ginger 'No Boots' Williams was running the line under sufferance and hadn't been watching.

In between, Jezz had fallen over nothing, nothing at all, as he turned to fetch the ball from the Sweet Turf brambles. Tuck laughed and I made a mental note to remind the keeper that falling over nothing was far more stupid then falling over a table.

Half-time. I crossed the pitch, a wasted walk. Nothing was said that anyone took in.

"This is it," I said to Jezz walking back. "The last 45 minutes."

"Ah," he replied.

Bran. Within 10 minutes, it had an end-of-term feel, so he shook a fist.

"We've got to want to know," he yelled. It would be his last plea of the season.

Mitch Gennard had taken the flag from Ginger but was relieved of his duty when Carl Evans, in a state of urgency, told the rehabilitated midfielder his dad wanted him to warm up, his first game since Barrel. Carl watched him sprint and round the top goal, loosening his muscles as he went, then turned to Jezz and me, giggling.

"Look at him, stretching!" he pointed. "Paul don't want 'im on at all!"

After 58 minutes, he was on, though, in place of Stan. I was by Carl as they swapped.

"They never give up, do they?" I pointed at the Merrivale lot. They hadn't. For a club that had won only one game all season – only one that counted, anyway, after Barrel and the Bengals quit – their attitude had been inspiring. They'd never moaned.

"We'd have give up a long time ago if we'd been losing all season," Carl added.

Eight minutes from time, Mark capped a 30-yard run with a shot the keeper could only help on its way. The 21-year-old ripped his shirt off in his celebration run, and halted, legs astride, before kneeling down to wipe the toe of his left boot.

"Ay, I've gotta wash that!" Jezz shouted. Then he yelled at the ref. "Book 'im for tekking his shirt off!"

The man in knee bandages waited for the celebration to end then, like a plod on point duty, called Mark over, and waved the yellow card. Jezz laughed till he cried. As the card went away, Mark drifted to the far touchline, head down. Jezz laughed more.

"Look," he could barely draw breath, close to a coronary again, though not stress-related this time. "He's sulkin'!"

The ref barely moved from the centre-circle in the final minutes.

"If you can't be bothered, what hope have the rest of us got?" Bran called to him. Carl had already jammed the lino's flag in his back pocket, disgusted that the man in black hadn't seen his last three waves. Eventually, he drifted in front of our back four to the far touchline. It took him 30 seconds, but they were the most incisive 30 seconds that part of the pitch had seen all morning. The ref never noticed that, either.

I adjourned to the pub and sat alone for a few minutes after the whistle. The TV wall had a picture of the 2000-2001 Yew Tree side on it, a foot above one of Albron taken a couple of years before. In my bag, I had new one. Most faces were in all three.

The 17 balls row was still simmering as the rest arrived.

"In four hours time, I 'ope Blues'll be in the Premiership," someone called to Jezz.

"So do I," he answered.

"I'll bet someone lets *them* have balls for the kick-in," Bran muttered, and Jezz started again.

Back in July, when I'd first ventured in to the Smoke Room, I'd been asked to draw the 100 Club. I did it again this day and pulled out John and Iris Acock's number. Then Paul picked Bran's, and Rob handed him his £30 winnings.

"I'll have some of that for new balls," Jezz said.

Landlady Lin Sanders appeared with the trays of chips and bread and butter, and Bran lifted one over. They were like gannets. I'd never grabbed before, but I did now. Well, rude not to. My first mouthful was interrupted by a moaning noise. It was Ginger. There was cheese all over the chips.

"Ginger's allergic to cheese," Bran laughed. He'd dropped in to the pub, the day before, and asked Lin to dig out the grater.

Then I asked Rob about Little Greeny. It was good news. He was out of hospital after his bone marrow graft. A couple of weeks before, he'd had mouth ulcers and his system had fought them off. Now he faced 18 months building his immune system. James had been to see him, and he was looking well. Maybe I could call them in a few weeks, after all, I thought. And that was it.

From: "jeremy dingley"
To: "Mark Higgitt"
Date: 14 May 2002 16:19
Hi Mark (ar bin ya) – Got up with sore head on Monday (cause), drink & burnt, that's the price for being bald. I'll post you some tickets for the presentation. I'm glad you've enjoyed yourself watching us. I hope it's what you was looking for and a little bit more. See you in June... JEZZ

Woodside Liberal Club's a fume-stained, brown-brick building on Dudley's busy Stourbridge Road, about 400 yards from 23 Malvern Crescent, Holly Hall, where Duncan Edwards was born on October 1, 1936. The tables are packed tight around the dance-floor and the house whisky's £1.99. For a double. My first round at the presentation do was £3.79

for four drinks and two bags of nuts. I counted and recounted the change from a tenner, and realised it would be cheaper to ditch The Hollybush and pay the petrol up here from now on.

No one had turned up in fancy dress, even though the tickets mentioned it. They must have thought I was born yesterday!

I sat down and started putting faces to the names Maggie had heard over the past nine months, those anyway who hadn't already welcomed her and moved furniture for me between the bar and table. Aaron Manning, the photographer who'd shot some action at the Selly Oak Eagles match and then tagged along most other Sundays after, sat down with his young lady, Kelly. They'd long since christened him Azza, and taken him in, as they'd taken in me.

Before the formal part of the evening, as thanks for the welcome they'd given a stranger, I presented my own awards, complete with certificates and cans of Banks's Bitter. There was one for Bran (*Fart of the Year*), another for Nige (*The Andrex Award*) and Gavin (*The You're Not on Telly, Ref! Award*). Rob won *The Belfast Boy Award*. There was the *Will Young Award* for Bass and Opple, *Gazelle of the Year* for Bowe, and the *Let's See Award* for Paul Gennard, the winning of which had begun on Sunday, September 9, 2001, Harborne vs Yew Tree Rangers, with the words "Let's see if we can defend this corner". If I'd had a pound….

There was something for everyone. Even Meesey. He took *The Silver Peg Award* for being the last out of the dressing rooms to avoid putting the nets up. Well, he would have taken it, if he'd turned up.

The real awards went to Gavin (*Player of the Year* and *Players' Player*) and Bowe, Bass and Tuck (*Clubmen of the Year*). There were flowers for Lin, Sam and Paula, the ever-presents, and for Lindsay Dingley, for turning dirty socks inside out and transforming green and brown back to orange and blue. The final bouquet brought a hush to the room. It was for a steadfast supporter, Jezz remarked, and he choked a little as he said it. She'd been having a tough time and everyone wished her a speedy recovery. He asked Tracey Wall to step forward, and the applause was deafening.

Half-an-hour later, I saw club chairman Ted Terry at the bar.

"What's the matter with Tracey?" I leant forward and spoke into his ear.

"They found a lump," Ted said.

Osgood-Schlatter and I were on our last legs long before Lindsay Dingley insisted on me joining a Queen medley.

"I'm a little on the big side, self-conscious, so I don't like to go," she'd told me about social events, after Jezz's heart-scare. You'd never have guessed it. She was meant to party. She didn't stop. For the next 20 minutes, only motor-memory kept my legs remotely near the beat but, fortunately, most people were too far gone to notice.

I had a can of Banks's left, so I escaped and took it over to Rob for James, a lame prop on a joyous night to ask a young husband about his sick wife. He explained. One thing led to another and, somehow amid the din, our conversation took us back a year, to the Harborne and Gornal games that had caused me to wonder whether I wanted to risk 20-odd more like them. It had been an empty feeling.

All I'd had to fight it was blind faith that this place and these people would come up with something to justify following my out-of-date A-Z round the Warley & District Sunday League. Then I'd shared that pub evening with Rob. Something burned deep inside him, and it warmed me.

In the end, they'd played 31, won 21, lost nine and drawn the other – the very first game I'd watched them play. They'd scored 94 and conceded 54, had 18 bookings and two reds.

While all this happened, the world had kept turning. On the road to Baptist End, and down the Memory Lane of Dad's childhood, my radio companion had brought me news of September 11, the reprisal attacks on Afghanistan, Gerard Houllier's health scare, the passing of The King – and the Queen Mother – the on-off soccer TV cash strike and the Nationwide play-offs. And the traffic lights outside the McDonald's drive-in at Halesowen had only ever been on green once.

Now, in a room that had witnessed a million conversations, we retraced our steps, my roots, Dad's roots, his, Hingley's Chain & Anchor Works, Titanic, Black Country folk, bonds, the simple life, football genetics, and the game itself.

Football. It was the one thing that had changed the least since Dad and his bunch of scruffy 11-year-olds played as Whiteheath Albion in the Nig-Nog league, 67 years before, or maybe even since the Strollers had walked to Wednesbury to buy a ball, 56 years before that.

It was the thing that had kept millions of lads and men occupied between tea and Ovaltine for the first half of the 20th Century, the thing that made men in their mid-20s rush around shouting "Bergkamp!" with their arses hanging out of their shorts at the start of the 21st. The thing that's only ever been a game. But always much, much more than one too.

"From Sundays, to Juventus to England, whatever," Rob had said in September. "It ay just 11 and 11. It's families and communities. It's brilliant, ay it?" Brilliant, ah.

The reminiscing went on. That night, I lay in bed, let my mind meander, then tried to work my way back to where I'd started. My ears still echoed to YMCA and I went back to the icy day, 18 months before, when I'd wandered round the pitch at Lion Farm and bumped into Jezz, dressed like an orange man-overboard dummy, sizing up Tree's next two opponents. In minutes, we'd been laughing.

I'd found him again months later. I'd put my idea to him in the Smoke Room one Sunday. If we can muster a team, he'd said, come along. The rest you know.

Those first few, awful days had gradually given way to something better, and so had Dad's recovery from cancer. Rob had mentioned Hingley's and Titanic, then unfolded the Dudley News cutting and shown me Parkdale's 1952 line-up. If fate hadn't already taken a hand at Lion Farm, that's where it had. The cutting led me to John Hingley and that foggy, spine-tingling February night when Duncan Edwards stepped in to the story. It's a night I'll remember the rest of my life, as I will the man I shared it with, and his honest answer to a hopeful question: "Did you ever play against him?"

"I can't quite remember." Not "Yes", even though no one could have proved him wrong.

And, after poring over Dad's memories of a Black Country childhood, Birchley Park, Pratt's Brickyard, the Blue Billy, West Brom winning the cup, was it a simple yearning to sit down in the kind of house he'd been born in that had sent us to the Black Country Museum a few months before? Or was fate working from a different plan?

I lay with my eyes open, staring at the darkened ceiling, replaying the moment we'd wandered round the museum's Hall of Fame, Dad reciting my grandfather's words about Ray Westwood, the Bolton Wanderers and England star of the 30s and 40s, Brierley Hill born and bred. I replayed the scene, as I've done dozens of times since.

"Granny Pendress was a Westwood," Dad had said. "At the time Ray Westwood played for England, I recall your grandad saying he was related to Mother's side."

I lay still in bed, but – in my mind – I was reopening the book in the souvenir shop, *Duncan Edwards – The Full Report*, the story of the tragic Busby Babe's football career.

"Both sides of the family had footballing connections," it had said of the young Edwards. "His uncle, Ray Westwood, played as a professional with Bolton Wanderers in the 1930s, and also represented England."

"Read this!" I'd told Dad, twice, before snatching it back and reciting it for him. I'd looked up as the light finally flickered in his eyes. "You know what this means?"

This was my thought-chain that night. All the way up, Lowes-Dingley-Yew Tree-Wall-Parkdale-Hingley-Edwards-Dad-Museum-Edwards-Westwood, and all the way back. Then, head still buzzing, I wondered if I'd done the right thing, urging Dad to explore the family tree, then urging him not to. If John Hingley had said "might have" when he could have said "Yes, I played against Duncan Edwards", then I'd rather go through life knowing we might be related to the Black Country's greatest sporting hero, than hunt for proof and find we weren't. Too much to lose after a year when I'd gained so much.

Then, I think, I fell asleep.

They say your team finds you. Four weeks after the presentation do, we gathered at the Yew Tree for a second team picture, this time in front of the pub, this time with Stan. I swigged an apple juice as they changed in the Lounge. At some point, I started to gather the pen-picture questionnaires I'd handed out in March, in anticipation of a cup final. We'd come close, hadn't we? I flicked through them anyway, and a few honest answers leapt out. A few dishonest ones did too. This was Ginger's (I think Jezz must have checked his spelling):

- Name: Clark Williams
- Age: 27
- Nickname: Ginger
- Career record: Brierley Hill Bullets, Halifax, Leeds Utd, Netherton Libs, Yew Tree.
- Best game you've played: Brierley Hill Bullets 19, Tividale 1
- Best goal you've scored: Free kick for Yew Tree about 40 yards out. Curl, speed, direction technicly perfect.

- Strengths: Everything.
- Weaknesses: None
- Marital status: Single.
- Occupation: Builder, Glynbuild.
- Family connections at club: Bran's my cousin.
- Favourite footballing star: Denis Bergkamp.
- Favourite meal: Crisps.
- Best friend: Loads, but not Mitch.
- Usual Yew Tree drink: Anything free.
- Worst mistake this year: Bran falling over and letting there forward in.
- Best thing you've seen this year: Bran's overhead goal.
- If you weren't you, which other Yew Tree player would you like to be, and why: Rob, cause his nearly as hard as me and he sleeps with Trace.

There were others, like this from Stan. Weaknesses: Fitness; Best Friend: Ginger; Favourite meal: Burger and chips; Usual drink at Yew Tree: Lager; The worst mistake you've seen made in the team this year?: Ginger not paying fines and subs.

Bran. Honours: Not many; Best friend: Mitch, John Hingley; If you were weren't you, which other Yew Tree player would you like to be?: Yosser. The things he can do with a ball, scary!

Sons of the Ten Yard Seam: Landlady Lin Sanders with the Yew Tree boys. Picture by Aaron Manning

Paul joined me at the bar at some point.

"They been training since the season ended. Paying for it themselves," he said. "Yoss looks like he's lost a few pound." Then he added "Jezz and I was wondering, if you're coming down on Sundays, if you'd like to mark the players for the Player of the Year award next year…."

A few minutes later, I was back to the pen-pictures with Tigs. Strengths: Running with ball; Weaknesses: Smoking; The worst mistake you've seen made with the team this year? Playing Ginger at left-back; Football Fantasy: Going professional.

Rob. Strengths: Pace; Best goal you've scored: Cubs 1971-72, lost 4-1 final, I scored a George Best special; Favourite footballer: George Best.

If he'd been born 30 years earlier, that might have read Ray Westwood.

That reminds me. I was flitting round the internet, one day, and stumbled on a picture of Westwood. He looked uncannily like my Uncle Fred's eldest son, Trevor. Alongside the picture was an extract from *Wartime Wanderers*, the story of the Bolton players who'd joined the 53rd Field Regiment Royal Artillery, in 1939, and fought with great distinction for six years in the Second World War.

"Ray Westwood was the first sponsored player when he accepted a contract to model for Brylcreem posters, a campaign which helped him become the first of the celebrity footballers," the extract said.

I bought the book. Three pages into Chapter 1, it reads: "The 14th of April, 1912, was a notable date in more ways than one. It was the day the Titanic sank after striking an iceberg in the Atlantic Ocean on her maiden voyage, and it was also the birthday of Ray W Westwood." I shivered and made a mental note to tell Rob.

Among other things, it also mentions that his dad's name was Sam, and that his wife was Fanny. She and Ray were married at 9am on Sunday, February 18, 1940. They had a son called Alan, and a daughter, Janet. A fair chunk of a family tree, for anyone interested in that sort of thing, I'd say.

24 A BIT DOWN AT THE MOMENT

FROM: JEREMY DINGLEY
To: Mark Higgitt
Subject:
Date: 21 October 2002 16:24

Hi Mark – We beat George Celtic 4-1 on Sunday, at last. Robin, Bass got the goals. It wasn't easy thou. Myself Robin, Ted and Lynn are a bit down at the moment. Young Greeny passed away last Tuesday. He's the lad who they had the sponsored head shave for last year. His funeral is on Wednesday... I'll give you a call on Friday. Hope to see you soon. JEZZ

25 DAD AND LITTLE GREENY

I WAS GOING TO LEAVE YOU WITH RAY WESTWOOD, but the e-mail arrived a minute after I finished the final paragraph. So let me tell you about David Green. Little Greeny.

On his bedroom wall, hanging on top of black-and-white striped wallpaper, opposite a bed made with a black-and-white striped duvet and pillow, there's a framed black-and-white striped Newcastle United shirt, signed by Alan Shearer. In the frame next to it there's an orange-and-blue Yew Tree shirt, signed by a bunch of blokes Shearer doesn't even know exist. Little Greeny treasured them both. His parents still do.

If you walked in, you'd think it was a normal teenager's room, until you wondered about the photos on another wall, and his dad explained they were friends in Ward 15 at Birmingham's Children's Hospital who'd battled leukaemia too.

I'd passed June and Eric Howell's unassuming Victorian terrace dozens of times, little realising who lived there, or that it was where James Wall's 15-year-old mate had beaten the disease he called Eric Cantona twice, but lost to it once.

His name had been spoken at least once in every pub conversation with Rob, Ted and James since the previous winter. I'd waited for a chance meeting, reticent about trying to judge the moment to knock on their door and find out for myself – beyond the warming notion that, in these parts, you looked after your own – what it was about the lad that had made him such an important part of the Yew Tree family. Eventually, I sat in the Howells' kitchen as they chain-smoked and told me.

His natural father walked out after a row when June was pregnant. He saw David when he was born, stood at the gate for 10 minutes, and never saw him again. Instead, David grew up thinking June's second husband was his dad. When he was eight, and they split up, she met Eric and they told him the truth.

By 10, he was fed up with people asking why he was Green and his brother Luke was Hill, so he decided to be a Hill too, until he came home from school one day.

June thought his uniform was hanging off him, and he was pale. So she walked him to the doctors, a mile-and-a-half he should have breezed, except it made him so tired he kept needing to sit. The GP did some tests and sent him to Russell's Hall Hospital.

"His spleen's enlarged," a doctor said. "Are there blood disorders in the family?"

"Only my brother," she told him. "He's had leukaemia."

It was 11.30 in the morning. By 4.30, they'd found abnormal cells in his blood.

"March 13, 97," she added before I'd half-spoken the word 'when'.

Within 24 hours, they were at Birmingham Children's Hospital, and the 'Hill' surname plan went west as the ink dried on David's record with 'Green' written. Consultant Phil Derbyshire explained how bad it was and asked if they wanted David to know.

"He won't trust anyone if he finds out they've been lying," they said, and they told the truth, almost till he died. From then on, the clock that governed their lives wouldn't run for 90 minutes a time, it would run according to some frank, fundemental new rules.

Like induction, the four-week period of chemotherapy that would end with a bone marrow test and a prayer that all evidence of the disease had gone. Remission.

Like the three periods of intensification, when more drugs would be pumped into him to kill off any undetected leukaemic cells. Then two years of maintenance, daily medication and monthly chemo injections.

Frank information like this, as Eric recalls it. The toxic vincristine injected into a vein through a cannula in his hand at his first treatment: "To you it's a needle. But if I give it you, it'd be the same as holding a lit cigarette on your hand for 15 seconds."

There were no beds that Friday, so he was admitted to Ward 6 on the Saturday. He had a blood transfusion, then a lumbar puncture on the Monday, to see if the disease was heading for his brain. They were the first entries in diaries and charts that, on and off, would govern their lives for the next six years, like "Mostly tired, ate like a horse (pizza £1.99) woke up in a sweat at midnight 36C" and "First injection in leg".

When they walked in that first Saturday, Eric expected to see half-a-dozen kids. There were around 200, he recalled. June went to the desk to check in and he ran out, crying.

"She day even cry," he nodded at her across the table. "I was breaking me heart. She didn't even shed a tear, and I'm thinking 'What's the matter with you?'"

He knew, of course. She'd watched her brother, Martin, fight acute myeloid leukaemia, and win. He fell apart again when David's treatment to beat acute lymphoblastic leukaemia started. His bone marrow was producing too many immature lymphocytic white blood cells, causing cancer in the lymphoid line. I didn't know the science of that grim process then, but I do now.

He reacted like any 10-year-old scared of needles would. It took the patience of a nurse, Sue Smith, to calm him for that first, searing infusion. It took her five hours. Five hours? I spent three with Eric and June and I was drained, 180 minutes of conversation about times, dates, drugs, procedures, reasons to celebrate, reasons to fear, memories to raise a laugh, thoughts to make you pause before the next question.

Like this. On March 25, *Dudley News* journalist Richard Allen heard David's story and, 12 days after his diagnosis, a ball signed by Alan Shearer arrived. He'd made it happen quickly because consultant Mr Derbyshire had told them time wasn't on their side.

Little Greeny wanted to be treated normally, but the old normal had gone. The new normal meant June coming home from work, taking him to hospital, checking his central line was clean – she felt her chest – and handing out pills.

They can both reel off the sequence, "four hours apart for one tablet, three hours for another, six hours for another, Mondays and Tuesdays another". They wrote a chart showing what to take and when, until David didn't just know the order, he could recite the names of the drugs, how to spell them and tell you what they did.

June reached across to show me a list of drugs.

"Dexamethadone, ranitidine, chlorhexydine, cotrimoxovol. He used to have that injected into his back…." she ran a finger against another name I couldn't pronounce.

"…. 'cos they don't want it to go through the lymph gland to the brain," Eric completed her sentence. They could do this in their sleep. Probably do.

Every Wednesday, for two years, June would take him to Brum for blood transfusions and platelets, or the 'intensification' chemo blocks, guided by another chart that guaranteed he didn't have an infection. If he did, that was another week back on Ward 15, when June would stay at the hospital, when Eric would slide in to a relentless round of work, going home, washing, cleaning, going up to the hospital.

Every week they grew to depend on sister and brother-in-law Garry and Vanessa.

"Absolutely fantastic," Eric said. "Never any petrol off you or anything. He'd knock the night off work to tek you. Vanessa and Garry."

He handed me a 26-week chart. It was like the A-level timetable I'd hung in our kitchen in 1976, a tick each day, written evidence that I was prepared to wish my life away simply to reach the end of what I regarded as torture, and still do. Pathetic, now I think about it.

There were moments which still made them rock with laughter. David had a moulded, transparent face-mask to protect his skin in treatment and soon found it had unintended uses. He'd put it on in the car and stare at motorists. He'd laugh like a drain. I could see how it provided them with a memento, but I felt a shudder grow as Eric held it in front of me. It was the closest I'd come to seeing Little Greeny.

Inevitably, there were also days when David would go to bed and cry.

"I'd say 'I can't cope'," June said, and shrugged, to underline that nearing the end of your tether was a fact, not a crime. "He'd say 'I don't want this Mom', and I couldn't listen to it. He had a lot of anger. I had to fetch Eric. He did that side of things. I did all the taking him to hospital, basically looking after him with that feeding tube up his nose.

"Some days, he'd say 'I don't want it'. I'd throw it. He'd say 'No need to be like that!' and I'd say 'You won't do nothing for me, I won't do nothing for you."

He knew what June was doing, though. If the spelling on his Mother's Day card, six months into his treatment, was a typical 11-year-old's, the message wasn't.

"Thank you for everything you've done in my life," he wrote next to a poem. "If it wasn't for you I probably wouldn't be alive. I can't thank you enough for it."

Sometimes, he and Eric would sit up till three in the morning, talking, and Eric would be knackered when he started work at the warehouse a few hours later.

"He was hyperactive. Something was needed to make him focus. He hates Man United. 'You've got to call it som'at'. So it was the Eric Cantona disease."

Little Greeny eventually asked if he could join Yew Tree chairman Ted Terry's ballpark team with James Wall and his mates. They said 'No' and he hit the roof.

"If I go down there, they'm walking me back," he told them.

"You ay walking back, not with a line and whatever," Eric told him. "You know what the ballpark's like. What if there's a scrap? If someone's bringing you back, that's okay."

So that's what happened. Robert Greswell's mum started picking them up.

David went in goal, central line and all, because he couldn't keep up with the others. It was like standing on eggshells for Eric and June.

But it didn't stop at the ballpark. Eventually, he turned out for Rob's Sunday afternoon side, too. They went to watch. He was on to start with, but he was subbed after a few minutes. Next thing, he was back on.

"He's been subbed," Eric called to Rob. "What's going on?"

"We arranged it," Rob called back. "I can sub him any time I want. If he gets tired, I'll fetch him back off. When he's okay, I'll put him back on." Typical Rob.

"I couldn't believe it," Eric recalled. "Our nipper Chris is playing for a church team. He tries his hardest and he's getting two minutes at the end. They should be 'Give the underdog a go'. And here's a pub team, all the little roughnecks in it, and they'm doing it!"

"Was that a hard decision to let him play?" I asked.

"No," they chorused.

"I'd have been frightened to death."

"No, you wouldn't. 'Cos the alternative was to say 'no'. And he couldn't hack that."

He went into remission for the first time seven weeks after treatment began. Then everything was devoted to keeping him there. But, one night in May, 1999, he came home from the ballpark and his legs were black. June knew they weren't football bruises.

They were at Russell's Hall Hospital until three in the morning, then he was transferred to Brum and they began again, the four-week induction period, the lumbar puncture, the marrow test, the prayer that the disease had gone, the chemo blocks.

"He'd come back and he'd cry," June recalled, "because he thought he'd beat it."

When that happened, Eric would tease out the fighter in him, a streak they knew. It didn't take much to drag him into a ruck, not because of the hair loss, or the feeding line, or the bloating, though the last two embarrassed him. His closest Hillcrest mates were Robert Greswell, James Wall and Carl Beasley, a lad everybody picked on.

"David used to think it was wrong. He always used to stick up for him."

But there were fallings-out. Greeny and Robert were watching football on TV, one day, when a goal was scored. Robert jumped on him, and he told him to stop. He didn't.

"David lost his temper. Bang! Walloped him. Told him to get out. And he went."

During his second round of treatment, David went to a school for children who'd been disrupted by illness or problems. His teacher knew Wolves' Robbie Dennison and, at some point, David must have told her of his dream of a Shearer shirt.

"Her told Robbie Dennison," Eric said. Shearer had played in Dennison's testimonial and had signed a shirt. Soon it was in a frame on David's bedroom wall.

A couple of months before his name first cropped up in my touch-line conversations with Ted Terry, he started having headaches. They took him for a lumbar puncture on Sunday, October 8 – the day Ginger saw red against George Celtic – and found the disease had reached his brain. He went in again on October 10 and was given a drug to stop it. But tests showed the Philadelphia chromosome. It had come back as a different leukaemia.

June showed me his diary, brief ballpoint entries that barely scratched the surface. For three-and-a-half years, the furthest they'd dare to plan ahead was the seven days after his weekly blood tests. Once, it was a bad result from St James' Park. Now other figures would tell them what kind of week they'd have.

I ran my eye down the page, discreetly trying to work out how ill he'd been when Rob, Jezz, Ted and the lads had done their sponsored head-shave. June watched me.

"He relapsed on the eighth of October," she lit another cigarette, shuffled her seat closer to mine and guided me down the list: Oct 17, chemo; Oct 22, throat swab; Oct 24, chemo; Nov 6, chemo, Nov 17, home; Nov 26, Day Care Unit chemo.

I let my eye run into December. The head-shave had been in late November.

"Ted had been round and told us it was a couple of hundred quid," Eric said. "When he bought the money, he tipped the bag on the table and there was 640-odd pound."

A few nights later, the evening I'd met John Acock, Ted had told me June and Eric were searching for a donor. The second relapse had left them with one hope, finding someone to donate stem cells via a bone marrow transplant or from their blood.

June was tested as a potential donor, and so was David's half-sister, Amanda. To their surprise, the 18-year-old was the better match. He was supposed to go back in on Boxing Day, 2001, for more chemo, but there were no beds in Ward 15, and he wouldn't go anywhere else. It was four days before he began the cycle again.

In mid-March, transplant co-ordinator Sara Kirk visited Church Road to explain what lay ahead. Because no complete match had been found, Amanda was David's only hope. As she was only a half-match, the fight would be tougher.

"The longer we wait for a transplant, the more risk he has of the leukaemia coming back," Sara was gentle but clear. "He has a high risk of a relapse."

A couple of weeks after my first visit to June and Eric, I'd go back to check dates and names, and they'd lend me two tapes of Sara's conversation, and my simple pub chats with James and Ted would suddenly seem shallow.

I would spend the coming days listening to those tapes while driving to and from work, two hours of Sara, June and Eric going over page after page of what might happen, some of it vague, a year or two ahead, some of it cut and dried, and timed to the minute, a practical conversation, as if D-Day was a week away.

One second, they'd swap the names of medical procedures and drugs like battle-hardened veterans reading maps. The next, they'd be thinking of the what-ifs, the equivalent of being on Sword Beach at 0600 in six days time, praying, wondering about enemy positions, and what might go wrong afterwards, maybe on the outskirts of Arromanche, maybe the suburbs of Berlin. Too much to take in.

I'd hear the budgie whistle and the back door open and close, and the word "football" would echo around the conversation as much as "injection" and "anti-viral". They'd be laughing a moment before Sara asked "Have you signed consent?" and, if you'd been in the car with me, listening, we'd have both realised they were talking about David's last chance.

Then, suddenly, I'd hear David's voice for the first time, not yet a man's, but not a boy's either, down-to-earth, like he was taking part in a pre-match team-talk.

He went into hospital in late March to prepare for the transplant.

"And then Amanda," I started reading aloud from David's diary.

"She was given an injection to boost her white cells," June finished my sentence. "They put a needle in each arm, one to take the blood, the other to put it back. Three times she had to do it. It was painful. Like that" – she held her arms out straight – "for four hours. But they ay normal needles what they have in their veins."

"Ten mill," Eric said. I've never been metric, but 10 mill said 'blunt pipe' to me. June handed me a photo. We winced.

"That's all it is," she turned the page to a picture showing a small bag of liquid.

"That's all it is?" I asked. She nodded.

David cried when he saw how small that bag was. He'd imagined something bigger after all they'd been through. Yet here it was, packed with the life-giving stem cells that had taken 12 long hours to harvest and filter, platelets one way, T-cells another, white cells another, a mini refinery. It took 10 seconds to infuse.

"The white cells," June underlined the vital ingredient, three single syllables.

"What day was this?" I asked.

"April the second." Two days after Tree had defeated Swan in the WBA Cup.

Then we arrived at photos with

A cherished picture from the family album: Little Greeny with Amanda during his treatment

faces I knew, Greeny with Ted and Lin Sanders in the Bar, surrounded by mates. Just five minutes later, that night, I'd poked my head round the door. I realised how close I'd come to meeting him.

"Some of them talked about going clubbing," June smiled, "but he used to say 'I ay going clubbing when I'm older. I'm going to be a pub man'. That's the way he was."

After six weeks, he came home. It was the start of a long, hot summer they'll never forget, and one night that will outshine all the others.

"There was me, her, Nessa and Garry, their three lads, our kids, all in the garden till four in the morning," Eric nodded beyond the open kitchen door. "We were all lying on blankets, watching the shooting stars. It was brilliant. Nobody played up. The kids was swapping laps. I had my arm round 'em. We was counting 'em. 'No lying! Only count the ones you actually see'. We had a brilliant night."

Then, one day, David noticed a swollen testicle as he was showering and called June. They took him to see Mr Derbyshire, who examined David.

"You do realise we're looking at a relapse here?" he took Eric and June to one side.

"Yes," June said. They ran more tests and waited all day for the results.

"Am you worried?" David asked her.

"No, am you?"

"Yes."

Then a doctor came in and sat down. Before she told them, her eyes filled up. Then Mr Derbyshire sat with them again. They could take David home and leave it at that. Or he could be an outpatient, which would give him a little bit longer. Or he could go for the "heavy dose", bring it under control and live a little longer still.

They were hoping he'd make his 16th birthday, on December 22, and Christmas. Eric wanted to delay treatment till the Tuesday, so that they could go to Blackpool. But David didn't want to wait. On the Monday, there were no beds. Tuesday, no beds. Wednesday, no beds. There were no beds on the Thursday, either, but they took him as a day-patient.

"He was home by 5.30," Eric said. "By seven, he was so hot we had to phone for an ambulance to take him back. He never come home after that."

The doctors told them he had three weeks to live. They explained to David that there was nothing that could be done, and told him it was between three and 12 months.

"It ay like I've got run over," he told his dad. Then they talked about his funeral, and he told them exactly what he wanted. No suits. Everybody in football tops. No Sunderland shirts. He wanted his mobile phone. He wanted a bottle of pop. Dr Pepper. No other brand. A bag of crisps. He didn't want a piss-up after.

"Just go to the Yew Tree."

One day, Greeny turned round to Eric and told him he didn't want to die.

Eric sat there thinking "What am I supposed to say now?"

Three weeks became two and he was still fighting, but some days were dark. They recalled the moments matter-of-factly.

"They had to sedate him," June said, starting a final sweep through the album.

"He day want to be put out," Eric took over the commentary. "He grabbed me and says 'They ay gonna do that to me!' The pain he was in. You couldn't let him suffer."

"Constant diarrhoea," June said and touched another shot. "This is the bed, wor it? He'd sit in the bed here and, whoosh. Five times a day he went in the bath."

On his last Saturday, half-brother Ricky said: "Dad, don't ask me to come again. I know he's dying, but I want to remember him as he is."

On the Sunday or the Monday, Eric bent down by David's bed and whispered: "Ricky says he loves you."

Two weeks passed and the drugs made it darker still. Then three weeks passed and, eventually, after being pumped with enough morphine to fell a rhino, he drifted deep into unconsciousness.

"I know he's going to die," Eric told June one day, "but I wish I could hear his voice."

Later that day, David suddenly propped himself up on his elbows, and stared at his step-brother, Lee.

"Where am I?" he asked. Eric looked at him. He hadn't woken for a week.

"You'm in hospital."

Another time, he started looking into the corner of his room.

"His eyes were like that," June opened hers wide. "'I'm coming in a minute'."

"You've had enough now," his mum told him, eventually. "Someone else needs the bed. Let go now."

"How long did he fight for?" I asked, a few minutes later.

"He died on the 15th, the Tuesday morning, at 20 to one," June said.

Eric was talking to him, alone, about a footballer on TV, Mendieta.

"He'd look great in a Leeds top, wouldn't he, Dave?" Eric said, holding his hand.

Then June came back in the room, and Eric started to rise from the chair.

David had been taking shorter breaths, but Eric had become used to waiting for the next gasp, feeling his hand twitching. This time, it didn't.

"He day look like a dying lad, did he? He day look poorly," June said.

"He died watching football," Eric added and, for a while, I didn't utter a word.

"He waited for me to leave the room," June looked at Eric. "He knew, because I told him ages ago that I day want to be there when he passed."

A couple of days after, Ted Terry rang and told Eric that the Yew Tree lads wanted a minute's silence before Sunday's game. He didn't feel like going, but he went.

It was a typically cold Hillcrest Sunday. The players laid their shirts round the centre-circle, and Ted put Little Greeny's Newcastle top in the middle.

"Was that your lad that snuffed it?" some bloke walked up to him on the line.

"Yes."

"How old was he?"

"Fifteen."

"Hadn't had much time, had he?" he added, then yelled "Come on, you lot!"

Four days later, Ted wore the Newcastle shirt to David's funeral. They followed his coffin into St Andrew's Church, and then followed his instructions. The Rev Billy Barnes, a Scouser, greeted Eric, June, Ricky, Lee, Amanda, Luke, Stacy, Chris and all of David's friends with a warning. Smiling was compulsory. Everyone had to be in a football shirt. And anyone wearing a Sunderland top must leave.

They sang *Jerusalem* and *All Things Bright and Beautiful*, and *The Blaydon Races*, the Magpies' anthem, filled the church as his coffin left.

They'd already kept one promise, dressing him in his Newcastle United shirt, with his mobile phone, his Dr Pepper, and a bag of crisps by his side because "What am I going to do if I wake up?" Afterwards, they kept another by driving to the Yew Tree, having a drink and enjoying themselves, as much as they could.

Three days before Christmas, on his sixteenth birthday, they gathered at Gornal Wood cemetery. The lads stood round his grave, as instructed, holding bottles of Stella. They took a swig each and poured the rest on his grave. Then they placed the empties round the edge, a flower in each. They'll do the same on his eighteenth and his twenty-first.

"You two seem to be quite together," I said to June, struck by how simply they'd told their story, but drained by the telling of it.

"He said to me before he died 'Don't mope, Mum. Have a cry, but don't mope'. But I had a bad week last week. First week I've had a bad week."

The day I took the tapes back, she showed me a book. When David died, they'd had the choice of a final reminder, a handprint, a footprint or a photo. His foot was too big for the page, and neither wanted a picture. Too morbid. They settled on the hand.

I put mine beside his to see how it compared. The creases and traces of fingerprint could easily have been pressed a few minutes before. It's the hand of a young man.

"Since David's died, most of his mates have gone too," June turned a page, and put names to a couple of pictures. "Then we found out about one of the nurses from Birmingham Children's, Sue Smith, who looked after David from day one."

I knew what she was going to say. I'd edited the story a few months before. Sue had died on a level crossing in Worcestershire. She'd parked her VW Golf on the track and waited for an inter-city to arrive. The inquest heard of a caring woman who'd finally found the stress of her job too great.

"Sue was the first nurse he ever seen. She was absolutely brilliant," Eric said.

"David idolised her," June finished. "They say they don't get involved. They do."

We talked on about support for the family, about honest Mr Derbyshire, a man David had worshipped. Then, don't ask me why, I asked if he'd had any ambitions, a throwaway question, the last one of the last interview of my odyssey.

"He was going to leave his mother, move to Newcastle and get a season ticket," Eric laughed. I'd heard worse.

It was only ever meant to be one season with Yew Tree but, while I'm here, tapping the final words of this snapshot, I might as well tie up some other loose ends.

The *Dudley News* reported on Friday, July 5, 2002, that moves to name the Primrose Hill bridge after Jeff Astle had failed. British Waterways weren't happy because all their maps read Primrose Hill. But ward councillor Frank Whitehouse went further. With so many people supporting other local teams, if it was renamed, it could "entice vandalism". He named the Villa but, why, I don't know.

Fat Stat had pulled on the old gold for Wolves' opening game of the 2002-2003 season at Bradford, admitting to being jaded by the past 12 months, but unable to quell the butterflies at the thought of another chance. The game ended 0-0.

Around the time of Greeny's funeral, Paul Gennard called it a day. I never found out exactly why. My guess – and, I imagine, yours – was that he'd finally accepted he might as well give his pre-match team-talk to the dog and save himself the petrol. Jezz took over as Tree kept themselves in the thick of the Division 1 promotion battle.

Tracey Wall finished her cancer treatment and went into remission. I was with Lin Horton, one Sunday morning, and I mentioned I hadn't seen Tracey for some time.

"They separated," she told me.

"Rob and Tracey?" I was stunned. She nodded. I glanced back down the hill at him.

A few weeks later, he wrecked his knee on a heavy pitch and his season was over. I saw him on the line at Merrivale. He said he was trying to perfect one-legged trench-digging and thinking of seeing a doc if it didn't improve. I watched him later. A footballer who ought to have made it, knocking 40, the man whose life I'd thought was pretty sound.

Tree lost 2-1, a match they'd have won by a country mile if they hadn't lost their composure. A couple of weeks after that, they went to title rivals Sandwell Borough, realistically needing a draw to keep the championship alive. The pitch was so big you could have camped on either wing and not interfered with play. Tree lost 3-1.

I drove to Worcester's Royal Hospital that afternoon.

Dad had a bad hip and congestion that had kept him awake for weeks. They'd done scans, hoping the bladder cancer hadn't spread. I told him the morning defeat meant that, if they were going to win the title, Tree had to win the return at Hillcrest the next week, and even then pray Sandwell didn't win their last game.

The first thing he asked me, the day after the big clash, was "How did they get on?"

"Ref didn't turn up. Postponed," I told him. "It's next Thursday."

His first question the following Friday afternoon was the same.

"Won, 2-1," I smiled. "Tense. Two breakaway goals, then The Alamo. If Sandwell don't win by two goals on Sunday, we've won the title!"

He smiled, something he hadn't done much for a few weeks. None of us had. We knew by then what the shadows on his x-rays were, but he didn't, because the doctors wanted to do a biopsy, to see if the cancer had invaded his bones. It had.

We were told he had weeks or months, not months or years. We settled for months.

The day after they told him, I lifted a *Daily Telegraph* from his bed to read about Graeme Hick's majestic 108 for Worcestershire against Kent.

"I wish I could have seen it," he said.

Later, I took a short walk down the hospital corridor with a man who used to spend 12 hours a day in a hell-fire drop forge, then play 90 minutes football on a Saturday afternoon with a Christmas-pud casey. At 78, a short walk was all he could manage.

"I'm not frightened of dying," he said. "It's not living that scares me."

There were good moments, too, though, including the Sunday afternoon we breezed in and told him that Sandwell had lost their final match. Yew Tree were Warley & District Sunday League Division 1 champions. He was chuffed.

A week later, he was overjoyed to be in a cottage hospital close to home.

We made plans for him to see his garden, but he wasn't well enough.

We plotted to kidnap him for a trip to New Road, and hope Sir Graeme would oblige. But he deteriorated rapidly, and he died in his sleep a few days after that, a couple of short breaths, a pause, then gone.

I was thinking of him when Maggie and I slipped into Woodside Road Liberal Club a few weeks later, still a few hundred yards from where Duncan Edwards was born, for the presentation evening. We were greeted like old friends.

I was thinking of him when Ted stepped up to collect a statuette for Little Greeny's folks.

I was thinking of him when, out of the blue, Jezz asked me to present the players' individual championship trophies and Bran – quitting before a back injury made a plasterer a cripple – led a round of applause for my shirt, a blue *Hawaii Five-O* number. It made my evening, old enough to be a father to most of them, a big brother to the rest, but treated like one of them. Dad would have enjoyed it too.

After that, Jezz announced he'd finished as manager. I wasn't surprised. Not in the least. Part of me was relieved, I must confess. Part disappointed.

"Most of you know what's been agoin' on," he said, "so I thought it was time I gave it a rest. Robin and Paula Tucker, they'm taking over, and I'm sure you'll give 'em your support."

"What's been agoin' on.... " could have referred to any number of things. I hoped it was the amount of hours he'd spent thigh-deep in brambles. I suspected it was the link between a near-stroke and a defence that occasionally showed a reluctance to defend – anything of that kind, rather than something more private.

So, no more hunting for balls in the thorny, wild patch where the Sweet Turf worshippers would one day hold their own Sunday communion.

No more finger-wagging cross-examination of refs lagging 10 yards behind the play.

No more hugs after a last-minute winner.

No more Sunday mornings living on the teetering edge between laughter and tears.

Mind you, I couldn't wait to hear what Paula would come up with, in her new official capacity, to match "Ref, yo'm a twat!" or "Yo couldn't hit a cow's arse with a banjo".

"You know, you're always welcome, even if the book's finished," Ginger had said to me a couple of minutes before, so I felt I had to pick up the mic and thank Jezz, again, for welcoming me into their world, from the moment I'd bumped into him at ice-bound Lion Farm to nights like this, the one that was about to become raucous.

I can't remember what music the DJ played, which is hardly surprising, given that the singing was awful and they danced the way they played, five seconds of poetry in motion, two minutes drifting to the left-hand side of the dance floor, en-masse, and another two standing stock still, glitter ball-watching. I didn't join in. I would have, but I'm waiting for an exploratory op on my knee. Osgood-Schlatter.

Printed by CreateSpace, an Amazon.com company

Proof

Made in the USA
Charleston, SC
23 September 2015